African Luxury

African Luxury
Aesthetics and Politics

Edited by Mehita Iqani and Simidele Dosekun

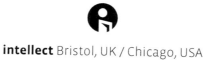

intellect Bristol, UK / Chicago, USA

First published in the UK in 2019 by
Intellect, The Mill, Parnall Road, Fishponds, Bristol, BS16 3JG, UK

First published in the USA in 2019 by
Intellect, The University of Chicago Press, 1427 E. 60th Street,
Chicago, IL 60637, USA

A catalogue record for this book is available from the
British Library.

Copy editor: MPS Technologies
Cover designer: Aleksandra Szumlas
Cover image: Copyright Sydelle Willow Smith, featuring ballet dancer
Londiwe Khoza.
Production editor: Faith Newcombe
Typesetting: Contentra Technologies

Print ISBN: 978-1-78320-993-4 (hardback)
Print ISBN: 978-1-78938-221-1 (paperback)
ePDF ISBN: 978-1-78938-024-8
ePUB ISBN: 978-1-78938-023-1

Printed and bound by TJ International, UK.

Contents

Introduction

The Politics and Aesthetics of Luxury in Africa

Simidele Dosekun and Mehita Iqani

S ome might assume that the phrase 'African luxury' is an oxymoron, certainly not considering the notion that Africans are the *consumers* of said luxury. At the time of writing, entering the search keywords 'Africa' and 'luxury' into Google Scholar resulted not in scholarly work that engaged critically, or indeed otherwise, with how luxury consumer cultures play out in African settings, but rather in numerous articles that use the idea of 'luxury' as a rhetorical device to ask whether certain developmental needs are necessities or 'nice-to-haves' for Africans. For example, one question raised is whether the availability of adolescent psychiatry is a 'luxury' for African communities (Robertson et al. 2010), and it is also considered how, in certain Aids-stricken African contexts, it might be a 'luxury' to grieve for loved ones lost to the disease (Demmer 2007).

While there is extensive scholarship examining various aspects of contemporary consumer cultures and identities in Africa, including those of elite actors and demographics (Dosekun 2020; Gott 2009; Huigen 2017; Iqani 2015) and those centred on expensive goods – and indeed their symbolic destruction, in the case of the South African township culture, *izikhotane* (Howell and Vincent 2014) – 'luxury' has been little considered as a distinct category thus far, moreover as distinct from 'conspicuous consumption'. Some attention to luxury can be found in work on other global south[1] locations – often, tellingly, more in relation to so-called 'new' middle classes than the 'elites' or 'super-elites' of concern in the global North (Brosius 2012; Fernandes 2006; Lange and Meier 2009; Southall 2016). There is, for example, work on luxury accommodation in gated communities in Bangalore, India (Upadhya 2009); on the growing popularity of luxury golf courses in China (Zhang et al. 2009); and on middle-class Thai consumers' savvy expenditure on affordable 'fast fashion', complemented with 'substantial investments in expensive western branded goods – a Prada bag, a pair of Gucci sunglasses', which gives them entry into elite consumer spaces, and which are often resold or traded at 'luxury goods exchanges' (Arvidsson and Niessen 2015: 9; Wattanasuwan 1999). At the same time, in both the larger and more established body of scholarship on luxury from business, marketing and management studies (Cavender and Kincade 2014; Dubois and Duquesne 1993; Kapferer and Bastien 2012; Truong et al. 2008), and in the emergent field of critical luxury studies concerned with the cultural and other politics of what is contemporarily deemed luxury (Armitage and Roberts 2016; Featherstone 2014), the focus is almost exclusively on the global North.

African Luxury: Aesthetics and Politics emerges from, and begins to fill, these multi-faceted gaps. With original case studies spanning the continent, from Togo to the former Zaire to Angola, the book moves beyond predominant imaginaries of Africa as a place to be 'saved' or 'aided', as well as more recent, teleological formulations of it as 'rising', to foreground and also historicize different extant forms of the production, consumption and representation of wealth, indulgence and lavishness on the continent, including self-declared luxury brands, services and industries. We know that, however precisely defined, luxury very much matters. It matters in our contemporary global moment of extreme income inequality; in a world in which we speak routinely of not just 'the 1 per cent' but smaller fractions thereof and, conversely, of 'surplus' or 'disposable populations', the many (and rising) on the sharp end of 'neoliberalism's power to define who matters and who doesn't, who lives and who dies' (Giroux 2008: 594). If in even the wealthiest and officially democratic of societies, 'food banks and Ferraris coexist in close proximity' (Armitage and Roberts 2016: 1), luxury becomes a matter demanding close scholarly attention and critique.

As John Armitage and Joanne Roberts (2016: 14) write in their delineation of critical luxury studies as an emergent, interdisciplinary field – one in which we situate this book – luxury is a site of power and of struggle. Luxury, in the first place, is a difficult property to define and fix, being highly relative and contextual. Literally, the word points to the non-essential, to that which is desired rather than strictly necessary, although this boundary between need and want is cleverly blurred by marketers. The tag of luxury assigns considerable symbolic meaning, rendering its referents not only symbols of wealth and status but also of the consumer's personality, taste and ability to access a world of exclusivity and superiority, from the craftsmanship of material goods to rarefied experiences of leisure. At the same time, luxuries are 'things which have power over us'; 'by offering a range of pleasures' they sway and move us (Featherstone 2014: 48). Luxury can serve, then, as a site and method to pose and answer critical questions *about* power. Through luxury we can trace, theorize and, in and across divergent sites, connect the complex political-economic, social, cultural and also subjective workings of global neoliberalist capitalism. Luxury points our attention to the sensory and affective, too, including as newly intensified realms of commodification and economic value (Böhme 2003).

From African and other global southern perspectives, luxury also matters and reveals, because the inequalities that enter necessarily into its meanings and marks centrally include the geopolitical. A key question that arises is the extent to which the very idea of luxury today, as well as the kinds of brands and commodities most associated with it, are wedded to ideas of the 'global', and the 'western' more specifically, such that global luxury economies can be considered new sites and vehicles of cultural imperialism. A cursory observation of elite consumer practices and tastes in key African cities might seem to confirm the cultural imperialism thesis: what we see most typically and visibly construed as luxury includes French champagne, Italian suits and fashion labels, American-style malls, German sports cars, private jets and the like. In recent years, western media outlets have also begun to see and take an interest in African elites and their spectacular consumption, often focusing on their travels to, and lifestyles in, the West – often in a patronizing and scandalous tone. 'The Nigerians have arrived' declares a 2014 article in *Tatler* magazine, for instance, that goes on to detail how much the wealthiest amongst the group in question have been rumoured to spend on champagne in nightclubs (over a million pounds), how many properties they own in the choicest of London neighbourhoods and the like (Jenkins 2014). The British television station Channel 4 followed up two years later with a documentary entitled *Lagos to London: Britain's New Super-Rich.* As discussed in Mehita Iqani's chapter in this book, global firms are also beginning to recognize that there are 'high net worth individuals' on the continent and, thus, luxury customers to be curried there, and markets to be developed and exploited.

The time is thus ripe, we believe, to pose critical questions about what exactly luxury means in and concerning Africa today: what does it consist of? Where does it reside? From where does it originate, and for whom is it available? How is it represented and contested? What are its politics, economics and stylistics? This collection does not pose such questions with a prior or strict definition or demarcation of luxury, in reference to particular brands or types of goods (say, Dior and diamonds). Rather it takes an exploratory approach, concerned precisely with what emerges in the name of luxury in relation to Africa as both a material and imagined place, understanding luxury as ultimately performative and perspectival. All the chapters proceed with notions and cases that variously encompass and emphasize values, signs and promises of 'first-class' quality, desirability and discernment, cultural elitism, expensive price points and scarcity. But in and by broaching and seeking to theorize these things from Africa, we do proceed with a series of political and historicized premises about the mere conjuncture of luxury *and* Africa; namely that the former is not antithetical, foreign or new to the latter.

Methodologically, conceptually and analytically, this starts us beyond taken-for-granted ideas that the West is the source and focus, beginning and end, of high-end, hyper-desirable and expensive material cultures. A central contribution of *African Luxury* (and this not only in relation to our particular continent) is to challenge and retheorize Eurocentric assumptions about what luxury is and how it comes to have value. Attuned instead to the factors of African agency and tastes, markets and histories, we may see and acknowledge unique and innovative processes of commodity production and cultures and forms of consumption on the ground; from the aspirational to the actual, and from the local to the regional and global. 'African luxury', as we call it heuristically, is equal in aesthetic, if not economic and cultural, stature to other formations of luxury, and it plays a constitutive role in the contemporary global luxury economy and its politics.

The Roots and Routes of African Luxury

Luxury, as we have begun to say above, is contrary to neither Africa nor 'Africanness'. Regardless of western or other perceptions, Africa is a place in which luxury is meaningful in more than simply metaphorical and watered-down ways, and in which luxurious commodities, experiences, spaces and practices have long been part of the cultural, moral and physical landscapes. From the intricately hand-woven, wild silk textiles of West Africa to early forms of gold mining and metal-craft in Southern Africa, from the elaborate, bespoke forms of jewellery and adornment across the continent to the monumental architecture of North Africa, Africa is rich in cultural and aesthetic forms of sumptuous materiality. And, as these few examples suggest, this luxury is not only available to, or extracted for, others, whether in the form of export to wealthier parts of the world, or for wealthy visitors to come and experience adventure. It is inherently addressed to and embraced by Africans too.

Precolonial luxury consumption was tied to both royal and charismatic authority, and manifested in and communicated via such indigenous values and materialities as volume or bulk (Boyer 1983), sheen (Douny 2013), exclusivity and cosmopolitanism (Gott 2009). This last value is especially important to underscore because, as remains the case today, luxury in Africa has often been imbricated with the new, foreign and 'exotic', and thus with trade and exchange from near and far; from north, east and west; by sea and by land (Gott 2009; Prestholdt 2007). The transatlantic slave trade, and later European colonial conquest, significantly impacted African cultures and practices of luxury consumption and production. On the one hand, they continued and deepened the integration of the continent into world markets, and with this continued and proliferated the supply of new luxuries on the ground – new fabrics and items of dress, new domestic and cosmetic goods, new alcohols and so on, which, as this indicative list would suggest, were deeply gendered (e.g. see Weinbaum et al. 2008). Access to such things was also increasingly expanded or levelled by the erosional effect of both colonial rule and market forces on customary sumptuary regulations (e.g. Gott 2009; Prestholdt 2007). At the same time, as with other European colonies, those in Africa were reorganized for extraction above all, thus becoming key sources of the raw materials, labourers and repatriated profit that drove modern consumer cultures in colonial metropoles. A key example is cocoa, which has since become a staple good, no longer a rarity, across the world (Leissle 2012, 2018).

Roberta Sassatelli notes that the 'thirst for luxury' (2007: 25) was a key factor in the rise of new retail geographies in European cities during the Industrial Revolution, and that this played a key role in colonial expansion and commerce:

> a large part of the goods which make up the growth in demand of early modernity are precisely [...] non-essential goods [...] in particular spices and drugs, perfumes, dyes, silk and linen, precious stones and then, from the late 16th century onwards, sugar, coffee, tea and cocoa.
>
> (Sassatelli 2007: 21)

Mike Featherstone writes, similarly, that 'European luxury demand was a crucial factor in opening up the Americas' (2014: 50) – for the conquest of the Americas, we would call it. If we consider the 'intimacies of four continents' (Lowe 2015) – the mutually structured and productive linkages between European trade and later colonial forays in the East Indies, China and Africa, settler colonialism in the Americas, the enslavement of Africans and later indenturing of East and South Asians to toil in the 'New World', and the rise of Euro-American modernity – we see that Africa is in fact at the constitutive heart and base of the very concept of 'modern luxury'. It must also be noted that the continent was a source of luxury for others long before the times to which we are referring here: Arab traders were crossing the Sahara in search of gold from the Ancient Kingdom of Ghana as early as the ninth century, for instance (Hilson 2002). Modern luxury has nonetheless become naturalized or 'propertized' as Euro-American through its globalization and due to the exercise of political-economic power acquired through colonial expansion and oppression; and it is on this basis that, in some quarters, Africans' desires or moves to also partake of luxury is considered imitative, derivative and so on.

In this book, we reject notions that Africans' pursuit and acquisition of luxury amounts to cultural mimicry or loss on our side, and western cultural imperialism on the other side. These positions are ahistorical, simplistic and disciplinary. We also seek to complicate related suggestions that where and when Africans partake of luxury or other forms of expensive or sizeable consumption, it boils down to 'conspicuous consumption', a sort of 'showing off', the more so when it is of western-originated goods and signifiers. In the call for papers for a 2014 conference on conspicuous consumption in Africa hosted at the University of Cape Town, the organizers posited that the notion of conspicuous consumption (Veblen 2007) was most relevant for framing 'aspiration, acquisition and conspicuous display' in Africa because:

> There are some striking resemblances between the America of the late nineteenth century that Veblen was writing about, and many parts of Africa today: buoyant economic growth, rampant and loosely regulated accumulation, along with rapid upward mobility in the higher reaches of the society coupled with abiding or deepening poverty and marginality for most, within states doing little to manage or ameliorate the inequalities.
>
> (Posel and Van Wyk 2014)

Beyond disagreeing with a historicist emplotting of the African present, which, amongst other things, implies oppositional stories of 'originals and copies' that we have already problematized, we would continue to insist that, both as practice and logic, extravagant materialism and display are neither new nor imported. The Veblenian concept of conspicuous consumption has also been subjected to critique in itself (Kistner 2015). For present purposes, we will only note that it offers a rather structuralist account of a social imperative to communicate material status above all, and carries more than a whiff of Calvinist judgement about the 'wastefulness' or 'non-industry' of the whole affair.

Historical, anthropological and political science literatures on Africa offer a range of alternative and/or complementary conceptual frames to situate what it is that Africans are doing when they expend extravagantly. Scholars of Yoruba culture, for instance, have noted that within the culture there is an imperative to not only accumulate money or disburse it in ways that might look industrious to a capitalist eye. There is also an imperative to *spend* money including, quite centrally, by way of hosting others and distributing gifts (e.g. Bascom 1951; Boyer 1983). The moral Yoruba subject:

> must spend money on his [*sic*] house and on his clothes so that he can be well dressed. He must spend money on entertaining at the time of his annual religious ceremony, contribute generously to the ceremonies and funerals of his close relatives by birth and marriage, and entertain his guests and the members of his club in a manner befitting his means. A principal rule of Yoruba hospitality is that a man must offer food and drink to anyone who comes to visit him.
>
> (Bascom 1951: 496)

Suzanne Gott writes of the importance of feminine fashionability in the traditional Asante cultural practice of *poatwa,* or 'sumptuary competitive display' (Gott 2009: 147). While it is certainly a sign or display of class status, it is also one of feminine maturity, respectability, initiative and discernment; in short, a sign that one is a 'big woman'. And it is *expected*: 'It is generally said that a woman who fails to wear a sufficient number of good-quality African-print ensembles or who wears only the cheaper grades of African-print cloth will be "laughed at," or ridiculed' (Gott 2009: 158). Amongst other things, this demands that women accumulate textiles and, as many other scholars have also noted of other West African contexts – including M. Amah Edoh in her chapter in this book – this accumulation becomes a form and source of feminine wealth. It is not just consumption, but also investment: accumulated luxury textiles represent a form of durable wealth that can be passed on to future generations.

Much more than the figure of the big woman is, of course, the 'big man' that has been discussed and theorized extensively in Africanist scholarship, most notably for his exercise and consolidation of political power through material splendour, display and patronage (Bayart 1993; Mbembe 2001). Achille Mbembe has argued that, in the African 'postcolony', the display of power:

> must be extravagant, since it has to feed not only itself but also its clientele; it must furnish public proof of its prestige and glory by a sumptuous (yet burdensome) presentation of its symbols of status, displaying the heights of luxury in dress and lifestyle, turning prodigal acts of generosity into grand theatre.
>
> (Mbembe 2001: 109)

According to Mbembe, this aesthetic of power, or indeed domination, very much includes waste. To this, Jonathan Cane's contribution to the book on the palatial gardens of 'big men', like Mobutu Sese Seko, adds the complex case of 'ruination'.

That an aesthetic and even rationality of waste may be part of luxury consumption and display in Africa is different from the moralized position that we touched upon above in reference to Veblen – that luxury is by definition wasteful, obscene and so on. As we see it, this kind of view may have a particular readiness and charge when it comes to Africa *because* it is Africa: because of the overwhelming poverty there, but also because of equally ready assumptions that, where there *is* wealth, it must be a product of corruption. In her contribution to the book, Claudia Gastrow shows how such suspicions complicate local perceptions of luxury housing estates in Luanda. Questionable and outright illegal sources of wealth in Africa must be critiqued unreservedly. Our point of caution here is that it should not be immediately assumed that corruption is the cause when Africans have, acquire or flaunt wealth, and that scholarly critiques should not begin or end with moralisms, including judgements of good and bad taste.

In Africa as much as elsewhere, luxury *does things*: it forges subjectivities, as shown by Alexia Smit's chapter on the role of luxury in televised romance discourses, and builds communities, as shown by Pamila Gupta's chapter on the makers and consumers of Marigold necklaces; it produces spaces, as shown by Jonathan Cane's chapter on the design and ruination of elite luxury gardens; it shapes and defines cultural practices, as explored in M. Amah Edoh's chapter on the marketing of Vlisco wax cloth; and it mediates social positions, as shown in Ndapwa Alweendo and Simidele Dosekun's chapter on the narratives of success shared by black women luxury shoppers. What, how and for whom luxury operates are the kinds of questions that concern us in this collection, not whether luxury in Africa is good or bad, if Africans have the mere right to it or what the moral character of those amongst us who indulge in luxury may be. Seeing luxury as just one of the many sites and practices through which African identities, materialities and signs are made, communicated and contested, our aim in this book is to provide rich and theorized accounts of its textures and effects. This calls for an interdisciplinary approach. Just as consumption is not mere sociological fact, so too is luxury more than simply an agglomeration of economic and political factors. It is also about beauty, pleasure, craft and style. Our particular focus in this book is on the politics and aesthetics of African luxury.

The Discourses, Practices and Spaces of African Luxury

African Luxury brings together nine chapters from a wide variety of disciplinary perspectives including anthropology, cultural geography, media studies and cultural history, and from diverse areas of the continent, as we have already noted. Grouped into three closely interconnected sections, across which the core analytic insights resonate and build, these chapters advance a discussion about mediated, especially visual, representations of luxury in or for Africa; the diverse material practices and forms of labour that shape and constitute it, from gardening to brand management to craft; and the spaces in which African luxury is located and performed.

Under the rubric of 'Africa Risen', the first section of the book brings together three chapters that concern both external and internal visions and projections of what Africans' luxury consumption does, will or could look like. Africa is the 'new frontier' for luxury marketing and brands – indeed the final one, according to the corporate briefs and reports of leading global consulting firms such as KPMG and Bain & Company that Mehita Iqani critically analyses. She shows that, while speaking of Africa in terms of the new, these reports recycle old western visions of it as a largely undifferentiated place to be conquered or penetrated for profit, and where desires for western brands can be presumed. Hlonipha Mokoena offers what she calls a retrogressive reading of a 2001 advertising campaign in South Africa by the denim brand Diesel, which depicts an Africa now topmost in the world, an Africa that extends charity to the West while its citizens luxuriate in hedonistic lifestyles. While seemingly 'Afro-optimist', the advertising campaign continues colonial negations of the historical wealth of Africa, Mokoena argues, including in its implicit suggestions that Africans do not know what to do (read: tastefully) with our 'new money'. Luxury is seen to be more 'aspirational' than 'achieved' in the case study that Alexia Smit presents of the South African reality television show, *Date My Family*. Nonetheless, the politics of 'good taste' versus 'excess', 'realness' versus 'fakeness', also come to the fore. Smit shows how the democratic/democratizing promise of love and romance is interwoven with that of luxury commodities on the show, and thereby (re)confirmed as tempered and bounded by class and the 'world of things', in practice. To put it quite simply, if love looks like a Mercedes Benz, not just anyone need apply.

The chapters in Section 2, '(Re)Crafting African Style', present three sets of diverse cases, sites and agents engaged in multifarious forms of labour and value-creation to render 'African things' luxurious. Based on fieldwork in Holland and Togo, M. Amah Edoh offers an ethnographic account of how Dutch company Vlisco has recently sought to rebrand and reposition its wax prints, so long tailored to West African consumers and tastes that they are known widely as 'African prints', as a global luxury product. She argues that the cloth's sedimented value derives from the longstanding investments by the very women whom the rebranding now moves to eclipse because they are 'too African' and they do not have the desired look for 'the global', much less the globally luxurious. By contrast, what does not fit the bill at Alára, a new luxury store in Lagos, is that which looks too '*un*African'. Reading and feeling her way through the store's highly aestheticized and atmospheric Instagram account, Simidele Dosekun argues that Alára stages itself as a kind of playground for the most moneyed and mobile of African elites to find the world of luxury at home, including via a certain re-enchantment of African arts and crafts. Luxury as 'return to craft' but not necessarily heritage – a key distinction – is the theme that Pamila Gupta takes up in a ruminatory ethnographic account that moves between Bulawayo and Johannesburg as, respectively, the fields of production and consumption of a line of bespoke beaded necklaces 'akin to ribbons of silk'. Reflecting upon the sensorial, affective and intersubjective value of the necklaces for women at both sites, Gupta offers a hopeful reading of them as surfacing new forms of African feminine self-making, empowerment and community.

The final section, 'Ambiguous Luxury Spaces', addresses the spatial manifestations and power dynamics of luxury in Africa. Ndapwa Alweendo and Simidele Dosekun consider the meanings of the exclusive Johannesburg store, Luminance, for black South African women.

They argue that such women's ability to buy into luxury, a post-apartheid ability, is thoroughly political even as it is not transformative or radical. Hence, they propose a conceptualization of the store as a 'crooked space' in the sense of a structurally skewed discursive, moral and material site in and through which a new black South African femininity is being fashioned. Exploring the divergent built landscapes of Luanda, Claudia Gastrow contrasts alternately aspirational and suspicious popular visions of the city's exclusive luxury estates with the realities of disrepair and shoddy infrastructure that lie behind their high walls. Her central argument is that the idea of luxury requires ongoing maintenance, both material and reputational, in contexts of vast socio-economic inequality. The final chapter by Jonathan Cane continues this line of contention that luxury contains within it the seeds of its own decay. Cane explores the ruination of three large-scale, luxurious gardening projects in central and southern Africa. Broaching landscape as process, he shows how these gardens materialize the inherent ambiguity and instability of power and lavish lifestyles in the postcolony.

Aspiration, Style and Friction in Critical African Luxury Studies

Individually and in combination, the nine chapters in this volume make a significant, Africa-centred contribution to the nascent field of critical luxury studies, developing analytical understandings of some of the specificities of African luxury cultures in the current moment, extending and deepening more global understandings of the politics of luxury, and also pointing to new avenues for further research. We would summarize the conceptual contributions of the book as a whole in terms of three intersecting themes: aspiration, style and friction.

Aspiration is key to understanding what consumption practices mean and do in contexts of stark and quite tangible economic inequality, which is a definitive characteristic of all African countries:

> It is the concept of aspiration that links the otherwise binary opposites of wealth and poverty, and that allows practices of consumption, no matter how extravagant or modest, to be theorized as part of a broader picture of humanist impulses for life to be better for individuals and their loved ones.
>
> (Iqani 2016: 47)

This book shows how luxury plays into various forms of aspiration. Most obviously, there exist desires for expensive, beautiful and exclusive commodities, experiences and spaces amongst African consumers, some of whom cannot necessarily afford them, or could not in the recent past. This is particularly evidenced in this volume in the chapter by Smit, in which desires for luxury lifestyles are integrated into dreams for romance; in Gastrow's chapter, where ordinary Angolans are prevented from even glimpsing how the privileged few live;

and in the contribution by Alweendo and Dosekun, where women narrate their desires for high-end branded goods, indeed what they deem their right to these things, as part of their experience of political, economic and subjective transformation.

What these and other chapters show is that – as contemporarily (re)produced by and, largely, in service to global capitalism and consumerism, but also as a deeply historicized and localized cultural and aesthetic formation – luxury is a crucial site through which the psycho-social processes of desiring, dreaming and (self-)imagining occur and are expressed. The chapters also push us to consider aspiration as not merely the junction between material possession and lack but also as mediating both social and subjective experiences of inclusion, belonging and citizenship. In turn, this broadens our critical view of what it means when aspirations to luxury are denied, or moralized, or editorialized by others – more powerful others, typically. If luxury looks like a quite brute denial of citizenship and material rights for most in Gastrow's chapter, other chapters in the collection show how similar logics are also in play in more representational and ideational realms. In the chapters by Iqani, Mokoena and Edoh, for instance, what we see is that even when Africans are being represented and interpellated as partakers of luxury – the terms of our inclusion and belonging may remain qualified, and a western supremacist narrative of African aspiration as a step in the road to 'development' may be reinscribed. Alweendo and Dosekun's chapter shows how this also happens at more local levels, in this case intersecting with gendered visions about who should remain where, in what place.

The case studies in the book complicate easy assumptions that where it is that Africans aspire to arrive is 'western-ness'. Likewise the book presents material that differs from views of 'lower-income consumers' as mainly interested in 'higher-status luxury objects to increase their perceived social status in the eyes of others' (Mazzocco et al. 2012: 520). In Africa, luxury might look like Gucci and Prada, but also like a favoured television show, a patiently hand-loomed necklace or a treasured length of wax print. As such, a central contribution of the book is to force us to rethink how we define and delimit luxury itself, and on whose terms. More research is required on the practices, values and priorities of African consumers, and how they define what luxury is and is not, in dialogue with or in resistance to what is being marketed and otherwise presented as such by external actors, local brands and local elites (the latter being considerations that call for further enquiry in their own right).

The book shows that the modality of aspiration to and inclusion in the global style is central to understanding how luxury is produced, plays out and signifies in contemporary African contexts. Style is without doubt central to many African cultures, which maintain detailed and sophisticated aesthetic sensibilities. But what the book also shows is that this style cannot be conceptualized adequately through simple, oppositional dichotomies of local/global, vernacular/imported, African/western, but rather needs to be framed within complex and historicized frameworks of transnationalism, hybridity and heritage or tradition, and closely contextualized notions of beauty, prestige and value. The chapters by Dosekun and Gupta each show how considered, embodied and agentic forms of stylization, crafting, curating and also investing in luxury take place in African contexts. Conversely, Edoh's chapter suggests how much can be lost in translation when European marketing executives try to impose an external definition and vision of luxury onto existing cultures and logics of accumulation and self-styling. These chapters and others point toward a crucial research trajectory that considers Africa as a contemporary source of luxury consumer cultures, items and tastes – not simply their destination – and that asks to what extent this is bound up with, but in some ways also exceeds or escapes, the dominant dictates and directional flows of global capital.

Finally, the chapters in this book also open up space for thinking about forms of tension and even disappointment that necessarily attend luxury in African contexts – and more globally, because *inherently*. The experience of luxury consumption, or the creation of a luxury discourse or aesthetic, is never smooth and uncompromised. It always includes some kind of contradiction, which, following Anna Tsing (2012), we find it fruitful to name 'friction' in the sense of the resistance, tension, even jumpiness that accompany the making and coming-into-contact of diverse bodies, trajectories, worlds.[2] The luxury condominium in Luanda may regularly have its water and power cut-off; the luxury car navigating unpaved streets in a South African township is promptly splattered with mud; the strongman is deposed and his palatial estates fall into decay and disuse. The frictions necessarily extend to the labour that subtends luxury. From the Bulawayo beading cooperative discussed by Gupta in this book to the workers at Alára invisibilized as players, the labour of luxury in Africa requires more research. In addition to the elite African actors who make luxury their business, who exactly works in luxury spaces? Who crafts, stitches or manufactures the products labelled, and priced, luxurious? How much of these employment practices are rooted in African contexts, and how and where do they stretch beyond these places?

How aspiration, style and friction continue to play out in the makings and meanings of luxury in Africa, the global south and beyond should remain on the agenda for future critical inquiry. This book shows that African luxury is multi-faceted, locally constructed as well as globally influenced, and that it ties into numerous political, cultural, economic and social structures and flows endemic to African cities, cultures and political sensibilities. Far from being mimetic of western styles and cultures, as writers fixated on the 'conspicuousness' of African consumption would have it, luxury in Africa speaks to deeply dignified histories of style, wealth and beauty, expert craftsmanship and worldly, aspirational forms of material culture, as well as the politics of how luxury often fails to live up to its promises. Just as it does elsewhere on the globe, in African contexts luxury shapes spaces, discourses and practices in ways both linked to and separate from historic inequalities. As the field of critical luxury studies evolves, it will be crucial to find a balance between recognizing the uniquely African factors and conditions that help us to understand luxury in ever more complex ways, and identifying the resonances and qualities of luxury that cross borders, temporalities and subjectivities in increasingly similar ways. This book aims to – and, we believe, succeeds in – putting Africa on the luxury map in a way that recognizes these complexities. It also sounds the call for opening up progressive and exciting new research agendas concerned with the meanings and importance of African iterations of wealth, elite consumption, design, style and taste.

References

Armitage, John and Roberts, Joanne (eds) (2016), *Critical Luxury Studies: Art, Design, Media*, Edinburgh: Edinburgh University Press.

Arvidsson, Adam and Niessen, Bertram (2015), 'Creative mass: Consumption, creativity and innovation on Bangkok's fashion markets', *Consumption Markets & Culture*, 18:2, pp. 111–32.

Bascom, William (1951), 'Social status, wealth and individual differences among the Yoruba', *American Anthropologist*, 53:4, pp. 490–505.

Bayart, Jean-Francois (1993), *The State in Africa: The Politics of the Belly*, London: Longman.

Böhme, Germot (2003), 'Contribution to the critique of the aesthetic economy', *Thesis Eleven*, 73:1, pp. 71–82.

Boyer, Ruth (1983), 'Yoruba cloths with regal names', *African Arts*, 16:2, pp. 42–98.

Brosius, Christiane (2012), *India's Middle Class: New Forms of Urban Leisure, Consumption and Prosperity*, London: Routledge.

Cavender, Raye Carole and Kincade, Doris (2014), 'Management of a luxury brand: Dimensions and sub-variables from a case study of LVMH', *Journal of Fashion Marketing and Management*, 18:2, pp. 231–48.

Demmer, Craig (2007), 'Grief is a luxury: Aids-related loss among the poor in South Africa', *Illness, Crisis & Loss*, 15:1, pp. 39–51.

Dosekun, Simidele (2020), *Fashioning Postfeminism: Spectacular Femininity and Transnational Culture*, Champaign, IL: University of Illinois Press.

Douny, Laurence (2013), 'Wild silk textiles of the Dogon of Mali: The production, material efficacy, and cultural significance of sheen', *TEXTILE*, 11:1, pp. 58–77.

Dubois, Bernard and Duquesne, Patrick (1993), 'The market for luxury goods: Income versus culture', *European Journal of Marketing*, 27:1, pp. 35–44.

Featherstone, Mike (2014), 'Luxury, consumer culture and sumptuary dynamics', *Luxury*, 1:1, pp. 47–69.

Fernandes, Leela (2006), *India's New Middle Class: Democratic Politics in an Era of Economic Reform*, Minneapolis: University of Minnesota Press.

Giroux, Henry (2008), 'Beyond the biopolitics of disposability: Rethinking neoliberalism in the New Gilded Age', *Social Identities: Journal for the Study of Race, Nation & Culture*, 14:5, pp. 587–620.

Gott, Suzanne (2009), 'Asante hightimers and the fashionable display of women's wealth in contemporary Ghana', *Fashion Theory*, 13:2, pp. 141–76.

Hilson, Gavin (2002), 'Harvesting mineral riches: 1000 years of gold mining in Ghana', *Resources Policy*, 28:1, pp. 13–26.

Howell, Simon and Vincent, Louise (2014), '"Licking the snake": The i'khothane and contemporary township youth identities in South Africa', *South African Review of Sociology*, 45:2, pp. 60–77.

Huigen, Brandaan (2017), 'Cadres and compatriots: An analysis of their good lives as presented by *Top Billing*', *Anthropology Southern Africa*, 40:3, pp. 172–84.

Iqani, Mehita (2015), 'The consummate material girl?', *Feminist Media Studies*, 15:5, pp. 779–93.

—— (2016), *Consumption, Media and the Global South: Aspiration Contested*, London: Palgrave Macmillan.

Jenkins, David (2014), 'The Nigerians have arrived', *Tatler*, 24 November, http://www.tatler.com/article/the-nigerians-have-arrived. Accessed 29 January 2018.

Kapferer, Jean-Noel and Bastien, Vincent (2012), *The Luxury Strategy: Break the Rules of Marketing to Build Luxury Brands*, London: Kogan Page Publishers.

Kistner, Ulrike (2015), 'Trading in freedom: Rethinking conspicuous consumption in post-apartheid political economy', *Critical Arts*, 29:2, pp. 240–59.

Lange, Hellmuth and Meier, Lars (eds) (2009), *The New Middle Classes: Globalizing Lifestyles, Consumerism and Environmental Concern*, London: Springer.

Leissle, Kristy (2012), 'Cosmopolitan cocoa farmers: Refashioning Africa in Divine chocolate advertisements', *Journal of African Cultural Studies*, 24:2, pp. 121–39.

—— (2018), *Cocoa*, Cambridge, MA: Polity Press.

Lowe, Lisa (2015), *The Intimacies of Four Continents*, Durham, NC: Duke University Press.

Mazzocco, Phillip, Rucker, Derek, Galinsky, Adam and Anderson, Eric (2012), 'Direct and vicarious conspicuous consumption: Identification with low-status groups increases the desire for high-status goods', *Journal of Consumer Psychology*, 22:4, pp. 520–28.

Mbembe, Achille (2001), *On the Postcolony*, Berkeley, CA: University of California Press.

Posel, Deborah and Van Wyk, Ilana (2014), *Conspicuous Consumption in Africa*, call for papers.

Prestholdt, Jeremy (2007), *Domesticating the World: African Consumerism and the Genealogies of Globalization*, Berkeley, CA: University of California Press.

Robertson, Brian, Omigbodun, Olayinka and Gaddour, Naoufel (2010), 'Child and adolescent psychiatry in Africa: Luxury or necessity? Guest editorial', *African Journal of Psychiatry*, 13:5, pp. 329–31.

Sassatelli, Roberta (2007), *Consumer Culture: History, Theory and Politics*, London: Sage.

Southall, Roger (2016), *The New Black Middle Class in South Africa*, Martlesham: Boydell & Brewer.

Truong, Yann, Simmons, Geoff, McColl, Rodd and Kitchen, Philip (2008), 'Status and conspicuousness – are they related? Strategic marketing implications for luxury brands', *Journal of Strategic Marketing*, 16:3, pp. 189–203.

Upadhya, Carol (2009), 'India's "new middle class" and the globalizing city: Software professionals in Bangalore, India', in H. Lange and L. Meier (eds), *The New Middle Classes: Globalizing Lifestyles, Consumerism and Environmental Concern*, Dordrecht: Springer, pp. 253–68, http://link.springer.com/chapter/10.1007/978-1-4020-9938-0_14. Accessed 10 December 2013.

Veblen, Thorstein (2007), *The Theory of the Leisure Class*, Oxford: Oxford University Press.

Wattanasuwan, Kritsadarat (1999), 'It isn't just for image: The lived meaning of luxury-brand consumption among wealthy Thai teenagers', *Thammasat Review*, 4:1, pp. 22–58.

Zhang, Yaoqi, Deng, Jinyang, Majumdar, Suman and Zheng, Bin (2009), 'Globalization of lifestyle: Golfing in China', in H. Lange and L. Meier (eds), *The New Middle Classes: Globalizing Lifestyles, Consumerism and Environmental Concern*, Dordrecht: Springer, pp. 143–58.

Note

1 Although many scholars capitalize the term as 'Global South', we prefer to think of the global south as an experimental and exploratory term rather than a paradigm-defining one, and as such we leave it uncapitalized.
2 Tsing's (2012) conceptualization of friction is in reference to globalization specifically, and articulated against the globalization theorists who claimed that the world was smoothly and seamlessly coming together as one.

Section 1

Africa Risen

Chapter 1

The Last Luxury Frontier? How Global Consulting Firms Discursively Construct the African Market

Mehita Iqani

Introduction

In line with neoliberal discourses championing the expansion of the global economic system around the world, in the past decade the narrative of Africa 'rising' (Mahajan 2011; Taylor 2014a, 2014b) has become a familiar trope in media coverage about the continent. Although a significant amount of consideration remains focused on the vast natural resources that non-African powers covet, increasingly more attention is being paid to the growth of consumer markets on the continent. This chapter contributes to a broader project of critically exploring how so-called 'new' luxury consumer markets in Africa are considered by the (still largely) western political-economy that drives global consumer capitalism. It does so by considering how the market for luxury goods in Africa has been explored and spoken about by actors who specialize in advising global consumer firms in how to access it. In the past several years, a number of reports and commentaries have been produced by consulting firms, including large global firms like KPMG, Bloomberg, Bain & Company and Deloitte as well as boutique agencies such as Africa Wealth Report, which in one way or another speak to the economic potential of the market for luxury goods in Africa.

Taking reports and briefings produced by these actors as the basis for analysis, this chapter sketches out the main ideological positions that are presented in the material, and puts those into critical context by theorizing what they mean in relation to the aesthetics and politics of luxury in African contexts in the current moment. This chapter is structured as follows. First, a brief discussion of how African consumer markets have been studied is offered in order to provide scholarly context for the study undertaken. Next, the analytical approach taken is discussed. Then, a thematic discussion of the content of the corporate reports on the African luxury market is provided. Finally, and in conclusion, this material is theorized in order to show how the discursive construction of the African luxury consumer market ties in to bigger questions about the operations of global neoliberal culture.

Regarding Consumer Markets in Africa: The Place of Luxury

Some historical writings have shown that precolonial Africa was not a place of poverty at all, but one in which wealth of various types was accumulated and shared in diverse ways

(Gott 2009; Diop 1988; Guyer 1993, 1995). It is worth considering as a starting point that before the brutality of colonial occupation, there were many forms of luxury that were produced, traded and enjoyed by Africans in many cultures, for example Kente cloth in the Asante region of West Africa, which remains a valuable item collected by enthusiasts around the world (Asamoah-Yaw and Safo-Kantanka 2017). Colonial powers did to an extent fetishistically admire the luxurious lifestyles of the precolonial elites, such as the Rajahs in India (Shome 2014: 110); and the collection of African objects in the museums of Europe bears testimony to the fetishistic desire exercised by colonial explorers. It is, however, impossible to consider how contemporary consumer markets in Africa are regarded without taking into account the deeply traumatic and damaging legacy of colonialism. Initially, as the continent was occupied and its raw materials and resources plundered by western powers, African peoples were seen both as sources of slave and cheap labour and as potential consumers of the many products being manufactured to serve western markets. Furthermore, the production and consumption of luxury commodities did not utterly exclude Africa. In fact, as Roberta Sassatelli (2007) has convincingly shown, it was precisely the demand for luxury items in Europe that served as the engine for modernization, and in turn it was imperial expansion that drove the production and consumption of luxury items worldwide: 'the consumption of luxury goods contributed to the accumulation of capital which constituted one of the material prerequisites for the development of modern industry' (Sassatelli 2007: 21). Luxury, therefore, played a critical role in spurring on global capitalism as we recognize it today. Historically situated as sites from which various luxury commodities voraciously desired in the metropole like sugar, tea, indigo and spices were extracted, colonies also became markets for goods manufactured in the West. Although racist laws and exclusionary economics often prevented indigenous peoples from accessing the pleasures provided by luxury goods, colonial settlers enjoyed 'lifestyles [...] full of luxury, associated with excessive food, drinks and adventurous explorations of the colony, a standard of living which would be quite impossible in Britain' (Hussein 2010: 410). While settlers enjoyed better lives than they could have at home, and as colonial powers entrenched their control over African territories, new missionary tactics were employed to turn African subjects into good consumers as part of a civilizing mission that included marketing low-cost commodities like soap to local consumers (Burke 1992, 1996; McClintock 2013).

In the postcolonial context, as political and economic strategies were put into place by new governments to address the legacy of colonial oppression, wealth became more accessible to Africans, and along with the growth in economic opportunity came new consumer desires, which played out differently in different contexts. For example, Kenya saw an urban pleasure-culture emerge (Spronk 2012) and South Africa saw a shift in residence from townships to suburbs (Ballard 2010). A growing literature about so-called 'new middle-classes' in Africa (and the global south more broadly) highlights the role of consumption and consumer identities (James 2014; Southall 2016; Melber 2016; Li 2010; Scrase and Scrase 2008). In some contexts, an affiliation towards 'luxury' items such as automobiles, televisions and refrigerators (items, by the way, that are considered unremarkable to consume in the West) is considered one indicator of middle-class status. In South Africa, the corporate interest in these 'new' black middle-classes (Iqani 2015a, 2015b) led to the construction of a new identity-category for black consumers: 'black diamonds' (Krige 2011) as coined by the University of Cape Town's Unilever Institute, a marketing research think tank.[1] As democracy dawned in South Africa, key players in the local magazine industry reportedly approached global luxury brands to encourage them to enter the local market so that there would be wider pool of advertisers to draw on for the booming glossy magazine market (Viljoen 2008: 338).

Recent writings have explored luxury markets around the world, particularly in the global south (Atwal and Bryson 2014; Atwal and Jain 2012; Cui et al. 2015; Wattanasuwan 1999). But little has been written about the luxury market in Africa, aside from minimal interventions focusing on South Africa's 'appetite' for luxury goods (Crosswaite 2014). Some marketing professionals write of the 'discovery' of the African consumer market with enthusiasm and a sense of excitement at learning that Africans, too, are ordinary people with perfectly normal hopes and expectations for material expressions of their lives and relationships. For example, the introduction to a book, written by a global marketing professional, aimed at motivating corporate actors to expand their global marketing plans to include the continent of Africa observes:

There will soon be a billion consumers on the continent of Africa, and this is one of the fastest growing markets in the world. Every day, they need to eat. They need shelter. They want education for their children. They would like to have soaps to wash their clothes. They desire cell phones, metal roofs for their homes, televisions, music, computers, movies, bicycles, cosmetics, medicines, cars and loans to start businesses. They celebrate marriages, births, and religious holidays and commemorate death.

(Mahajan 2011: xi)

Of course, those working in marketing are caught up within western structures of power, in which Africa and Africans are typically stereotyped. Although much has been written about how advertising and marketing play out globally, most of it from a managerialist perspective; only a little has been written about how marketing *to* African consumers takes place. Two marketing studies intervene in this major gap in the literature to attempt to map out the challenges and opportunities for marketing to sub-Saharan African consumers (Nwankwo 2000; Gbadamosi 2013), and another examines the plots in television adverts in Nigeria and South Africa (Oyedele and Minor 2012). Extending this is some critical work that considers what the main discourses and ideologies are that are preferred in promotional cultures in Africa. Unsurprisingly, colonial tropes and narratives about Africa are dominant in western commercial and advertising discourses, and the typical western consumer's imagination (Bonsu 2009; Ramamurthy 2003; Keim and Somerville 2017; Lutz and Collins 1993; McClintock 2013; Burke 1996). Although critical work on southern and African consumer cultures is growing (Iqani 2016; Howes 2002; Sinclair and Pertierra 2012; Newell 2012; Spronk 2012; Dosekun 2019), still missing are critical perspectives on the operations of marketing industries in Africa.

It is crucial that alongside proliferating managerialist accounts of the growth in African consumer markets, nuanced critiques of the links between global neoliberal power and African contexts are also developed. It is to this latter project that the remainder of this chapter aims to contribute. How do current key players in the global luxury industry regard Africa as a market for luxury goods?

Thematic Analysis of Consulting Firm Reports: Notes on Methodology

Consulting firms provide advice to organizations, not only but often those that are profit-oriented, for a fee. As such, they make their income by advising businesses in how to do business. In order to win contracts to provide this advice, the consulting firms need to come across as knowledgeable in key areas. This is achieved by producing briefings on what they consider to be key topics and areas, which are made publically available on the consulting firms' public online platforms. These documents are often put together by junior staff from publically available information, with the aim of winning the consulting firm consulting contracts from new clients. This study performed a thematic analysis of 23 such documents about the global or African luxury market produced by global consulting firms, including KPMG, Bain & Co, Bloomberg and Deloitte, which are some of the main players in the global consulting industry. The texts analysed are summarized in Table 1, and when quoted from in this paper are referred to by the document number noted in the first column.

These documents were located through exhaustive Internet searches. Most of these documents focus on Africa specifically, but a few of them look at the global luxury market and include some relevant commentary about Africa, and as such were included in the corpus for analysis. It should be noted that this list of documents is by no means exhaustive, but it is indicative of the majority of items that were publically available at the time of writing. It should also be noted that some relevant reports or briefings were not freely available (for example a few authored by Euromonitor that were protected by a £800 pay wall), and as such were not included in the material analysed in this study.

The reports were analysed by looking for cross-cutting themes to the ways in which the African luxury market was written about. These are presented in some descriptive detail first. Thereafter the political aspects to how the African luxury market is constructed by western economic power are explored. Note that not all of the 23 documents are quoted in the discussion that follows, but they are included in Table 1 to illustrate the breadth of the corpus analysed, and in which similar themes and discourses come up throughout.

Four key themes are evident, which deal with a homogenized market, individualized wealth, narratives of frontierism and an equation of luxury with the West.

Table 1: Consulting firm reports analysed in the study.

	Report Title	Produced By	Date	Length
1	*2012 Luxury Goods Worldwide Market Study*	Bain & Company	15 October 2012	47 pages
2	*Sizing Up Luxury Goods Opportunity in Africa's Frontier Markets*	Euromonitor	4 September 2012	3 pages
3	*Beyond China: Luxury Brands in Africa*	Euromonitor	4 March 2013	3 pages
4	*Luxury Goods Worldwide Market Study Spring 2013*	Bain & Company	16 May 2013	2 pages
5	*Luxury Goods Worldwide Market Study Fall 2013 Press Release*	Bain & Company	28 October 2013	1 page
6	*Luxury Goods Worldwide Market Study Fall 2013*	Bain & Company	October 2013	46 pages
7	*The State of the Luxury Market*	Euromonitor	October 2013	6 pages
8	*Sector Report: Luxury Goods in Africa*	KPMG	2014	16 pages
9	*Luxury Brands Turn to Africa as the Next Growth Frontier – Deloitte*	Deloitte	16 July 2014	2 pages
10	*African Wealth Briefing Vol. 1*	Africa Wealth Report	December 2014	36 pages
11	*Global Power of Luxury Goods: In the Hands of the Consumer*	Deloitte	2014	36 pages
12	*African Wealth Briefing Vol. 2*	Africa Wealth Report	March 2015	56 pages
13	*Untapped Africa Growth Potential Attracts Luxury Goods*	Bloomberg Professional Services	11 May 2015	6 pages
14	*UHNW in Africa Challenges and Opportunities*	Africa Wealth Report	21 May 2015	9 pages
15	*Global Power of Luxury Goods: Engaging the Future Luxury Consumer*	Deloitte	2015	52 pages
16	*Africa Luxury Goods Market: Full of Untapped Promise*	Bloomberg Professional Services	5 November 2015	2 pages
17	*African Wealth Briefing Vol. 4: Special Summit Edition*	Africa Wealth Report	January 2016	56 pages
18	*Global Power of Luxury Goods: Disciplined Innovation*	Deloitte	2016	54 pages
19	*Altagamma Worldwide Luxury Market Monitor*	Bain & Company	20 October 2016	53 pages
20	*Luxury Goods and Wealth Management in Africa*	KPMG	November 2016	56 pages
21	*Luxury Goods Worldwide Market Study, Fall-Winter 2016*	Bain & Company	28 December 2016	13 pages
22	*Luxury Goods and Wealth Management in Africa*	KPMG Blog	November 2016	3 pages
23	*Global Power of Luxury Goods: The New Luxury Consumer*	Deloitte	2017	52 pages

Mapping Corporate Discourse on the African Luxury Market

A number of similar themes came up across the corpus of texts analysed. Interestingly, consulting firm reports often reference one another as sources for their own statements, so there is a clear sense that the authors of the reports are acutely aware of one another's work and need to keep up with 'trendy' topics in business, and legitimize the arguments and statistics that they offer not by referencing peer-reviewed scholarship or other in-depth research but by noting that their peers in the industry have similar opinions. It is therefore important, at the outset, to note that the material being dealt with here is not being treated as a factual reflection of reality, but a set of representations, which, through their communicative labour, socially construct certain ideas as fact.

'Should we look at it as one market?'

Titled with this provocative question repeated as the heading for this sub-section, the discussion that follows, from Document 14, about whether the African market should be homogenized tries to argue that it should not be.

> Africa cannot be looked at as a single market, a common mistake made by a large number of international banks and financial institutions looking to benefit from the wealth creation that is taking place across the continent. The origin of the accumulated private wealth, the distribution of this wealth and the economic and political climates, vary from country to country. Additionally the ethnic and cultural diversity present within individual countries mean that having a strong understanding of the specificities of each market is crucial to doing business on the continent.
>
> (Doc 14: 2)

Ironically, throughout the discussion about how the African luxury market should not be homogenized, the author refers only to 'Africa' and never to any of the discrete names or politics of different African countries or local ethnic or cultural contexts. The tendency to speak of the African luxury market as a single entity was common across all the documents analysed. This is a common practice in colonial discourses about Africa in general, which treat it as a single place and often show little to no knowledge of the political, linguistic, religious and cultural diversity, homogenizing it as a 'dark continent' (Jarosz 1992). Although the reports sometimes demonstrated knowledge of particular national economies, Africa was typically lumped into one single entity: 'Among the more promising markets are Colombia, Mexico, Philippines, and much of sub-Saharan Africa' (Doc 6: 7). South Africa, Nigeria, Morocco, Angola and Cote d'Ivoire are mentioned by name to varying degrees, but the rest of the continent seems to be subsumed into the socio-economic patterns of the big players.

> As African wealth rises, luxury goods makers may target openings beyond Morocco and South Africa, which account for 86% of Africa's directly-operated luxury stores.
>
> (Doc 16: 1)

In Document 1, for example, only South Africa is mentioned as a 'new emerging market' with 'plenty of untapped potential' alongside Brazil, India and South East Asia, but the report then goes on to make several claims about 'African' markets, 'African' wealth and 'African' countries (19).

Celebrating the African UHNWI

A central figure in corporate narratives about the luxury market in Africa is the 'ultra-high net worth individual' (UHNWI). These individuals – often gendered as male – are the consumers over whom marketers of luxury items salivate.

> Demand for luxury watches, men's clothing and leather goods in Africa is driven by the higher spending power of men. In South Africa, women have just 60% of the disposable income of men.
>
> (Doc 13: 2)

An UHNWI is a millionaire or billionaire, and the consulting firm reports are unanimous in their praise and admiration for these individuals and their seemingly meteoric rise to wealth. Impressive statistics on the number of UHNWIs are presented (although their precise provenance not made clear):

> In 2011, the number of HNWI in Africa grew by 3.9%, more than twice the rate of growth in Asia. Africa also had the second-highest regional rate of growth after Latin America.
>
> (Doc 9: 13)

> Africa's ultra-high-net-worth individuals may expand 59% from 1,900 by 2024, the most of all regions globally. Ivory Coast tops the regional list, with 119% growth in the richest population predicted by 2024.
>
> (Doc 16: 2)

> Though the necessary data is currently thin on the ground [...] the number of African multimillionaires (those with a wealth of over $30 million) will double in the next ten years.
>
> (Doc 12: 7)

One briefing profiles Nigeria's Aliko Dangote – 'the first African to hit the £25 billion threshold!' – and praises the 'quintessential African business-tycoon' for his diverse interests in a variety of unnamed sectors (Doc 9: 11). In order to explain how these billionaires appeared and will continue to appear, it is explained that a 'combination of rapidly growing economies and youthful populations' and that 'a recent spate of oil and gas discoveries – and the high probability of more to come, for example in Ghana (oil) and in Tanzania (gas) – could provide a get-rich-quick spawning ground for a new generation of high net worth individuals' (Doc 4: 2). The reports are keen to contextualize their claims about African UHNWIs by pointing out that they are still not as numerous as those in Latin America and Asia, but temper this with enthusiasm about their future potential. Although it is also sometimes noted that African UHNWIs are 'un-financially savvy' (Doc 9: 5) and face 'some political hurdles' (Doc 9: 3), they are also respected for 'changing the social, economic and political landscape of this rich continent' (Doc 9: 3) as well as for their purchasing power. UHNWIs are lauded as extremely successful neoliberal subjects, who have a preference for private jet travel to London (Doc 16: 2), and who live in big cities like Lagos, Johannesburg, Cape Town, Nairobi and Marrakesh (Doc 9: 30). Embedded within these statements is an awareness of the increasingly global profile of the high-net worth African consumer, who travels frequently and spends money abroad as well as at home: 'Nigerians are among the top global spenders in the U.K., following only Middle Easterners and the Chinese. [...] Tourism is likely to continue benefitting luxury brand portfolios in the near future' (Doc 6: 10).

> There's a beautiful Yoruba adage that says 'otosi-talika di olowo nla' which in English means 'the rugged poor guy is now a money-bag'. That is the case of today's African wealthy individuals.
>
> (Doc 9: 19)

The African UHNWI – 'Mr Money Bags' – is a stand-in for the luxury consumer market in Africa in general. As implied in the material presented in this section so far, Mr Money Bags is a self-made millionaire, who enjoys the finer things in life and is happy to flaunt his wealth through luxurious consumption.

The Last Luxury Frontier

Although UHNWIs are celebrated, the business consultants caution that the savvy luxury retailer interested in 'smaller markets, such as Kenya, Angola and Morocco, [...] would be wise to look not just at multimillionaires, but further down the consumer hierarchy to find the next frontier fortune' (Doc 12: 8). In other words, the potential of people other than millionaires and billionaires buying luxury items is what could reap the more significant returns for luxury brands interested in Africa in the long term. These 'untapped' markets are referred to as the 'new frontier'.

> Having witnessed the impact that brand-obsessed nouveau-riche have on revenue, luxury brands are always on the lookout for the next frontier. There is really only one last frontier when it comes to luxury: Africa.
>
> (Doc 12: 7)

Africa provides a longer-term growth opportunity for luxury brands. Sub-Saharan Africa is second only to Asia-Pacific in growth of consumer markets […] albeit from a very low base. While the region is still considered 'frontier' and isn't likely to supersede the BRICs soon, it is worth nothing that Nigeria is one of the fastest growing markets for French champagne and digital televisions.

(Doc 6: 9)

[Sub-Saharan African] countries have improved governance, competitive industries, and favourable demographics. They should experience strong economic growth in the coming decade. As business develops in these countries, the number of upper income households will rise quickly, thus contributing to growth of the luxury market.

(Doc 6: 7)

Tellingly, African markets are also referred to as 'underpenetrated': limited retail locations from only half of 'Bloomberg Intelligence's luxury peers' suggests that there is scope for more 'penetration' into the African retail environment (Doc 13: 2–3). The reports emphasize how Africa is the last place on earth that does not yet have a formalized luxury consumption sector, unlike Asia and Latin America. It is precisely the absence, they argue, of an established luxury market that should make it appealing for retailers who might be reaching saturation in sales elsewhere: 'As Asian economic growth rates slow, luxury goods companies may accelerate their presence in Africa to capture untapped demand' (Doc 13: 1).

In 2013, investment interest grew further in the Sub-Saharan Africa region, which is set to become a key battleground for the luxury goods industry. Sub-Saharan Africa is experiencing the second-fastest global economic growth – behind Asia-Pacific – and is home to five of the 10 fastest growing economies in the world. This is set to translate into higher incomes and subsequent consumer spending growth. To this end, many African consumers will move into the categories of discretionary spending for the first time, offering significant potential investment returns.

(Doc 7: 2)

The characterization of the African market as an underpenetrated zone, as a new frontier ripe for exploration and profit-accumulation, brings to mind a kind of pioneer attitude underscored by patriarchal and masculinist attitudes, which can be linked to an imperialist ethic. Although no longer able to seek new territories to conquer politically, western power is keen to find new opportunities for economic expansion and profit-making.

Notably, this 'new frontier' is constructed as one that has more future potential than present actuality. Throughout the material analysed, the African luxury market is portrayed as marginal to the global industry. Africa is often only mentioned once or twice in some reports on the global luxury goods market. Often Africa is bundled in with 'rest of world' (e.g. Doc 19: 26) and sometimes it is bundled in with 'emerging markets (e.g. India, Africa,

Central Eurasia)', which 'are finally finding their own way to luxury' (Doc 1: 32). At other times, Africa is conspicuously absent:

> Consumers in emerging markets continue to drive luxury market growth. In China, Russia and the United Arab Emirates, markets that we have categorised as emerging luxury markets, the percentage of consumers claiming to have increased their spending stood at 70 per cent, compared to 53 per cent in the more mature markets (EU, US and Japan).
>
> (Doc 20: 1)

Despite its at-once marginal and frontier status, an optimistic attitude about the potential for selling luxury items to Africans is consistently communicated.

> Africa is increasingly demonstrating its attractiveness as a high-potential region, with 11% growth and expansion into new markets such as Angola and Nigeria beyond its traditional strongholds of Morocco and South Africa.
>
> (Doc 5: 1)

> With China slowing down, Africa is now poised to become one of the fastest growing economies. Luxury sales are still very concentrated in South Africa and Morocco, but brands are starting to expand in new markets (e.g. Angola, Nigeria).
>
> (Doc 6: 19)

The reports highlight that the 'African middle-class' have a predisposition 'to spend proportionally more on luxury items than what would otherwise be expected' (Doc 23: 1). Africa is represented as an exciting new location for luxury sales beyond the cash-splashing of the UHNWI: as a frontier that can be penetrated excitedly by western firms seeking new markets for their commodities. What is quite striking in this is that it is absolutely taken for granted that Africans aspire to own these items.

Luxury Means Western Brands

A striking omission in the documents analysed is any sense that there are goods created within African countries and cities by local artists, designers or craftspeople that could be considered luxuries by African consumers. A strong thematic throughout the material analysed is the assumption that luxury goods are synonymous with western products and brands.

> Nigeria was the second fastest growing market in the world for champagne between 2006 and 2011 [...]. Total consumption reached 752,879 bottles (75 cl) in 2011 (higher than

in Russia or Mexico), and placed Nigeria among the top 20 champagne markets in the world.

(Doc 4: 3)

Take Nigeria for example; the West African nation already has Africa's largest private jet market, champagne consumption and one of its biggest art markets. Luxury brands are also popping up: Ermenegildo Zegna famously set up shop in Lagos in 2013, as did Porsche, while there are already dealerships specializing in Aston Martin, Lamborghini and Rolls Royce (despite the city's infamous gridlocked traffic and potholed roads). Hotel chains, Marriott and Intercontinental are also betting on five-star guests with new hotels opening up across the country.

(Doc 12: 7)

Through partners in Nigeria and Angola, Cartier has seen a rise in sales. Breitling now distributes its watches through wholesalers in Ghana, Algeria and 10 other African countries. Louis Vuitton, Fendi, Gucci, Miu Miu and Prada all have outlets in Casablanca's first luxury mall, while Prada has also recently opened a store in Luanda, Angola. Senegal's new Sea Plaza mall is home to lower-end fashion labels Hugo Boss, Mango and Guess.

(Doc 12: 8)

These extracts reveal precisely how luxury commodities are defined by the business consultants: not as bespoke, handcrafted, artistic, beautiful items in general but as specifically those that are designed in the West, are mass-produced and are branded. From this perspective, the idea of luxury is fundamentally limited and an utterly Eurocentric definition preferred. No space is given to imagining forms of luxury originating in African cultures. Rather, luxury is seen as naturally emanating from the West and imported, like cases of champagne and shipments of sports cars, to African ports. Luxury is made synonymous with western brands and trademarked beverages. This conflation of western and luxury makes sense in terms of the strategic objectives of the consultants writing these briefings: their job is to help their clients, presumably western companies, to sell their wares to African consumers, rather than to suggest that local companies have equal stature or potential in those markets. The result of this discourse, however, is an assumption that the African luxury market is thereby limited to one that has an interest in 'German cars, European perfume and Swiss watches' (Doc 23: 9). Unsurprisingly, therefore, the reports also highlight the importance of brand awareness and loyalty amongst African consumers.

The median African consumer tends to be brand loyal, which provides the first mover with substantial growth potential. Luxury goods brands can, by establishing brand loyalty at an early stage, benefit from the evolution of the African consumer, especially in moving up the value chain.

(Doc 8: 11)

Although unsubstantiated with empirical evidence, the ideas that African consumers immediately conflate western brands with the idea of luxury and are loyal to the brands they prefer are taken for granted throughout the reports. Attention is paid to advising companies on how to achieve brand loyalty:

> Building brand awareness through a well-known local partner in emerging markets is a key to a profitable investment.
>
> (Doc 16: 2)

> It is therefore not a moment too soon to start creating the 'luxury idea' in Africa. Africa has the youngest population of any continent, which are more brand aware than their forbears. Investing in branding will therefore create aspiration for your brand among a growing class of urban and wealthy consumers.
>
> (Doc 12: 8)

The practice of equating western brands with luxury goods and the argument that African consumers are, or should be groomed to become, brand loyal are arguably central to this western vision of the challenges and opportunities offered by the African luxury market.

Offensive or Sympathetic? Navigating the African Luxury Market Discourse

The analysis has made clear that there is a great deal of repetition within and across the reports, alongside an even greater vagueness: the source data is not provided for the statistics offered and often the reports simply reference one another as sources for 'fact'. The factuality and empirical robustness of the reports and briefings is not the question here, however. What is more interesting is to consider how what is both present and absent in the reports paints a picture of the African luxury market, and also what it says about the painters of that picture.

To sum up, corporate consulting firm discourses about the African market for luxury goods are characterized by four key narratives. The first erases diversity within the continent's consumers and homogenizes the African market into a single, definable essence. The second privileges an individualistic narrative of masculine wealth and celebrates a predicted boom in African billionaires. The third pictures the continent as unexplored territory ripe for domination by western corporate adventurers and extols the economic opportunity linked to the growth of African middle classes. The fourth firmly equates the idea of luxury with western brands and suggests that African consumers are enthusiastic and uncritical consumers of those brands. The four themes described in this chapter at once offer new and old versions of western portrayals of Africa and Africans; they simultaneously re-inscribe certain colonial ideas and try to make new arguments about the place that Africa might have at the 'table' of global consumer culture.

It could be argued that the reports contain strands of discourse that are aimed at making strong arguments about how Africa needs to be taken seriously by luxury global brands, and no longer treated like the 'poor cousin' of global consumer culture. This sympathetic view makes an argument for the spending power of the African consumer – both the high-net-worth millionaires and members of the growing middle classes – and can be interpreted as a demand for recognition and respect. Recognizing the interest that African consumers have towards global brands is also important, and validates their desires, aspirations and practices. Claims that Africa represents a huge untapped potential consumer market could be interpreted as paying homage to the increasing stability on the continent and its long-awaited entrance to the global economy as an equal player, as a mass of consumers and not only as a source of resources and exploited labour. Although these interpretations certainly have some validity, it is important to contextualize them within an awareness of the structural conditions within which the reports were produced, as well as the global political-economy that sees African countries still largely marginalized from broad-based economic empowerment. As such, although there is space for recognizing the positive aspects of the celebratory 'Africa Rising' ethic, and it must be recognized that marketing professionals are least likely to take a critical stance on the work that they do, it is important to consider the extent to which the myopic and Eurocentric aspects present in the consulting firm discourse are problematic. A scholarly critique of these problematic aspects may in future feed into more thoughtful representational work by those in the industry. It should be noted that the critique that follows is not of the individual consultants and marketing professionals who authored the reports, but of the systemic discourse produced by the industry. This reveals some important insights about global cultural and geopolitical imbalances and the power of discourse to construct social reality.

A more critical stance would argue that many of the attitudes evident within the material could be considered offensive. The discourse of Africa as the new frontier of luxury consumption can be seen as problematic, in that it echoes colonial attitudes to Africa as a place that could be conquered and plundered for wealth destined to return to the West. Instead of raw materials and minerals, the 'natural' resource now being coveted by western economic powers is the buying power of African consumers, thus ushering a new age of economic exploitation. Producers and marketers of luxury goods seek to use that mass buying power in a way that is aimed at benefitting their bottom line. The uncritical celebration of an individualistic narrative of wealth and success is arguably an extremely western paradigm, which does not take into account the diverse, often very collectively situated, cultures and ethics that might define consumption differently in various African contexts. The homogenization of the billions of African consumers into 'one market' is also problematic, in that it shows no interest, never mind insight or care, in the hundreds of languages, religious belief systems and cultural practices that are present on the continent. The extent to which similar homogenizing discourses are deployed to 'analyse' other non-western regions is an important question for future research. And perhaps most offensive of all is the idea that luxury is an idea owned by the West, exported to Africa to consumers who are assumed both to be loyal and to need educating about the importance of brands. These western values and potentially abusive attitudes towards Africa might not come as a surprise. After all, the organizations producing the reports are firmly rooted within a western neoliberal political-economy, and their *raison d'etre* is to support the economic activity of other profit-oriented firms. As various debates on cultural appropriation have shown, it is in the nature of neoliberal culture to only include difference when it is profitable to do so (Rogers 2006), and the attention being paid to the African market for luxury items is undergirded by a strong motivation for financial gain.

In the material presented in this chapter, we have seen both sympathetic narratives, and offensive forms of stereotyping. There is a complex interplay between ideologies committed to African wellbeing and advancement, at least in the limited sense framed by economic development and consumer markets, and those that see Africa as a playground for profit-making. Both require further critical attention in future research projects. As a contribution to this research agenda, this chapter has shown that attention paid to consumer markets in Africa, specifically those for luxury goods, from corporate analysts should motivate further critical research into the subject. Future enquiry should continue to explore not only how African markets are discursively constructed by corporate actors, but also their actual marketing practices and strategies on the ground, as well as of course how African consumers of luxury themselves give an account of what their consumption means to them culturally, politically and socially.

References

Asamoah-Yaw, Ernest and Safo-Kantanka, Osei-Bonsu (2017), *Kente Cloth: History and Culture*, Bloomington, IN: Xlibris Corporation.

Atwal, Glyn and Bryson, Douglas (2014), *Luxury Brands in Emerging Markets*, New York: Springer.

Atwal, Glyn and Jain, Soumya (2012), *The Luxury Market in India: Maharajas to Masses*, Basingstoke: Palgrave Macmillan.

Ballard, Richard (2010), '"Slaughter in the suburbs": Livestock slaughter and race in post-apartheid cities', *Ethnic and Racial Studies*, 33:6, pp. 1069–87, https://doi.org/10.1080/0141987090 3477320. Accessed 4 November 2016.

Bonsu, Samuel K. (2009), 'Colonial images in global times: Consumer interpretations of Africa and Africans in advertising', *Consumption Markets & Culture*, 12:1, pp. 1–25, https://doi. org/10.1080/10253860802560789. Accessed 4 November 2016.

Burke, Timothy (1992), 'Nyamarira that I loved: Commoditisation, consumption and the social history of soap in Zimbabwe', *Collected Seminar Papers: Institute of Commonwealth Studies*, 42, pp. 195–216.

—— (1996), *Lifebuoy Men, Lux Women: Commodification, Consumption, and Cleanliness in Modern Zimbabwe*, Durham, NC: Duke University Press.

Crosswaite, Inka (2014), 'Afro Luxe: The meaning of luxury in South Africa', in G. Atwal and D. Bryson (eds), *Luxury Brands in Emerging Markets*, London: Palgrave Macmillan, pp. 187–200, https://link.springer.com/chapter/10.1057%2F9781137330536_18. Accessed 4 November 2016.

Cui, Annie Peng, Wajda, Theresa A. and Walsh, Michael F. (2015), 'Luxury brands in emerging markets: A case study on China', *Entrepreneurship in International Marketing*, 25, pp. 287–305, http://www.emeraldinsight.com/doi/abs/10.1108/S1474-797920140000025013. Accessed 4 November 2016.

Diop, Cheikh Anta (1988), *Precolonial Black Africa*, Chicago: Chicago Review Press.

Dosekun, Simidele (2019), *Fashioning Postfeminism: Spectacular Femininity and Transnational Culture*, Champaign, IL: University of Illinois Press.

Gbadamosi, Ayantunji (2013), 'Consumer involvement and marketing in Africa: Some directions for future research', *International Journal of Consumer Studies*, 37:2, pp. 234–42, https://doi.org/10.1111/j.1470-6431.2012.01096.x. Accessed 4 November 2016.

Gott, Suzanne (2009), 'Asante hightimers and the fashionable display of women's wealth in contemporary Ghana', *Fashion Theory*, 13:2, pp. 141–76, https://doi.org/10.2752/175174109X414259. Accessed 4 November 2016.

Guyer, Jane I. (1993), 'Wealth in people and self-realization in equatorial Africa', *Man*, 28:2, pp. 243–65, https://doi.org/10.2307/2803412. Accessed 4 November 2016.

—— (1995), 'Wealth in people, wealth in things: Introduction', *The Journal of African History*, 36:1, pp. 83–90, https://doi.org/10.1017/S0021853700026980. Accessed 4 November 2016.

Howes, David (2002), *Cross-Cultural Consumption: Global Markets, Local Realities*, Abingdon: Routledge.

Hussein, Nazia (2010), 'Colour of life achievements: Historical and media influence of identity formation based on skin colour in South Asia', *Journal of Intercultural Studies*, 31:4, pp. 403–24, https://doi.org/10.1080/07256868.2010.491275. Accessed 4 November 2016.

Iqani, Mehita (2015a), 'A new class for a new South Africa? The discursive construction of the "black middle class" in post-apartheid media', *Journal of Consumer Culture*, 17:1, pp. 105–21.

—— (2015b), 'Agency and affordability: Being black and "middle class" in South Africa in 1989', *Critical Arts*, 29:2, pp. 126–45, https://doi.org/10.1080/02560046.2015.1039200. Accessed 4 November 2016.

—— (2016), *Consumption, Media and the Global South: Aspiration Contested*, London: Palgrave Macmillan.

James, Deborah (2014), *Money from Nothing: Indebtedness and Aspiration in South Africa*, Stanford, CA: Stanford University Press.

Jarosz, Lucy (1992), 'Constructing the dark continent: Metaphor as geographic representation of Africa', *Geografiska Annaler: Series B, Human Geography*, 74:2, pp. 105–15, https://doi.org/10.2307/490566. Accessed 4 November 2016.

Keim, Curtis A. and Somerville, Carolyn (2017), *Mistaking Africa: Curiosities and Inventions of the American Mind*, London: Hachette.

Krige, Paul Friedrich Detlev (2011), 'Power, identity and agency at work in the popular economies of Soweto and Black Johannesburg', Ph.D. thesis, University of the Witwatersrand, Johannesburg, http://wiredspace.wits.ac.za/handle/10539/10143. Accessed 4 November 2016.

Li, Cheng (2010), *China's Emerging Middle Class: Beyond Economic Transformation*, Washington, DC: Brookings Institution Press.

Lutz, Catherine and Collins, J. C. (1993), *Reading National Geographic*, Chicago: University of Chicago Press.

Mahajan, Vijay (2011), *Africa Rising: How 900 Million African Consumers Offer More Than You Think*, Upper Saddle River, NJ: Pearson Prentice Hall.

McClintock, Anne (2013), *Imperial Leather: Race, Gender, and Sexuality in the Colonial Contest*, London: Routledge.

Melber, Henning (2016), *The Rise of Africa's Middle Class: Myths, Realities and Critical Engagements*, Johannesburg: Wits University Press.

Newell, Sasha (2012), *The Modernity Bluff: Crime, Consumption, and Citizenship in Côte D'Ivoire*, Chicago: University of Chicago Press.

Nwankwo, Sonny (2000), 'Assessing the marketing environment in Sub-Saharan Africa: Opportunities and threats analysis', *Marketing Intelligence & Planning*, 18:3, pp. 144–53, https://doi.org/10.1108/02634500010327935. Accessed 4 November 2016.

Oyedele, Adesegun and Minor, Michael S. (2012), 'Consumer culture plots in television advertising from Nigeria and South Africa', *Journal of Advertising*, 41:1, pp. 91–108, https://doi.org/10.2753/JOA0091-3367410107. Accessed 4 November 2016.

Ramamurthy, Anandi (2003), *Imperial Persuaders: Images of Africa and Asia in British Advertising*, Manchester: Manchester University Press.

Rogers, Richard A. (2006), 'From cultural exchange to transculturation: A review and reconceptualization of cultural appropriation', *Communication Theory*, 16:4, pp. 474–503, https://doi.org/10.1111/j.1468-2885.2006.00277.x. Accessed 4 November 2016.

Sassatelli, Roberta (2007), *Consumer Culture: History, Theory and Politics*, London: Sage.

Scrase, Ruchira Ganguly and Scrase, Timothy J. (2008), *Globalization and the Middle Classes in India*, Abingdon: Routledge.

Shome, Raka (2014), *Diana and Beyond: White Femininity, National Identity, and Contemporary Media Culture*, Champaign, IL: University of Illinois Press.

Sinclair, John and Pertierra, Anna Cristina (2012), *Consumer Culture in Latin America*, Basingstoke: Palgrave Macmillan.

Southall, Roger (2016), *The New Black Middle Class in South Africa*, Woodbridge: Boydell & Brewer.

Spronk, Rachel (2012), *Ambiguous Pleasures: Sexuality and Middle Class Self-Perceptions in Nairobi*, New York: Berghahn Books.

Taylor, Ian (2014a), *Africa Rising? BRICS: Diversifying Dependency*, Woodbridge: Boydell & Brewer.

—— (2014b), 'Is Africa Rising?', *Brown Journal of World Affairs*, 21, pp. 143–62.

Viljoen, Stella (2008), 'Masculine ideals in post-apartheid South Africa: The rise of men's glossies', in A. Hadland (ed.), *Power, Politics and Identity in South African Media: Selected Seminar Papers*, Cape Town: HSRC Press.

Wattanasuwan, Kritsadarat (1999), 'It isn't just for image: The lived meaning of luxury-brand consumption among wealthy Thai teenagers', *Thammasat Review*, 4:1, pp. 22–58.

Note

1   See http://www.unileverinstitute.uct.ac.za/uui/research/black-diamond. Accessed 4 November 2016.

Chapter 2

African Utopianism: The Invention of Africa in Diesel's *The Daily African* - A Retrogressive Reading

Hlonipha Mokoena

The beginning of the twenty-first century coincided in South Africa with the end of apartheid and the Cold War.[1] No sooner had democracy arrived, previously unavailable brands arrived also. As a consequence of sanctions and cultural boycotts, South African consumers had lived for several decades in a consumption bubble in which the only available products were produced in the Republic. At the end of the 1990s, therefore, the 'global brand' was still a novelty in South Africa. The absence of the 'global brand' had touched mundane consumer goods (Canada Dry, 7up, IKEA)[2] as well as luxury brands (Gucci, Louis Vuitton, Bentley). Thus, with the end of apartheid and the liberalization of the South African economy, the latter concept of luxury was also liberated from exclusivity and black South Africans were, in theory, availed of the luxury goods that they had been denied.

The 2001 Diesel 'Le Chic Afreak' campaign is an example of this 'overdue' invitation.[3] Combining newsprint from a fictional newspaper entitled *The Daily African* with glossy and staged tableaux featuring black South African models in a series of hedonistic scenes, the advertisements visually and textually incorporated Africa and Africans into the world of fashion by inverting the binaries of the old/apartheid/Cold War order,[4] as it were, especially the black-poor and white-luxury binary, to place Africa on top.[5] Although the ad campaign was targeted at Diesel's global market, it used only black and South African models. The narrative of the adverts borrowed from the 'Africa Rising' discourse.[6] In Diesel's version of this discourse, fashion functions, linguistically, as a historical intervention. The Diesel Africa campaign uses history or, more graphically, the future of history to create the 'scene' as described in Barthes' statement that in fashion photography, 'the world is usually photographed as a décor, a background or a scene, in short, as a theater' (1983: 301). In the adverts, the real history of Africa becomes a fiction, as the copy of the adverts inverts the signs that have been used to understand Africa.

Conceptually, the analysis in this chapter relies on several ideas regarding contemporary Africa and its relationship to the history of the continent. In using the term 'retrogressive', the chapter wants to suggest that the Diesel campaign can only be read backwards since at the time, readers would only have seen a single advertisement at a time. Thus, to read the campaign as a moment in the history of the 'Africa Rising' discourse is to perform an examination that was not possible at the time. 'Retrogressive' also refers to the manner in which the physical copy of the ads resuscitates the history of newspapers in Africa. Some readers of the adverts would no doubt be familiar with the latter history, but some would not have been. Thus, by creating fictional newsprint, the Diesel advertisers were both creating history and retrieving it from the past. The creative process involved constructing an alternative image of Africa while the excavating project involved 'remaking' the history of wealth in Africa through suggesting that the 'contemporary' wealthy were a novelty and therefore worthy of the exposé that becomes the written narrative of the adverts. In addition to contributing to the Africa Rising discourse, the adverts could also be said to have borrowed from Afropolitanism, or what this chapter chooses to call 'African Utopianism'. The term 'Afropolitanism' was coined and popularized by the novelist Taiye Selasi who declared, '[w]e are Afropolitans […] not citizens but Africans of the world' (Bady and Selasi 2015: 149). As an assertion of worldliness and a transcending of borders, boundaries and bounded identities, the term has been criticized and sometimes rejected by those who describe it as an expression of bourgeois aesthetics (Bady and Selasi 2015: 149). For our purposes, the term is still useful because it has been taken up by others, specifically by Achille Mbembe who posits that,

> Afropolitanism refers to a way – the many ways – in which Africans, or people of African origin, understand themselves as being part of the world rather than being apart […] Afropolitanism is a name for undertaking a critical reflection on the many ways in which, in fact, there is no world without Africa and there is no Africa that is not part of it.
> (Mbembe and Balakrishnan 2016: 29)

In combination, the Selasi and Mbembe definitions captured the mood of the turn of the century but also simultaneously posed the question of what is next for Africa and its diaspora of Afropolitans. It is in this sense that the chapter uses the term African Utopianism to define an Afropolitanism that is also oriented towards the future of Africans.[7] The contention of the chapter is that in 2001, Diesel created its own version of African Utopianism by curating a visual feast of decadence, hedonism and plenitude through which it attempted to sell designer jeans and accessories.

The other introductory point is that Diesel is not the only Afro-optimist, or wasn't at the time. Even the prestigious *The Economist* made an about-turn from Afro-pessimist to Afro-optimist in the space of a decade (Havnevik 2015). The discourse on Africa's future can be best summarized as a continued engagement with the provocative thesis encapsulated in Walter Rodney's book, titled *How Europe Underdeveloped Africa* (1974). In other words, the contestation is not only over what became known as dependency theory but over whether dependency theorizing is still applicable to contemporary Africa. For the Afro-pessimists, Africa's misery is eternal; Africa's woes will never be over and several versions of the narrative offer their own varied explanations for why Africa's problems persist. On the other hand, the Afro-optimists' position has been visually and politically condensed in the concept of 'Africa Rising'. The latter concept has been portrayed on the covers of *Time* magazine and *The Economist*, and both publications were taken to task by the economist Grieve Chelwa on the popular blog, 'Africa is a Country' (Chelwa 2015). In 2001, Diesel clearly took the Afro-optimist narrative to its logical conclusion. In its images, not only is 'Africa Rising', Africa is luxuriating.

The choice of a 'newspaper' as a carrier of the message of a luxurious and wealthy Africa is no accident. *The Daily African*,[8] even though fictitious, represented what certain Africans had been asking for – that is, media that represented Africa in a positive manner. However, this was no mere shift from a positive to a negative; it was an inversion, since even the map of the world in the masthead of *The Daily African* was upside down. This cartographic charity translates into a linguistic one as the 'articles' in the copy demonstrate – Africa is now so wealthy that it dominates the tobacco industry and even the currency, the 'afro' is stronger than the US dollar. The inversion, or invention, of a new language to speak about Africa was however not a complete fiction since the issues raised by the articles are actually real. In a 2001 meeting of OAU (Organisation for African Unity) leaders, the former governor of the South African Reserve Bank, Tito Mboweni, jokingly suggested that the common currency of the proposed African Union could be called the 'afro', which is the name used in the advertising (Anon. 2001). Thus, in 2001, Diesel took advantage of the contemporary wave of African utopianism and optimism and portrayed it as a historical intervention. However, it should also be first pointed out that the advertising campaign was produced by the advertising agency DDB Stockholm.

A Luxury of Words

By their hybrid nature, the Diesel adverts present several theoretical conundrums. In this chapter, for example, they are being interpreted as a collection whereas in reality an individual consumer would have seen one advert at a time. Second, in themselves the adverts could be seen as commentary in place of the newspaper, in what was then the emerging landscape of social media and electronic advertising and consumption. Thus, it becomes difficult to write about the adverts from within a 'consumption theory' of popular culture since they are now mostly 'artefacts' of a particular moment in history, namely the end of the twentieth and beginning of the twenty-first century. Specifically, theories of media consumption are themselves limited, since they often presume a distinction between 'consumption' and 'consumerism' (Iqani 2012: 2). Due to the passing of time and the method used in this chapter, the latter distinction is insufficient for interpreting what Diesel and its advertising agencies were attempting to do in 2001. This is mainly because the first 'consumers' of an advertising campaign are the individuals and firms who produce the campaign to begin with. Before a campaign can be placed in a magazine, it has to be created for and vetted by the customer (in this case Diesel) and the advertising agency (DDB Stockholm). The preference in this chapter is to zoom in on the conceptual keywords of 'luxury' and 'Afropolitanism' with the former term being applied to not only the object being sold in the advertising campaign (denim jeans) but also to the self-definition of Diesel as a company that is in the business of producing 'designer jeans'. Both the concepts of luxury and designer jeans are not defined by consumers, but arrive pre-packaged by the advertisers and their customers (the fashion houses). In the foreword to his *The Fashion System,* Barthes summarizes the paradox of clothing as language in the question, 'why does fashion utter clothing so abundantly?' (1983: xi). In other words, by drawing an equivalence between clothing and language, Barthes asserts that what is sold in advertising campaigns and in the copy of fashion magazines is not clothing in its *functional* sense but a mediated object or objects. The medium is language. As he elaborates,

> Why does it [fashion] interpose, between the object and its user, such a luxury of words (not to mention images), such a network of meaning? [...] [I]f clothing's producers and consumers had the same consciousness, clothing would be bought (and produced) only at the very slow rate of dilapidation.
>
> (1983: xi)

This 'luxury of words' is directed at more than just the consumer. It becomes, in retrospect, a language in which Diesel announced its relationship to 'Africa' and all things African. Based on the images and tableaux alone, it is actually not possible to identify the advertising campaign as being about denim jeans. The object of the advertisements is what was then a nebulous and inarticulate version of African consciousness that was later given the name 'Afropolitanism'. The 'invisibility' of the denim jean as the object of the advertising campaign is purposeful, in that denim jeans have been around for decades and therefore from a 'functional' perspective, they don't need to be advertised.[9] The denim jean occupies a contradictory position in the language of fashion. Although the denim jean never lost the reputation of 'work' clothing, it also signifies leisure (Barthes 1983: 264–65). This tension between work and leisure functions as the frictional narrative against which Diesel's models play out their roles as 'Afropolitans' (Mbembe and Balakrishnan 2016; Bady and Selasi 2015). The narrative provided by faux headlines and stories from *The Daily African* further intensifies the sheen and lustre of what this chapter is calling African Utopianism that is, the reorienting and repositioning of Africa as the 'future' and, more importantly, as the *desirable* future.

As shall be argued below, however, the Diesel advertising campaign is about a different kind of leisure, that is, the leisure of postcolonial subjects.[10] In the traditional literature on leisure (Karl Marx, Theodor Adorno and Max Horkheimer and Thorstein Veblen),[11] the assumption is that the history of labour and leisure is universal. More importantly, the assumption is that leisure is offered as a respite, imagined or real, from the drudgery of work across the world. What these theorists do not explore is the racialized, as opposed to the capitalized, histories of work. Colonialism racialized work and created the dichotomies of leisure as 'white' and work as 'black' (at least in the case of Africa). In this way, colonialism complicated its own ending as, with the end of colonial rule, independent African countries found that they had to continue to 'work' (through producing the world's raw materials) even though they were no longer the 'working class' of the imperial world. In the postcolonial context, leisure becomes difficult to justify since, by prior definition, only masters and madams would enjoy 'leisure time'.[12] So, to enjoy leisure in a postcolonial context necessarily implies usurping the erstwhile position of the master. This complex history of labour, idleness and leisure is animated in J. M. Cotzee's 'Idleness in South Africa', in which Coetzee describes the role of travel writing in creating the image of the lazy and indolent 'Hottentot' and how this history of condemnation has shaped labour relations in contemporary South Africa (Coetzee 1982). Thus, to write about the luxury inherent in a pair of denim jeans is to touch on not just the history of commodities in Africa but also the history of leisure and the latter's relationship to colonialism and its aftermath, independence.

The Daily African

Although it has become commonplace to trace the emergence of African consumption to the encounter with missionary ideology (Comaroff 1989a, 1989b; Comaroff and Comaroff 1991, 1997; Marks 1986), it is by no means the only site where Africans were 'converted' to modern goods or were exhorted to acquire novel needs and expenditures. The African newspapers, what Les Switzer called 'The Black Press', were littered with advertisements that not only presented indigenous languages but also often surpassed the racial and cultural boundaries of their time in order to present their readers with a spectacle of modernity that was often denied to them by colonial society (Switzer 1983, 1997). It is doubtful that the creators of *The Daily African* knew or understood the history of the black press since they present their newspaper as a novelty. As a fantasy and a revival, *The Daily African* is thus an ahistorical object – it doesn't actually contain acknowledgements of its provenance. Yet, as a barometer of how an African newspaper could be written and read, the fictitious print functions as a commentary on the notion of 'Black Diamonds',[13] or '*Les Nouveau Riche des Afrique*' as *The Daily African* prefers to dub this group. Although the history of African newspapers cannot be elaborated here, it should be pointed out that *The Daily African*'s conception of black wealth was not as novel as the advertisers may have imagined. The newspaper's anticipatory and imagined future Africa was a reality in the late nineteenth century when Africans established, printed and controlled their own newspapers. Thus, there is actually very little difference between the fictional *The Daily African* and the bilingual newspapers such as *Inkanyiso* and *Ipepa Lo Hlanga* that were created to serve a nineteenth-century and mission-educated African elite who were as aspirant as the 'Black Diamonds' of Diesel's campaign (Davis Jr. 1997; Hughes 2001; Marable 1976; Switzer 1983; la Hausse de Lalouviére 2000; Peterson et al. 2016).[14] The marked and foundational difference is that these newspapers were created and owned by their readers, whereas the Diesel campaign is an outsider's view of what black aspiration looks like. More importantly, these aspirant nineteenth-century newspapers did not shy away from advertising luxury goods as well as including reportage on African extravagance at, for example, weddings. Thus, when interpreting the scenes created by the confluence of image, text and fantasy, the analysis below will take it as a given that *The Daily African* is simultaneously contemporary and retrospective. While in 2001 the newsprint may have been based on an imagined aspirant black super-rich class, such a class was, in the past, not only imaginable but actually existed. Such lifestyles were described in the newspapers of the nineteenth century. For the sake of brevity, some tableaux will be described in detail while others will be summarized.

Scenes of Pleasure[15]

The 'scene' of the African advertising campaign, to use Barthes' word, is contained in the tableau created around the following words: office, golf club, party, car and kitchen. This is the order in which the images from Diesel's advertising campaign are archived by DDB Stockholm (Jonason 2017). Each word encapsulates a 'mood' evoked in the *mise en scène* of each image. Contrary to the expectation that the models are clad in denim jeans, a variety of clothing and accessories is also being sold, from flip flops to jackets to clutch handbags. In fact, Jocke Jonason wrote that the advertising agency DDB Stockholm only has images of the denim advertising archived, not the images of the accessories advertising (Jonason 2017). In other words, Diesel and DDB Stockholm created two advertising campaigns, one that specifically focused on selling denim jeans and the other on selling Diesel's accessories (sunglasses, watches, bags, footwear and underwear). The tableaux created to depict 'Africa' are, however, important for another reason. It is the items that are not on sale that are exceptionally striking and hard to ignore: the zebra skin rugs, the fake afros,[16] the door-knocker earrings, the taxidermied mounts and the ever-present shimmer of gold 'bling'. It is these luxury items that complete the image of Africa that Diesel and DDB Stockholm tried to fictionalize. Thus, it is important to examine each of the scenarios while closely reading the 'news' that accompanies each scene. As noted earlier, the advertising campaign is not about absolute torpor since this would be a re-enactment of the 'indolent Hottentot' stereotype.

The Birth of the Kool[17]

In the office scene (Figure 1), a traditional wood-panelled office is occupied by male and female models in various stages of undress. They are putatively working since some are on computers or speaking on the phone (an old-fashioned landline one). In the hazy background, there are two couples: one couple is standing on a desk dancing and another is standing closer to one of the walls, also dancing. Of the six models (male and female), five look like they are wearing 'afro' wigs. There are two nods to conspicuous consumption. The first is the champagne flute that is placed next to the computer screen and the young male model who is presumed to be working on the computer. The second nod is the words that appear as the computers' screensavers: at least two of the computers in the image are scrolled with the words 'kool.kom'. This Internet destination or URL would not make sense without *The Daily African* headline announcing 'Kool.kom global launch delayed. Kool celebrates with delay party'. This headline gives meaning to not just the current scene being depicted in the image, but to also the background of the reported 700 Kool.kom workers who were

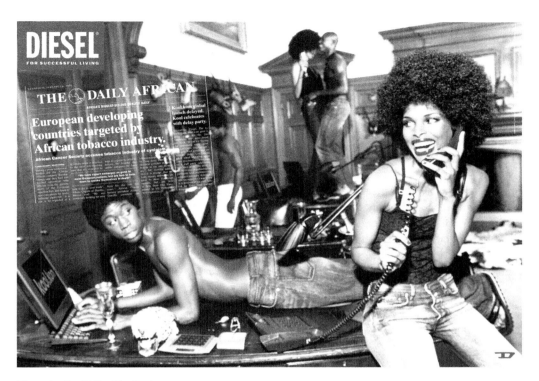

Figure 1: The Birth of the Kool.

the attendees of the reported party. For a South African readership, the hostname contains an added joke since in Afrikaans 'kom' means 'come', so the full web address would have read as 'kool dot come', implying that coolness is on its way - 'cool doth come'. There is also a second possible interpretation since many of South Africa's state-owned enterprises or parastatals end with the word '-kom'. The national electricity supplier is called 'Eskom' and the telecommunications one 'Telkom'. For a non-South African audience, the substance of *The Daily African* reportage would be the contrast between the lavish amounts being spent on the delay party versus the headline stating that 'European developing countries targeted by African tobacco industry'. The latter article is about the opening of two cigarette factories in Italy and Spain by the African tobacco company, Bumba Monga. In keeping with the spirit of inversions, *The Daily African* has a pull-quote from the president of the African Cancer Society, Allingo Gorella, pointing to the irony that, '[w]e have export embargos [*sic*] on guns to most European nations, but are free to help them to smoke themselves to death'. Notwithstanding the close relation between 'Gorella' and 'gorilla', the fact that what was once European paternalism has now been Africanized is the crux of the concept here. In the same way that Europe currently concerns itself with Africa's health problems, the decadent

Africa of *The Daily African* wants to rescue Europeans from themselves. More importantly, the implied dominance is not just in the area of business (in the form of the tobacco company) but also in the domain of munitions (since Africa is now not supplying Europe with guns). Thus, the news that the kool.kom launch has been delayed becomes the gossip or society pages story as opposed to the globally urgent and pressing lead story on tobacco and guns.

The Club House

The golf club as a site of pleasure, leisure and privilege is one of colonialism's least discussed legacies. From an aspirational perspective, being 'admitted' to a golf club was and is a marker of social mobility; it marks entry into the 'boys club' from which Africans were excluded during colonial times (Southall 2016: 173; JBHE 2000). In the case of colonized Africa, the golf club was also the place where white men were served by liveried staff (mostly black men), and this reputation is clearly the focus of *The Daily African* edition dated Monday

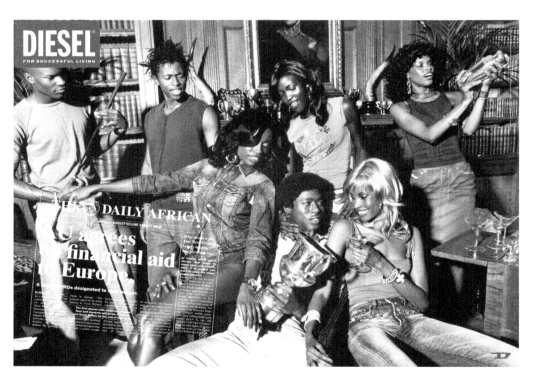

Figure 2: The Club House.

19 February 2001 (each edition has a unique date). The headline reads, 'Who needs a job? (Figure 2). The new economy brings wealth, but 'poor service', and the scene in the image is one of the golf club – presumably after the playing of a tournament, since the main male model is seated and holding a glistening trophy in his hand. What defines this as a golf event, however, is a second male model in the far-left corner of the image who is holding a golf club, and a female model seated on an armrest who leans on an upside-down golf club. Without these two hints, the scene would simply look like that of a man receiving excessive amounts of attention from three female admirers with a fourth on the right corner holding a cocktail shaker aloft and making martinis. This, therefore, is a celebratory scene: the winner wears an afro to authenticate his Africanness while the four women in the image wear synthetic weaves and wigs. Thus, the 'poor service' story serves to remind the readers of *The Daily African* that there is a reason why *'Les Nouveau Riche des Afrique'* still prefer the place of privilege created by their colonizers rather than visit the ones created by their own class (that is, other nouveau-riche Africans).

Africa Going Wireless

The party scene can, using the classical clichés, be described as a frozen bacchanal (Figure 3). The main ingredient of this revelry is the champagne that is being poured into and drunk from the same flute glasses used in the office tableau. There are nine male and female models grouped in triads, and each of these tells its own story. Other clichés also abound – leopard and zebra skin, gold bling, fake afros, one of the female models is even wearing an appliquéd map of Africa on her t-shirt. One triad of models is descending a staircase and entering the scene of the party. They are the newly arrived or arriving revellers, together with the abundant vegetation form the background of the scene. Although, like everyone else in the image, the trio is wearing informal and relaxed styles, the male model is also wearing a fake afro while one of the female models wears a fake blonde weave or wig. The former is the only male who is fully dressed; the other three male models are either fully topless or they have their shirts unbuttoned. Thus, the sense of reckless abandon and perhaps debauchery is implied by the abundance of well-toned pectorals and abs. What can also not be missed are the mid-strides that nearly all the models are in. This is to create the impression that the camera has stumbled onto a party that is in full swing: the camera is thus catching a conversation in mid-flow, a dancer doing his seductive moves, a woman who is either leaning on or being supported by two males while she positions herself on a skin-covered ottoman. The overall effect of this revelry is that it functions as a counterpoise to the good/bad news being reported in this edition of *The Daily African* (which is dated Saturday 26 May 2001). As with the previous images, the newspaper reports two stories; one is of a disaster unfolding in Europe and another is of the good fortune being enjoyed by Africans. In the case of the party scene, the good/bad news juxtaposition is about soaring birth rates in Europe and a Mozambican telecommunications company that has just scored a deal with

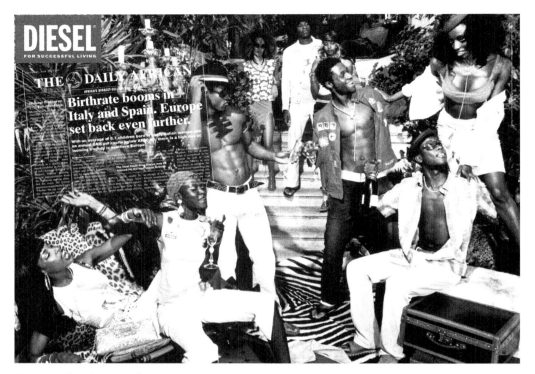

Figure 3: Africa Going Wireless.

Germany and England. This company is Ololongo Wireless, and the paper reports that its profits have gone up by 47 per cent due to its signing a deal to supply functioning telephone systems to Europe. The mirroring of the champagne bottles and glasses in the Ololongo story, with the reportage that affirms the place of champagne in nouveau-riche Africa, not only sets Africa and Africans apart – it also reinforces the image of Africa's modernity, in which raucous parties happen regularly and the human body is 'freed' from the burden of fertility, breeding and overpopulation.

Zebra Crossings

The place of the 'car' in the acquisition of wealth becomes the focal point of the fourth tableau that *The Daily African* tells us was released on Monday 16 April 2001 (Figure 4). The three models, two female and one male, are travelling in a car whose interior is luxuriously upholstered in azure-blue leather. This interior of the car then reflects and mimics the various other blues worn by the models, especially the indigo-blue of the bermuda shorts

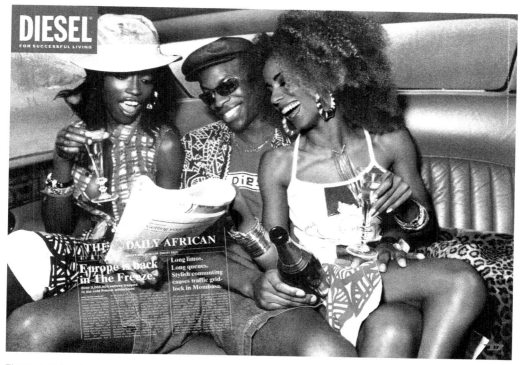

Figure 4: Zebra Crossings.

and peak cap on the male model. The fecundity of the gold metaphor also repeats itself – gold chains, gold bangles, gold doorknocker earrings and most importantly the golden hue of the fluted champagne. The three characters are all mirthfully reading a newspaper, presumably *The Daily African*. Rarely do newspapers inspire happy faces, so these three Afropolitans are obviously enjoying the story. The headline, 'Long limos, long queues: Stylish commuting causes traffic gridlock in Mombasa', is clearly about people like them.

This levity is echoed in the report itself, in which the 'old' Africa is represented by the mode of transport that used to be the norm, in this case 'zebra carriages', while the 'new' Africa is represented by stretch limos that now number 89,967 and are so lavishly stocked and supplied with champagne-filled fridges, Internet access and DVDs from 'Hollyvoodoo' that, according to the reporter's ironic tone, '[l]ife is tough in the back seat'. The latter comment sums up the image of the advert itself. The creation of non-existent stereotypes also adds to the notion of 'old' Africa that is now being discarded by the nouveau riche. The idea of the zebra carriages is a kind of old colonial joke, since zebras cannot be domesticated despite many past attempts (Anon. 1894; Swart 2003). Thus, zebra-drawn carriages are a stereotype that only exists in the annals of zoology. Similarly, the idea of 'Hollyvoodoo' is a nod to 'Nollywood', a term that also emerged in the early 2000s to describe homegrown Nigerian cinema (Alabi 2013). In the latter case, therefore, *The Daily African* was making unreal an African reality that was coming into being, or better yet, was becoming noticed by the rest of the world, since Africans had been making films for decades before the advent of Nollywood. The simulacrum between the image and the text is, however, broken with the second story. In this disaster story, Europe is back in the ice age with 'white tribes' descending the mountains, '[w]earing only cow hides and fox furs to protect them'. In this scenario, it is the Africans, representing an organization called the Red Spear who are rescuing and/or supplying Europeans with life-saving succour.

Caviar & Chill

An Afro-optimist future would not be complete without a domestic scene in which we are introduced to the new African gastronomy (Figure 5). The kitchen scene was the final image of the advertising campaign since, according to *The Daily African*, the date was Wednesday

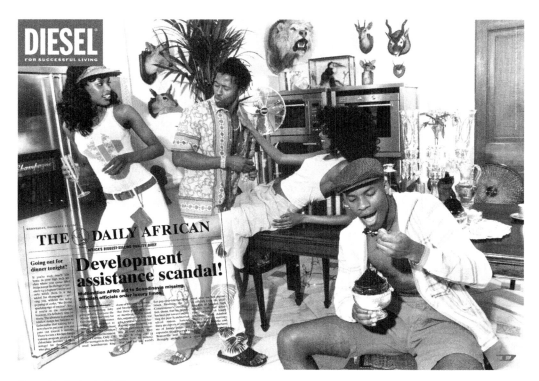

Figure 5: Caviar & Chill.

12 December 2001. Without much imagination, this image presents the African nouveau riche gorging themselves on caviar and champagne. Where normally a high-end double door fridge would dispense chilled water and ice cubes, the Afropolitan version also has the word 'champagne' scrolled in gold cursive script. In case there is some doubt about what is being celebrated in this image, the article in *The Daily African* confirms what the image depicts: the headline 'Going out for dinner tonight?' only makes sense once you start reading it and realize that the real question being posed is 'who would want to go out for dinner when you have such a well-kitted-out kitchen?' Hedonism is the other implied reason for staying at home; not only can you eat copious amounts of caviar, but it will be in the company of sexually alluring partners. The fictitious article confirms that the aspirational appliances in the kitchen are for the sole purpose of keeping 'the Beluga at precisely 14.7 degrees celsius' and that this could put restaurants out of business. The punchline of the article is that kitchen design has not only become a lucrative career, with customers waiting for their bespoke kitchens for up to six months, but that the Mombasa Institute of Technology (MIT) now offers a kitchen design programme.

Conclusion

Beginning with the notion of 'prestige ornaments' as defined by Kennedy (1991), it is possible to read the 'luxury' of the Diesel advertising campaign backwards in time. In her article, Kennedy singles out the status and rank afforded to Zulu kings, nobles and warriors by the wearing of brass ornaments. Such evidence of an indigenous and sub-regional trade and exchange of metals (like brass and the artisanal and metallurgical skills that circulated on the southeast of present-day South Africa) is often not at the forefront of historical narratives. The overall effect is to erase the history of luxury goods and instead to replace it with the 'grass skirt' stereotype of African aesthetics. More importantly, this narrative is often strengthened by the additional assumption that all African societies were egalitarian and without distinctions of class and status, what has been referred to in the literature as 'acephalous' societies (Parker and Rathbone 2007: 27–28). This latter broad-stroke assumption has not only defied evidence that Africans have lived under a variety of social organizations, but it has also sustained an assumption that luxury goods are always exotic and imported. Contrary to evidence such as the Igbo-Ukwu in Nigeria and Mapungubwe in South Africa, there continues to be an assumption that luxury goods in Africa should be studied as not only a 'foreign' idea but also as being made of 'foreign' materials and resources (Shaw 1973; Craddock et al. 1997; Woodborne et al. 2009). The idea that Africans could have created, sourced and even fought over precious objects is often not entertained. Thus, it is that the conception of Africa has largely revolved around 'want' and 'lack' rather than surfeit. It is from these assumptions that Diesel's Africa campaign derives its power and effectiveness. By portraying a new class of Africans as hedonistic, champagne-drinking moguls, the campaign solidified the idea that 'wealth' was a novelty in Africa and that Africans were prone to exaggerate and flaunt this new-found wealth. However, in 2001 this was a risky proposition since even at the time, the very idea that a new Africa was 'rising' was a novelty. A decade or so later, studies of Africa's 'new middle class' or even by extension other 'southern' elites, have proliferated (Southall 2004, 2016). What has changed? For one, the inequality gap has increased in those decades and the study of inequality itself has become the stuff of bestsellers and magnum opuses (Piketty 2014). Thus, whether inequality is examined from the perspective of the new vocabulary of BRICS (Brazil, Russia, India, China and South Africa) or the old vocabulary of 'developing countries', there is a renewed focus on what income and wealth gaps actually mean. As with the previous vogue of dependency theory, this new focus on inequality has the effect of occluding the role played by notions and desires for luxury goods in the creation of identity and selfhood. When luxury goods get bypassed, so do all the attendant culture industries such as advertising, fashion, music and, closer to home, precious metals. Thus, for example, the continued popularity of 'bling' becomes totally inexplicable if one focuses on the '1 per cent' and their supposed share of global wealth. How then is a 'bling' culture made? Surely, it cannot be assumed that it is the '1 per cent' who are solely responsible for driving the market for conspicuous consumption. Indeed, part of the argument of this chapter has been that luxury goods are not just the commodities and 'things' that are offered for purchase. What makes the Diesel African campaign effective is that, in its fictional guise, *The Daily African*, it presented a lifestyle in conformity with Diesel's aspirational slogan: 'For successful living'.

This 'new' definition of aspiration means that even if the advertising campaign didn't sell that many jeans, it sold the idea of the African nouveau riche as a possible future reality. Even in the case of the construction of *The Daily African* as the voice of Africa's nouveau riche, the Diesel campaign was working from an anticipatory position since the Africa of 'Africa Rising' was a utopia-to-come that, in 2001, was yet to manifest. This is not to laud the campaign as forward-thinking. Rather, it is to question why African wealth is almost always depicted as an inversion of European wealth despite archaeological evidence to the contrary.[18] By depicting Afropolitanism as a form of hedonism, Diesel and DDB Stockholm succeeded in resuscitating the missionary discourse of 'respectability', even though they were actually aiming for the opposite. By playing with inversions and thus presenting African luxury as ersatz, the campaign was negating the actual history of African luxury aesthetics and African newspapers.

References

Adorno, Theodor (2005), *The Culture Industry: Selected Essays on Mass Culture,* London and New York: Routledge.

Alabi, Adetayo (2013), 'Introduction: Nollywood and the Global South', *The Global South,* 7:1, pp. 1–10.

Allwood, Emma Hope (2016), 'Making the world's most controversial ad campaigns', *Dazed & Confused Magazine,* 18 November, http://www.dazeddigital.com/fashion/article/33763/1/making-the-worlds-most-controversial-ad-campaigns-diesel-jocke-jonason. Accessed 30 December 2017.

Anon. (1894), 'The training of zebras', *Scientific American,* 71:16, p. 251.

—— (2001), 'Lead boots: Can traders' prejudice explain the Rand's latest slump?', *The Economist,* 13 December, http://www.economist.com/node/905740. Accessed 27 September 2017.

Bady, Aaron and Selasi, Taiye (2015), 'From that stranded place', *Transition,* 117, pp. 148–65.

Baldick, Chris (2015), 'Farce', *The Oxford Dictionary of Literary Terms,* Oxford: Oxford University Press.

Barthes, Roland (1983), *The Fashion System,* Berkeley, Los Angeles and London: University of California Press.

Chelwa, Grieve (2015), 'Is Africa really rising? History and facts suggest it isn't', Africa is a Country, 18 June, http://africasacountry.com/2015/06/is-africa-really-rising-history-and-facts-suggest-it-isnt/. Accessed 27 September 2017.

Coetzee, J. M. (1982), 'Idleness in South Africa', *Social Dynamics,* 8, pp. 1–13.

Comaroff, Jean and Comaroff, John L. (1991), *Of Revelation and Revolution: Christianity, Colonialism and Consciousness in South Africa,* Vol. 1, Chicago: University of Chicago Press.

—— (1997), *Of Revelation and Revolution: The Dialectics of Modernity on a South African Frontier,* vol. 2, Chicago: University of Chicago Press.

Comaroff, John L. (1989a), 'The colonization of consciousness in South Africa', *Economy & Society,* 18:3, pp. 267–96.

—— (1989b), 'Images of empire, contests of consciousness: Models of colonial domination in South Africa', *American Ethnologist,* 16, pp. 661–85.

Craddock, Paul T., Ambers, Janet, Hook, Duncan R., Farquhar, Ronald M., Chikwendu, Vincent E., Umeji, Alphonse C. and Shaw, Thurstan (1997), 'Metal sources and the bronzes from Igbo-Ukwu, Nigeria', *Journal of Field Archaeology,* 24:4, pp. 405–29.

Davis Jr., Hunt R. (1997), '"Qude Maniki!" John L. Dube, Pioneer Editor of *Ilanga Lase Natal*', in L. Switzer (ed.), *South Africa's Alternative Press: Voices of Protest and Resistance 1880s–1960s,* Cambridge: Cambridge University Press.

Havnevik, Kjell (2015), 'The current Afro-optimism: A realistic image of Africa?', *FLEKS: Scandinavian Journal of Intercultural Theory and Practice,* 2:2, n.pag.

Horkheimer, Max and Adorno, Theodor (1973), *Dialectic of Enlightenment* (trans. J. Cumming), London: Verso.

Hughes, Heather (2001), 'Doubly elite: Exploring the life of John Langalibalele Dube', *Journal of Southern African Studies,* 27:3, pp. 445–58.

Iqani, Mehita (2012), *Consumer Culture and the Media: Magazines in the Public Eye,* Basingstoke and New York: Palgrave Macmillan.

JBHE (2000), 'Black colleges with White golfers', *The Journal of Blacks in Higher Education,* 30, pp. 78–79.

Jonason, Jocke (2017), personal e-mail to the author, 11 September.

Kennedy, Carolee G. (1991), 'Prestige ornaments: The use of brass in the Zulu Kingdom', *African Arts,* 24:3, special issue: 'Memorial to Arnold Rubin', Part II, pp. 50–55, 94–96.

la Hausse de Lalouviére, Paul (2000), *Restless Identities: Signatures of Nationalism, Zulu Ethnicity and History in the Lives of Petros Lamula (C. 1881–1948) and Lymon Maling (1889–C. 1936),* Pietermaritzburg: University of Natal Press.

Marable, Manning William (1976), 'African nationalist: The life of John Langalibalele Dube', Ph.D. thesis, Ann Arbor, MI: University of Michigan Press.

Marks, Shula (1986), *The Ambiguities of Dependence in South Africa: Class, Nationalism, and the State in Twentieth-Century Natal,* Johannesburg: Ravan Press.

Marx, Karl (2004), *Capital: A Critique of Political Economy* (trans. B. Fowkes), London: Penguin Books.

Mbembe, Achille and Balakrishnan, Sarah (2016), 'Pan-African legacies, Afropolitan futures', *Transition,* 120, pp. 28–37.

Mokoena, Hlonipha (2010), 'Anybody can be a maid', Africa is a Country, 6 December, http://africasacountry.com/2010/12/anybody-can-be-a-maid/. Accessed 28 December 2017.

—— (2017), '…If Black girls had long hair', *Image & Text,* 29:1, pp. 112–29.

Nuttall, Sarah and Mbembe, Achille (2008), *Johannesburg: The Elusive Metropolis,* Durham, NC and London: Duke University Press.

Parker, John and Rathbone, Richard (2007), *African History: A Very Short Introduction,* Oxford and New York: Oxford University Press.

Peterson, Derek, Newell, Steph and Hunter, Emma (2016), *African Print Cultures: Newspapers and Their Publics in the Twentieth Century,* Ann Arbor, MI: University of Michigan Press.

Piketty, Thomas (2014), *Capital in the Twenty-First Century,* Cambridge, MA and London: Harvard University Press.

Prashad, Vijay (2007), *The Darker Nations : A People's History of the Third World,* New York: W.W. Norton.

Rodney, Walter (1974), *How Europe Underdeveloped Africa,* Washington, DC: Howard University Press.

Shaw, Thurstan (1973), 'The Igbo-Ukwu bronzes', *African Arts,* 6:4, pp. 18–19.

Southall, Roger (2004), 'Political change and the Black middle class in democratic South Africa', *Canadian Journal of African Studies,* 38:3, pp. 521–42.

—— (2016), *The New Black Middle Class in South Africa,* Auckland Park: James Currey & Jacana.

Swart, Sandra (2003), 'Riding high: Horses, power and Settler society, c.1654–1840', *Kronos,* 29, pp. 47–63.

Switzer, Les (1983), 'Reflections on the mission press in South Africa in the 19th and early 20th centuries', *Journal of Theology for Southern Africa,* 43:1, pp. 5–14.

—— (1997), *South Africa's Alternative Press: Voices of Protest and Resistance, 1880s–1960s,* Cambridge: Cambridge University Press.

Thomas, Lynn M. (2006), 'The modern girl and racial respectability in 1930s South Africa', *The Journal of African History,* 47:3, pp. 461–90.

Veblen, Thorstein (2009), *The Theory of the Leisure Class,* Oxford and New York: Oxford University Press.

Weinbaum, Alys Eve, Thomas, Lynn M., Ramamurthy, Priti, Poiger, Uta G., Dong, Madeleine Yue and Barlow, Tani E. (eds) (2008), *The Modern Girl Around the World: Consumption, Modernity, and Globalization,* Durham, NC and London: Duke University Press.

Woodborne, Stephan, Pienaar, Marc and Tiley-Nel, Sian (2009), 'Dating the Mapungubwe Hill gold', *Journal of African Archaeology,* 7:1, pp. 99–105.

Notes

1   South Africa's role in the Cold War was defined by its alliance with Margaret Thatcher's Britain and Ronald Reagan's America. Thus, when apartheid and the Cold War ended, the trade, cultural and sport sanctions also ended; the anti-communist wars in the neighbouring countries of Mozambique, Namibia and Angola ended; and South Africa's isolationist or 'pariah' status in Africa also ended. With all these endings came the beginning of the World Wide Web, satellite television and the 24-hour news cycle.

2   The social and linguistic implications of sanctions, especially the flight of international brands, are aptly expressed in Jeremy Taylor's 1962 satirical song 'Ag Pleez Deddy' (also known as 'The Ballad of the Southern Suburbs'). For a description of the song and its hit status, see the Wikipedia entry: https://en.wikipedia.org/wiki/Ag_Pleez_Deddy. Accessed 15 March 2019.

3   The original details of the campaign, and its title 'Le Chic Afreak', appeared on page 23 of the September 2001 edition of *Elle* magazine (the South African edition).

4   The terms 'South Africa' and 'Africa' will be used interchangeably throughout the chapter since the advertising campaign 'covered' the whole continent in *The Daily African* articles, while the models used for the campaign were mostly South African.

5   As a brand, Diesel also seems to have only started actively advertising and marketing itself in the post-Cold War world. In an interview with *Dazed & Confused*, Jocke Jonason states that the company's ad campaigns 'started because Diesel hadn't done any official advertising before – this was back in 1991' (Allwood 2016).

6   With the demise of 'Third Worldism' (see Prashad 2007), each of the blocs that used to comprise this political unit – India, Asia, Latin America, Africa – has been reconfigured into a new focal point of growth, development and political influence. Thus, the 'Africa Rising' discourse is a mirror-image of the 'Asian Tigers', or even 'China Rising' discourses. The 2006 formation of BRICS (Brazil, Russia, India, China and then later South Africa) is another expression of the changing geopolitics of the post-Cold War world and the valorization of 'growth' as the main measure of actual and potential world dominance.

7   There are other possible terms such as 'Afrofuturism', but this has also created its own supporters and detractors.

8   *The Daily African* is the fictitious newspaper that served as the copy for Diesel's 2001 ad campaign. The newspaper's masthead consists of an inverted image of the globe and reads 'Africa's Biggest-Selling Quality Daily' (in capital letters), and each 'edition' of the fictitious newspapers consisted of two articles of news. The first article was 'global', focusing specifically on a disaster in Europe, and the second was a local news article focusing on the lifestyles and excesses of Africa's wealthy elites.

9   In their chapter, 'The culture industry: Enlightenment as mass deception', Adorno and Horkheimer observed that, '[t]he triumph of advertising in the culture industry is that consumers feel compelled to buy and use its products even though they see through them' (Horkheimer and Adorno 1973: 167).

10 Alternatively, the campaign could be interpreted using Sarah Nuttall's notion of 'Y culture' (*'loxion kulcha'*) as described in her chapter 'Stylizing the self' (Nuttall and Mbembe 2008: 91ff).

11 The literature on leisure and its link to capitalism has focused on the two interrelated concepts of 'fetish' and 'commodity', and many arguments are directly or indirectly the descendants of arguments presented in Karl Marx's *Capital* (2004: 125). For other iterations, see Adorno (2005), Horkheimer and Adorno (1973) and Veblen (2009).

12 On the relationship between maids and madams, see Mokoena (2010).

13 For a history of how this term was coined in South Africa, see Southall (2016: 44–47).

14 This comparison is limited to the nineteenth-century newspapers that were often black owned and edited, and circulated amongst an exclusively black and literate readership. The limits in technology also meant that many of these newspapers didn't print photographs or colour, so they were mostly black and white. This is the 'aesthetic' borrowed and mimicked by *The Daily African*. By the twentieth-century, many of these newspapers had been absorbed into larger conglomerates. Thus, for example, studies that focus on the emergence of the 'modern girl' are situated within the context of the latter historical era. For examples of this focus on the creation of the 'modern girl', see Thomas (2006) and Weinbaum et al. (2008).

15 Although it is possible to describe these subsequent scenes as farcical, strictly speaking 'farce' is a specific genre that is defined by Chris Baldick in the following terms:

> A kind of comedy that inspires hilarity mixed with panic and cruelty in its audience through an increasingly rapid and improbable series of ludicrous confusions, physical disasters, and sexual innuendos among its stock characters. Farcical episodes of buffoonery can be found in European drama of all periods since Aristophanes, notably in medieval France, where the term originated to describe short comic interludes; but as a distinct form of full-length comedy farce dates from the 19th century.
>
> (Baldick 2015)

16 In the following analysis, there are several references to hair and most of them are estimates since there is no way of knowing whether a model is wearing a wig, a weave or if their hair is natural. On the difficulties of writing and speaking about 'black hair', see Mokoena (2017).

17 All images are used with the kind permission of Jocke Jonason and DDB Stockholm.

18 The term 'archaeology' is preferred here since the literature cited above on Mapungubwe and Igbo-Ukwu concerns archaeological digs rather than historical narratives.

Chapter 3

For Love or Money? Romance, Luxury and Class Distinction on Mzansi Magic's *Date My Family*

Alexia Smit

This chapter explores the original South African reality television series *Date My Family* (Mzansi Magic, 2015–). As a dating show, *Date My Family* is organized around a quest for love. It stages this quest through a series of often-comedic encounters in the family home. The show contrasts and foregrounds tensions between different ways of thinking about love, juxtaposing a certain romantic ideal – aligned with luxury consumption, idealized leisure practices and classed performance – with a more humble approach to love that is linked to family values. This chapter will explore how an idealized romantic discourse of love as luxury spending is both celebrated and challenged in *Date My Family*. The romantic script that structures the series offers not only a reflection of love and family but – through the conflicts over branded fashion, luxury cars, romantic gifts and leisure practices featured on the show – a means of working through a range of potentially contested values relating to wealth for the show's audience. I contextualize my alignment of romance and luxury in relation to the show's distribution on the pay-television network, DSTV's Mzansi Magic channel.

Date My Family: The Format

Date My Family is an original reality television format. The show was developed in close consultation with the Mzansi Magic channels and was guided by intensive audience research (Sibeko 2016). On *Date My Family*, eligible singles are invited to have dinner with the families of prospective partners. Each episode's story is guided by a comical voice-over narration. In every episode of the show, an eligible 'bachelor' or 'bachelorette' is selected to 'date' three different families. Typically, the person selected as the eligible date is an ambitious person who represents themselves as relatively successful or on an upward career trajectory. This ambitious or 'aspirational' identity is often demonstrated through clothing, cars and other forms of consumption that might be understood as 'luxurious'. The week's bachelor or bachelorette meets only with the family members of their potential date. Each family prepares a meal for the guest and is expected to impress their guest on behalf of their absent family member. This prospective love interest is hidden from view and watches the evening's proceedings on a television screen in another location. By the end of the episode, the bachelor/bachelorette must select a final date based only on their experience with each participating family. The *Date My Family* car then pulls up to the home of each of the rejected families and delivers a bottle of wine. Finally, the car picks up the chosen date and the two singles meet for the first time before they go for dinner at an upmarket restaurant to see if they are compatible. My observations in this chapter are supported by analyses of a selection of *Date My Family* episodes: specifically, I consider Season 1, Episode 5, featuring bachelorette Asanda; Season 3, Episode 7, featuring bachelor Mduduzane and Season 4, Episode 5, featuring Sibonakaliso.

Luxury, Distinction and Reality Television in South Africa

Reality television is often understood as 'low-culture' trash TV (Hill 2015: 3). However, these shows frequently have a thematic interest in wealth, luxury lifestyles and conspicuous consumption. Viewers are invited to vicariously enjoy the extravagant lifestyles featured onscreen. For example celebrity lifestyle shows such as *Keeping Up with The Kardashians* (E!, 2007–) and *The Real Housewives of Orange County* (Bravo, 2006–) offer their viewers an intimate look at the lavish lifestyles of the wealthy; lifestyles that might otherwise not be accessible to 'ordinary' people. These American examples are readily available on South African pay television alongside local shows with a similar interest in wealth and lifestyle.

In the post-apartheid years, South African television has been focused on public service messages of nation-building and unity. However, Sarah Ives (2007) and Loren Kruger (2010) have both noted that this investment in nation-building is increasingly accompanied by a turn toward neoliberal messages via the national broadcaster, the SABC. For Ives, representations of new black wealth on South African television tend to represent national transformation in terms of individual aspirations to that wealth in a neoliberal capitalist order (2007: 167). The neoliberal mode of much contemporary programming is arguably further intensified on pay television, where programming is not bound to a public service remit. On DSTV's local channels, Mzansi Magic and Vuzu, there is a particular focus on wealth, celebrity and aspirational lifestyles. For example, DSTV broadcasts shows such as *Our Perfect Wedding* (Mzansi Magic, 2011), which documents lavish weddings, *Rich Kids* (Vuzu, 2015–), which reveals the lives of wealthy young South Africans, *Diski Divas* (Mzansi Magic, 2015–), a show about footballers' partners, and *Being Bonang* (Vuzu, 2017–), which documents the daily life of glamorous celebrity and businesswoman, Bonang Matheba.

Date My Family is produced by ConnectTV, a television production house headed by media mogul Basetsana Kumalo. The entrepreneur and former Miss South Africa has long been associated with luxury lifestyle television. She produced the highly successful long-running lifestyle magazine show *Top Billing* (SABC3), which has aired on the public broadcaster from 1996 to the present. Since the birth of the Mzansi Magic channels on DSTV, Kumalo's company, ConnectTV, has been working in close collaboration with the pay broadcaster to produce reality shows suited to an emerging black middle-class audience. These ConnectTV shows share a combination of glamour, romance and the foregrounding of 'real' South African lives with *Date My Family*.

Reality television certainly engages in the fantasies of affluence, but also important to the pleasure of the form is the way in which the mode plays on knowledge economies, deriving much of its entertainment value from class judgement and distinction. Commenting on British reality TV, Bev Skeggs, Helen Wood and Nancy Thumin contend that class distinction is one of its core fascinations. They write: 'One of the main functions of Reality TV is to symbolically and morally mark and value persons and to visualise that value' (2007: 13). I will show that similar operations are at play in South African reality television.

This interest in examining and marking out class distinction has resonance with theoretical work that describes the concept of luxury as defined by distinction. Mike Featherstone understands luxury in terms of two types of knowledge: on the one hand, identifying and experiencing luxury goods calls upon a sensory knowledge 'gained in close contact with the object' (2014: 54). The pleasure of distinguishing luxury goods relies upon an intimate sensory engagement. On the other hand, the concept of 'luxury' intersects with less tangible knowledge systems. Luxury goods 'may also be seen as representative of a class, a category located in a classificatory grid and offering pleasure in the play with distinctions and permutations' (Featherstone 2014: 54). I argue that this second attribute of luxury, pertaining to cultural distinction and status, is crucial to the comedic pleasures of *Date My Family*.

As a reality dating show that involves the selection of an ideal partner, judgement and distinction are built into the formula of *Date My Family*. Skeggs et al. explain that reality television shows 'make' class through certain techniques within their formula, such as 'event, competition [and] judgement', which work by 'exposing different levels of emotional, cultural awareness and knowledge in the participants' (2007: 14). The formula of *Date My Family* builds on these principles. The date functions as the primary 'event', structuring the show and guiding the 'competition' for love, while the ending of each episode is driven by suspense about what 'judgement' will be made. As my analyses will show, luxury items feature in the programme as tools for navigating, assessing and performing class distinction.

DSTV, Mzansi Magic and the 'New' Black Middle Class

While satellite television was once the preserve of wealthy, mostly white South African audiences, in the post-apartheid years the satellite broadcaster DSTV has radically expanded its reach to include audiences across Africa and a growing number of black subscribers in South Africa. In 2010, the Mzansi Magic channel bouquet was launched on DSTV, targeting the emerging black South African market. The channels are available via the relatively affordable 'DSTV compact' and 'DSTV compact plus' packages, making this programming available to viewers from a range of income brackets. In 2017, viewers had access to *Date My Family* through monthly subscriptions starting from R365. In a 2013 study, the Unilever group at the University of Cape Town established that the average household income of the black middle class is R20,583 and that 3 per cent (about R600) of this household income is spent on recreation and culture, including television (UCT 2013: 47–48). Between 2004 and 2012, the study reports a tremendous rise in DSTV viewership amongst its survey group, from 9 per cent to 62 per cent (UCT 2013: 144). These statistics need to be read with an understanding that the study in question categorized someone as middle class if they had an income between R16,000 and R50,000 per month, or if they met one of the following criteria: owns a car, has a tertiary education, has a white collar job or lives in a metropolitan area paying rent above R4,000 (UCT 2013: 4).

The Unilever study presents just one set of measures for understanding what 'middle class' means in South Africa, where other factors such as self-identification, vulnerability, home ownership and global class structures may also need to be considered. I maintain that the category of 'middle class' is constantly open to discursive interpretation rather than being a stable and manageable descriptor of identity. Indeed, I am interested in how ideas of 'middle-classness' are constructed and contested within the television show I examine. In particular, this chapter will maintain that this discursive work is mediated through the display of luxury objects and leisure activities.

However, I also acknowledge the very real material determinants shaping both market responses to this group and concepts of identity amongst those identifying as middle class. These ideas about the definition of an emerging 'new' middle class are the result of substantial changes to material living conditions for many black South Africans who were excluded from jobs, education, financial services, housing, transport and education during the apartheid years. After 1994, the African National Congress Government (ANC) was committed to increasing black involvement in the economy (Southall 2016: 65). Many black South Africans have benefitted from widened access to job opportunities aided by affirmative action programmes and the ANC government's Black Economic Empowerment initiatives, along with increasing access to education (Southall 2016). The Unilever institute estimated that South Africa's middle class grew from 1.6 million in 2004 to 4.2 million in 2012 (UCT 2013: 38). The study claims that, since 1994, the black middle class has grown by 240 per cent (UCT 2013: 39). It is interesting to note that this study was partially sponsored by DSTV, a company with a significant stake in understanding this market. While the Unilever group may not present the only way of understanding what constitutes the black middle class in South Africa, they do present a useful indicator of how DSTV is imagining this audience in the years preceding the launch of *Date My Family*.

The emergence of new black wealth in post-apartheid South Africa has been the subject of a great deal of interest, excitement and speculation. For many, the growth of the 'new black middle class' has been aligned with the promise of consumer-led economic growth for the nation. The social mobility of South Africa's middle class has also been celebrated as an indicator of the fulfilment of promises of freedom and transformation in democratic South Africa (Iqani 2016: 88–89; Southall 2016: xiv–xvii). DSTV might be understood as one of many companies that has identified and capitalized on the potential for growth in this market.

Questions of how wealth is performed, displayed and integrated into existing value systems are salient on Mzansi Magic because of the transitional nature of class identity for many amongst its audience. According to the Unilever group, for the black middle class, '[l]ifestyle choices are being made amidst tensions' (2013: 108). Because its target market is understood as aspirational or upwardly mobile, Mzansi Magic might be understood as exploring and negotiating intermedial spaces for its viewers, addressing the movement between differently classed spaces and subjectivities. Exploring representations of luxury products, clothes and experiences on *Date My Family* offers a way of mapping how ideas about new economic freedoms, aspiration and identity are negotiated for this audience. Luxury items have been key to the display and signification of new black wealth and have also been the focus of critical and moralistic responses to the apparent 'excesses' of newly wealthy black South Africans (Southall 2016: 163–64).

In her influential article on consumption in South Africa, Deborah Posel argues that – given the ways in which consumption and access to the market was restricted for black South Africans during the apartheid years – it is not surprising that new post-apartheid freedoms have been celebrated through spending and displays of wealth (2010: 159). Furthermore, Posel describes how the concept of luxury was racialized, with appropriate black South African spending understood in terms of necessities. Even the aspiration to luxury was regarded as a transgression against the apartheid order (Posel 2010: 170). Consequently, as opposed to 'necessary' spending, luxury purchases might be seen as a way of styling the self to demonstrate freedom and economic emancipation for the black middle class in the 'new South Africa'.

The Luxury of Love

Just as luxurious spending has been understood as an assertion of inclusion in South Africa's emerging democracy, representations of romance might also be read in terms of claims to full personhood and inclusion in the aftermath of the brutal and dehumanizing effects of the apartheid regime. The apartheid system of migrant labour was particularly devastating for personal relationships, as the system broke apart black South African families by sending men into cities to work away from their families, who were not allowed to join them (Ramphele and Richter 2006: 74). Thomas and Cole describe love as 'a crucial idiom through which people in Africa have debated generational and cultural distinctions and made political claims to inclusion, often by engaging in new forms of media' (2009: 13). In her study of wedding photography in South Africa, Danai Mupotsa (2015) explores how romantic practices are discursively tied to expressions of freedom and inclusion within a newly democratic South Africa. Mupotsa argues that, for black brides, producing the wedding spectacle (and styling oneself for this spectacle) can be read as a way of imagining and negotiating belonging and human ness in the post-apartheid public space (2015: 185–86).

Like the wedding spectacle described by Mupotsa, *Date My Family* brings both romantic discourse and the display of luxury consumption into a public arena for the representation of post-apartheid identities. On *Date My Family*, romantic love is bound up in the neoliberal and 'aspirational' narratives of new wealth and rising class mobility, which have emerged as a key feature of the post-apartheid television landscape (Ives 2007; Kruger 2010). As my analyses will show, the intertwinement of romantic and economic aspiration is discursively constructed through the display and discussion of wealth, aspiration and luxury goods.

While popular romance narratives have presented romantic love as a transcendent affect (something that overcomes material problems, class politics and differences between people), romance narratives have also long been aligned with concerns about exchange, class compatibility and, since the emergence of capitalism, the mass market. Eva Illouz (1997) addresses the relationship between romance and the market, with specific reference to the history of late capitalism in the United States. For Illouz (1997), the development of romantic discourse in the United States was entangled with a utopian vision of the American capitalist future. I will argue that these insights linking romantic discourse to utopian promise have particular resonance in the South African context, where the post-apartheid period has been defined by attempts at imagining modes of togetherness, prosperity and freedom.

Illouz describes how 'the meaning of romance became enmeshed with that of consumption, commodities and technologies of leisure' (1997: 26). This can be understood in terms of two parallel processes: 1) romantic discourses imbued products and leisure activities with mystical appeal and utopian promise in a process that Illouz (1997) describes as the 'romanticization of commodities'; 2) romantic practices became increasingly reliant upon consumer spending and luxury goods, which Illouz calls ' the commodification of romance'.

Similarly, Russel Belk and Gregory Coon argue for the importance of 'a material system of ritual gifts' (1991: 526) in romantic courtship. They write: 'American dating, mating and courtship activities employ money and tangible gifts as key ritual elements and as focal symbolic vehicles. Gifts and dating expenditures "say" what cannot be said in words' (1991: 521). In romantic practices, luxury items and experiences, whether they be clothing, bottles of wine, cars or dates, are a form of communication between romantic partners. These objects and experiences are used to map two different sets of meaning pertinent to the courtship process. On the one hand, the luxury trappings of romance help partners to read the relative affluence, social standing and cultural capital of a love interest. On the other hand, luxury can also be read as an indicator of the intensity and sincerity of a prospective partner's feelings.

Illouz (1997) argues that romantic discourses in the United States reflect some of the key contradictions of the capitalist system. I want to focus on one particular contradiction that she highlights, and to examine how it might be useful for understanding the play of discourses around capital, democracy and inclusion in a South African context. Illouz notes that discourses of romantic love manage a tension between 'the classless utopia of affluence and the dynamics of "distinction"' (1997: 11). Romantic love offers a utopian promise: the idea that class tensions can be overcome. 'Romantic love has become an intimate, indispensable part of the democratic ideal of affluence that has accompanied the emergence of the mass market, thereby offering a collective utopia cutting across and transcending social divisions' (Illouz 1997: 2). The notion that a utopian promise of romance can overcome class tensions is useful for an analysis of South African romantic culture. Indeed, it is in keeping with both Mupotsa's (2015) and Thomas and Cole's (2009) arguments that situate love as a key theme in the discursive construction of democracy and political inclusion in Africa.

I argue that *Date My Family* derives its comedy and conflict from capitalizing on the tensions Illouz (1997) describes between transcendence and distinction. *Date My Family* can be understood as addressing a utopian sensibility. The show champions the 'inclusive, populist, transgressive and egalitarian' (Illouz 1997: 13) promise of romance, representing love as a means of uniting people despite the diverse lifestyles, habits, cultures and class backgrounds that characterize South Africa's black viewing population. Participants also demonstrate their capacity to show love through the display of luxury gifts and experiences. This is significant in a post-apartheid context in which such luxury spending has historically been denied to black South Africans. The show might be seen as representing the desire for an affluent utopia in which the inequalities of the past have been replaced by collective access to new forms of wealth.

However, romance narratives also work to reinforce the very social divisions they apparently circumvent (Illouz 1997: 13). This is because of the reliance of romantic practices on both cultural and economic capital. Furthermore, alongside modes of consumption, romantic success relies upon a familiarity with appropriate manners and an ease with middle- to upper-class tastes. Thus, it is not enough to be able to purchase luxury items and experiences; romantic success also depends on being able to select, identify and engage with the appropriate luxury objects in a way that displays social status. *Date My Family* produces entertainment by foregrounding debates centring on class distinction.

In the analysis section that follows I will demonstrate how representations of romantic luxury on *Date My Family* derive conflict and entertainment by exploiting both dimensions of the romantic paradox; on the one hand, romantic spending is celebrated as a claim to freedom, aspiration and social mobility, while, on the other hand, much comedy and controversy is derived from failed performances of class, suspicions of 'gold-digging' and in classed mismatches of values and taste. In the analyses that follow, I will consider how both the democratic impulse of love narratives and the interest in romance and class distinction are mediated through luxury items and luxury spending.

Driving the Narrative: The *Date My Family* Car

Date My Family does not have an onscreen host, relying only on voice-over commentary, so the series' driver is the primary visual embodiment of its machinery within the discourse of the programme. The central role that luxury vehicles play in the show's format gives an indication of the extent to which *Date My Family* is structured upon an alignment of ideal romance and luxury consumption. In the first few seasons, the show used a Volkswagen sedan but, in Season 4, the *Date My Family* driver has switched to a Volvo sedan. These are both desirable global brands associated with quality and status. The driver is shown dropping the date off at each of the locations he or she visits. The final choice of partner is also mediated by the *Date My Family* car, which drops off bottles of wine to rejected partners and brings the final pair together, ultimately delivering them to their romantic date. Thus, the first space in which the prospective partners encounter each other is within the interior of a luxury vehicle. This is the show's chosen setting for the romantic encounter. Visually, the *Date My Family* car is a salient and recurrent motif for the show. Each stop at a date's house is introduced with a low-angle shot of the car arriving. The personalized licence plate, reading '#Date' (another status-signalling luxury expense), and the car's logo are central and dominate the visual field of these shots.

The car is a somewhat literal symbol of mobility, signifying the luxury of being driven around when many of the participants and viewers at home may rely on public transport. Megan Jones (2013) argues that the car is also a signifier of social mobility and inclusion in post-apartheid South Africa. She writes:

> The social capital of the car in the South African imaginary is substantial; cars disclose the contours of difference and exclusion that persist in our cities but also offer up possibilities for testing the status quo. The friction between drivers and nondrivers, between haves and have-nots, is coded in the ways in which cars are consumed.
>
> (Jones 2013: 212)

Here, Jones describes the car as an essential signifier of wealth-based distinction and also an object upon which the possibilities of social mobility can be performed and tested.

On *Date My Family*, the foregrounding of the luxury car is indicative of the way in which the show aligns romance with the promise of social mobility and luxury lifestyles. But at the same time, when we consider debates and utterances of the shows' participants, the luxury car also operates as a contested object through which values related to class positionality, success and aspiration are explored. In my subsequent scene analyses, cars are a recurrent and important theme through which aspirational identities are both imagined and contested.

Sibonakaliso: Negotiating Romance as Consumption

The car is a pivotal feature of the heated interaction in a popular episode of *Date My Family*, featuring helicopter pilot Sibonakaliso, who is taken aback by the directness of the questions asked by his hosts, the friends and family of prospective date, Nadine (SE4, EP5). In this episode, Nadine's friend Daren explicitly conflates romance with commodities in her discussion of Sibonakaliso's car. During dinner, Daren asks Sibonakaliso what car he drives. He seems shocked by this candid question. Secluded in her room and watching via the television, Nadine throws up her hands in embarrassment at Daren's brazen question. Sibonakaliso initially evades the question, answering that it's 'a nice one', but Daren is determined to find out the brand of the car. He eventually tells her it is Volkswagen. Sibonakaliso's hosts exclaim in delight: 'There's just something about a Volkswagen [...] it seems you have got your match'. Here the women understand romantic compatibility as directly discernible from the shared love of a luxury car. Later, in an interview to the camera, Daren comments that she believes Nadine and Sibonakaliso will be a good love match because 'both of them love the same car [...] and they really adore it'.

Sibonakaliso is an example of an appealing 'eligible bachelor' who potentially represents concepts of aspiration, success and having 'made it', which are part of the post-apartheid imaginary. It would seem that Daren sees him as an appealing romantic prospect for her friend because he represents a certain aspirant lifestyle and his car is taken as a symbol of his suitability as a partner. However, there is an obvious conflict between the way in which Daren and Sibonakaliso understand love. The well-off Sibonakaliso is embarrassed by conversations about money, cars and gifts. He thus finds Daren's questions crass. Daren is looking to make a financially rewarding match for her friend and does not distinguish between love and money. This alignment of romance with material spending becomes particularly explicit later in her exchange with Sibonakaliso about gift giving.

Daren tries to find a way to ask Sibonakaliso if he gives his girlfriend gifts. She stumbles a bit in her use of English (something remarked upon with hilarity by some users on Twitter) and asks him if he is 'guy's gift'. Sibonakaliso is initially confused by Daren's question. There is a cut away to the shocked face of her friend and prospective date, Nadine, watching in an adjacent room. 'Ah! Romantic!' she comments, putting into words what she thinks Daren is trying to ask. Back in the family living room, Sibonakaliso also seems to have understood Daren's message. He asks if she means 'romantic'. And then he responds, 'no I'm not romantic'. To this, Daren responds, 'or are you gigantic? If you are not romantic it means you are gigantic'. Here Daren's statement seems to suggest that if Sibonakaliso is not going to be 'romantic' by buying gifts for his girlfriend then he will have to make up for it with sexual prowess. It is interesting that, for all three participants – Daren, Nadine and Sibonakaliso – the word 'romantic' signifies lavish gift giving, but they display divergent responses to this idea. In this example from *Date My Family*, luxury spending is represented as an essential part of romantic discourse.

The 'romantic/gigantic' moment comedically stages one of the key paradoxes within romantic discourse. Sibonakaliso would like to think of love as something beyond class differences and the petty world of things; as a wealthy person, he has the luxury of thinking this way. Daren's pursuit of wealth reveals her to Sibonakaliso as lacking in the appropriate manners that he expects in the courtship ritual, and this in itself is an example of class judgement. The scene described above is punctuated by awkward pauses and lingering close-ups on the facial expressions of the visiting bachelor as he expresses shock. The mechanisms of the reality television show thus encourage viewers to identify with Sibonakaliso's position and offer judgement on Daren's indelicate references to luxury objects and gifts.

Mduduzi: Clothing and Classed Performance

Several episodes of *Date My Family* have featured guests who appear to be caught out in lies about their wealth, status or background. A key example is an episode featuring a bachelor named Mduduzi, or Mdu (SE3, EP7). Each of the families he visits is perplexed by his accent, which seems to change frequently throughout the night. In addition to speaking with a 'posh' accent, Mdu also speaks about himself in the third person throughout the episode. Mdu's long-winded and evasive answers caused Twitter users to lament his 'lies' (Kekana 2017: 1). The family encounter on *Date My Family*, in many cases, becomes a means of routing out class pretenders and 'gold-diggers'. The family members play a role in countering the lofty self-representations of the guest, either by catching them out in their lies or by offering contrasting values of 'realness' and humility. Thus, in the show, the family encounter provides a productive frame for the pleasures of judgement and class distinction that Skeggs et al. (2007) have argued are so essential to reality television discourse. Interestingly, it is not just Mdu's words that mark him as a liar for the families he visits; his choice of clothing is remarked upon by almost all of the family members he encounters as an indication that he is misrepresenting himself.

Potential date Pauline, watching via a video feed, comments: 'My first impression when I looked at the guy is that he looks like a blesser and that is a no for me'. The word 'blesser' describes a typically older man who bestows lavish gifts and financial support on a younger woman. As Roya Varjavandi explains, 'blesser' is a recent South African term similar in meaning to 'sugar daddy' (2017: 3). She comments that the term 'became popularized virally in 2016 through social media hashtags penned by women who claimed to be beneficiaries of a "blesser" who has "blessed" them with luxurious gifts' (2017: 3). Varjavandi directly links blesser culture to luxury consumption. Given that Mdu is only four years older than Pauline (he is 36) and that this is her first impression of him before he has even spoken, we can assume that her response is very much informed by Mdu's clothing. For this 'date', he is wearing a white floral blazer with a Versace belt. What interests me about Pauline's reference to blessers on *Date My Family* is that she identifies a certain mode of self-stylization through which a blesser might advertise his wealth to younger women. Thus, luxury clothing is understood as a way of signalling the offer of transactional sex. Pauline's statement is indicative not just of her opinion of Mdu but of how she sees herself within the love and money nexus. That is, just as much as the statement is a rejection of Mdu's apparently sleazy style, so too is it an assertion that she is not a 'gold-digger' or the type of woman to be tempted or taken-in by Mdu's extravagant display of personal wealth through clothing.

Pauline's family members share her discomfort with Mdu's dress, commenting to the camera that his outfit makes them think of 'izikhothane'. This term describes a subculture involving street dancing, extravagant dressing and conspicuous spending. *Izikhothane* became notorious for buying luxury items and then destroying them. The subculture has been the object of much media attention and has also garnered a great deal of academic interest (see Jones 2013; Mnisi 2015; Chipp et al. 2016; Mchunu 2017). Jabulani Mnisi understands this subcultural practice as 'aspirational consumption' (2015: 343). This is because the spectacle of destruction is underpinned by a gap between the actual wealth of the *izikothane* and the apparently wasteful practice of destruction. He comments 'When *izikhothane*, who are known to be poor, engage in conspicuous consumption, the end perception is that they are wasteful and not wealthy, since their condition is known. However, their consumption is taken to mean that they aspire to be different, to be wealthy' (2015: 345). For the interests of my project, it is the gap between the *display* of spending and actual wealth that is significant. The family members are identifying a sense in which Mdu's excessive performance of style and wealth is not backed by material prosperity. His style is so flashy that it is read as a lack of social status rather than the impression of high social status that apparently Mdu wishes to signal.

On the third date with Thokozile's family, Mdu arrives wearing an entirely white suit. This family compares his appearance to that of a charismatic pastor, 'the famous one with all the white suits'. In all the descriptions of Mdu offered by the show's participants there is a suspicion that the overly showy nature of Mdu's clothing signals not wealth but an intention to mislead. Here it is important to note that while Mdu characterizes himself through expensive dressing, 'posh' language and claims of material wealth, the families he visits push back against these excesses and essentially 'bring him down a peg' by exposing his lies. Through the mechanisms of social media, viewers at home can also engage with the families in this process.

In terms of a broader theorization of luxury in South Africa, this episode seems to suggest that luxury items are not always read as signifiers of real wealth. Indeed expensive clothing purchases can be read as gauche and sleazy. These judgements about the gap between real wealth and the display of wealth through clothing might indicate an awareness of what Southall describes as the 'precarious positionality of the black middle-class' (2016: 189) and of the very real gaps between aspiration and its fulfilment.

Asanda: The 'Snooty' Bachelorette

Another recurring feature of *Date My Family* is the 'snooty' bachelor or bachelorette who considers themselves as superior to the families they visit. The pretensions of a visitor are often thrown into comic relief when their behaviour and values are contrasted with those of the families they visit. A good example of this process can be found in the episode featuring bachelorette, Asanda (EP5, SE1). She introduces herself as an entrepreneur and the manager of a nail bar called A-List Couture. In her first on-camera appearance she is dressed in pearls and seated on white lawn chairs in a luxurious garden setting as she explains her aspirations, tastes and the way she likes to spend her time. Asanda is somewhat typical of the kind of candidate selected to visit families on this show. That is, she self-identifies as hard-working and upwardly mobile in describing the clothing brand that she runs. But more than simply being ambitious and upwardly mobile, Asanda reveals herself as somewhat conceited. This personality trait becomes a key source of comedy in each of her family date scenarios as Asanda is paired with families who appear to fall short of Asanda's standards in terms of wealth, dress and taste.

Asanda describes her 'date' with family number one as 'a disaster'. Upon arriving at their home, Asanda surveys the surroundings and comments that the visit is a 'waste of an outfit', noting that she should have worn a bucket hat instead of the stylish clothing she is wearing. Here Asanda directly uses products, in this case clothing, to measure her class status in relation to her hosts.

Asanda also locates her class status in relation to her urban lifestyle. When she is driven to date number three, Bongani's family home in Hammanskraal, she comments: 'What on earth would I do out here?'. Despite Asanda's distaste for Hammanskraal, Bongani's family wins Asanda over and she chooses Bongani for her date. She also makes her decision partly based on the fact that Bongani owns a German sports car and is involved in the fashion industry. Bongani's possession of a luxury car is a detail repeated by the voice-over artist at the end of the episode when Asanda makes her choice. The narrator announces: 'The winner is, the champion on paper, the owner of a German sports car'. Once again, the luxury vehicle operates as a sign of potential romantic compatibility but by describing Bongani as a 'champion on paper' the narrator also hints that this materialistic way of selecting a date might not produce a compatible match.

It is important to understand the discursive construction of luxury on *Date My Family* in relation to contrasting objects and practices. Asanda's sense of style is something that she explicitly contrasts to spaces and clothing items she feels to be below her class status. Thus her outfit is at odds with her environment and is contrasted to the 'bucket hat'. A similar contrast occurs when Asanda and Bongani have their date, when the pair has a dispute about a *skaftin* (a plastic container or item of Tupperware). At the end of Asanda's date, Bongani's family gave her food to take home in a *skaftin*. Bongani claims that the Tupperware has sentimental value for him as it was given to him by his mother and he asks Asanda to bring it back. Asanda is appalled at this request and notes that she had to keep looking down at her meal to hide her embarrassment.

This *skaftin* exchange was met with an uproarious online response. A slew of Twitter tags, memes and articles were devoted to the *skaftin* controversy. For example, Zalebs.com titled the episode 'The Battle of the *Skaftin*', while *The Daily Sun* released an article entitled 'I want my Tupperware' (Nxukumeshe-Makhubo 2015). The subheading of the article read 'If you know what's good for you, you will not come between a black man and his Tupperware' (Nxukumeshe-Makhubo 2015: 1). Here, a complex set of understandings about cultural practice, class and race are centred on a domestic item. The Tupperware becomes the locus for a certain sense of shared identity and understanding with many online commentators identifying with the importance of Tupperware in black South African households. Asanda is, notably, unable to relate to these discourses about the meaning of the *skaftin*. She is thus marked out as something of an outsider – the subject of a shared joke.

Furthermore, beyond the contestation of classed identity operating in relation to the *skaftin*, there is also a tension between two different types of love: romantic luxury versus the humility of family love. Bongani is sensitive about the Tupperware because it reminds him of his mother's love and its value is based not on money but on more intangible and humble properties, such as memories of the domestic home, an attachment to his roots and his love for his mother. Asanda appears unable to see value beyond the monetary cost and status-signalling role of luxury items. The exploration of value and love on this show is thus mediated through the contrast between luxury spending and objects that signify humility and family values.

Conclusion

In the episodes analysed in this chapter, I have explained the role played by luxury items in the representation of romance on *Date My Family*. I have shown that romantic practice and luxury consumption are often conflated in the discussions featured on the show. This conflation is particularly notable in relation to the romantic appeal of luxury cars. This understanding of romance as luxury suggests that the concept of luxury might be seen as a central component of discourses of romantic love on South African television. *Date My Family* provides a fertile site for exploring representations of luxury in South Africa because it at once celebrates luxury as a key facilitator of romance and subjects luxury displays to suspicion and criticism. While the fantasy of romance-as-luxury-spending underpins some of the pleasures of the show, there is also a contradictory discourse at play in the programme: one that enters into the heart of the paradox of love described by Illouz. Love in *Date My Family* offers the promise of transcendence and aspiration associated with the democratic ideals of the 'new' South Africa. However, at the same time the codes of love rely heavily on material means and luxury discernment. Luxury items, gift giving, clothing and cars are key index points for the negotiation of tensions between love, class and aspiration. This romantic paradox is rich material for the reality television format that is in turn driven by both fantasies of luxury and the more cynical pleasures to be derived from judgement and class distinction. The narrative of *Date My Family* is driven by the lure of a romantic future with an ideal partner, a future marked by luxury spending, shared ambition, career success and middle-class affluence. However, *Date My Family's* foregrounding of the family home plays a levelling role, contrasting the aspirational ideals of romantic discourse with an investment in humility and more grounded values; or subjecting the excessive displays of style and luxury clothing to a scrutiny in which excessive style is understood as a mask for the absence of real, stable wealth. The show speaks to the unstable, 'in-between' spaces of transitional post-apartheid class identities as prospective partners are caught out in the gaps between their real lives and the luxury lives to which they aspire.

References

Anon. (2015), 'Battle of the *skaftin*', Zalebs, 22 June, https://www.zalebs.com/post/reviews/date-my-family/. Accessed 28 June 2017.

Being Bonang (2017–present, South Africa: BME).

Belk, Russell and Coon, Gregory (1991), 'Can't buy me love: Dating, money and gifts', *Advances in Consumer Research,* 18, pp. 521–27.

Chipp, Kerry, Kapelianis, Dimitri and Mkhwanazi, Penelope (2016), 'Ukukhothana: The curious case of conspicuous consumption and destruction', in K. Plangger (ed.), *Thriving in a New World Economy, Developments in Marketing Science: Proceedings of the Academy of Marketing Science,* Cham: Springer, pp. 161–63.

Date My Family (2015), Season 1 Episode 5 (21 June, South Africa: ConnectTV).

—— (2017a), Season 3 Episode 7 (15 January, South Africa: ConnectTV).

—— (2017b), Season 4 Episode 5 (16 April, South Africa: ConnectTV).

Diski Divas (2015–present, South Africa: ConnectTV).

Featherstone, Mike (2014), 'Luxury, consumer culture and sumptuary dynamics', *Luxury,* 1:1, pp. 47–69.

Hill, Annette (2015), 'Studying reality TV', in G. Creeber (ed.), *The Television Genre Book,* London: Bloomsbury Publishing, pp. 161–63.

Illouz, Eva (1997), *Consuming the Romantic Utopia: Love and the Cultural Contradictions of Capitalism,* Berkeley, CA: University of California Press.

Iqani, Mehita (2016), *Consumption, Media and the Global South: Aspiration Contested,* Pietermaritzburg: University of KwaZulu-Natal Press.

Ives, Sarah (2007), 'Mediating the neoliberal nation: Television in post-apartheid South Africa', *ACME: An International Journal for Critical Geographies,* 6:2, pp. 153–73.

Jones, Megan (2013), 'Conspicuous destruction, aspiration and motion in the South African Township', *Safundi,* 14:2, pp. 209–24.

Keeping Up with the Kardashians (2007–present, USA: BMP Productions).

Kekana, Chrizelda (2017), 'Mdu's the dude with the "come and go" British accent', *IOL Entertainment,* 16 January, http://www.iol.co.za/entertainment/tv/dmf-mdus-the-dude-with-the-come-and-go-uk-accent-7418298. Accessed 20 July 2017.

Kruger, Loren (2010), 'Critique by stealth: Aspiration, consumption and class in post-apartheid television drama', *Critical Arts: A Journal of South-North Cultural Studies,* 24:1, pp. 75–98.

Mchunu, Koyi (2017), 'Izikhothane youth phenomenon: The Janus face of contemporary culture in South Africa', *African Identities,* 15:2, pp. 132–42.

Mnisi, Jabulani (2015), 'Burning to consume? Izikhothane in Daveyton as aspirational consumers', *Communication,* 41:3, pp. 340–53.

Mupotsa, Danai (2015), 'The promise of happiness: Desire, attachment and freedom in post-apartheid South Africa', *Critical Arts,* 29:2, pp. 183–98.

Nxukumeshe-Makhubo, Phumla (2015), 'I want my Tupperware', *The Daily Sun,* 22 June, http://www.dailysun.co.za/News/Entertainment/I-want-my-Tupperware-20150622. Accessed 27 July 2017.

Our Perfect Wedding (2011–present, South Africa: ConnectTV).

Posel, Deborah (2010), 'Races to consume: Revisiting South Africa's history of race, consumption and the struggle for freedom', *Ethnic and Racial Studies*, 33:2, pp. 157–75.

Ramphele, Mamphela and Richter, Linda (2006), 'Migrancy, family dissolution and fatherhood', in L. Richter and R. Morrell (eds), *Baba: Men and Fatherhood in South Africa*, Cape Town: HSRC Press, pp. 73–82.

Rich Kids (2015–present, South Africa: Something's Cool).

Sibeko, Sphumelele (2016), telephone interview, 18 September.

Skeggs, Beverly, Wood, Helen and Thumin, Nancy (2007), 'Making class through moral extension on reality TV', Umeå Universitet, http://www8.umu.se/medfak/cgf/bev%20warwick%20 with%20edits%20_2_.pdf. Accessed 5 December 2017.

Southall, Roger (2016), *The New Black Middle Class in South Africa*, Johannesburg: Jacana.

The Real Housewives of Orange County (2006–present, USA: Dunlop Entertainment).

Thomas, Lynn and Cole, Jennifer (2009), 'Thinking through love in Africa', in L. Thomas and J. Cole (eds), *Love in Africa*, Chicago: University of Chicago Press, pp. 1–30.

Top Billing (1996–present, South Africa: Tswelopele Productions).

UCT Unilever Institute for Strategic Marketing (2013), '4000,000 – and rising: The latest chapter in the meteoric rise of South Africa's black middle class', PowerPoint presentation, African Studies Library, University of Cape Town, 26 August.

Varjavandi, Roya (2017), '#Blessers must fall: Youth-led participatory action research and photo story creation on teenage pregnancy, transactional sex and gender-based violence', *Agenda*, 31:2, pp. 1–12.

Section 2

(Re)Crafting African Style

Chapter 4

From African Print to Global Luxury: Dutch Wax Cloth Rebranding and the Politics of High-Value

M. Amah Edoh

[*The young woman walks towards the camera. She is brown-skinned. Her face has Barbie doll qualities: features delicate, eyes almond-shaped, skin smooth and even-toned. She smiles softly at the camera and her gaze lingers as she sashays across the frame and along the bed, before she finally looks away sensuously. She is wearing a floor-length sleeveless dress cut from two classic Dutch wax cloth designs. As she glides past the bed, the camera pans from her face down to the bed, where folded pieces of iconic Dutch wax prints are spilling out of what looks like a large gift box. Stopping in front of the dresser, the woman reaches for framed black and white pictures of herself holding a baby. The voiceover begins:*]

A mother's beauty is passed on to her daughter.

[*The voice is a middle-aged black woman's, her accent a crisp British-West African suggesting high social status or education level. A quick succession of shots follows. The woman is now with two young children, an infant and a toddler. She rubs noses with the infant, strokes the fabric on the bed.*]

Her love of life and wisdom, bestowed as gifts.

[*The woman is now twirling and bouncing the infant as the toddler looks on; all three are clad in the same fabrics.*]

And that is why a mother passes on…

[*It is now the toddler's turn to be twirled and bounced, holding the laughing woman's hands.*]

…that there is only one Wax Hollandais.

[*Woman and baby turn to face the camera in time with the words 'Wax Hollandais'. The woman smiles knowingly towards the camera, as the baby gazes off-frame.*]

Vlisco Wax Hollandais.

[*The woman, alone once more, sashays back the way she came, past the bed and out of the frame. The shot lingers for a second after she has walked off, and the container holding the fabric on the bed is revealed to be not a gift box, but rather an ivory-colored suitcase, lying open atop immaculate white sheets and pillows in what looks like a high-end hotel room.*]

Vlisco, the true original since 1846.

[*A white background, with the words THE TRUE ORIGINAL and Vlisco's logo fades into the shot of the suitcase on the bed, eventually covering it.*]

A mind-blowing new collection, now also available in shorter lengths.

(Vlisco 2015)

Often referred to as 'African print', wax cloth has become a marker of Africanness since its introduction by European merchants to West Africa in the late nineteenth century. The Dutch company Vlisco is the sole remaining manufacturer of wax cloth from this era, and its flagship textile, featured in the advertisement above, is known as Dutch wax cloth, or Wax Hollandais.[1] This 30-second advertisement, intended for English-speaking West African television and uploaded to YouTube in 2015, exemplifies Vlisco's brand communications following the company's decision to reimagine itself from a maker of 'African print cloth' into a global luxury design and fashion brand. Indeed, in the late 1990s, after over a century of producing textiles for West and Central African markets and enjoying a privileged position in this trade, Vlisco found itself facing the cumulative effects of overwhelming competition from lower priced Chinese-manufactured wax cloth on one hand, and decreased purchasing power in much of West Africa on the other. With the competition unrelenting, and profit margins continuing to shrink, Vlisco decided in 2006 to target new, non-African markets with its products, by remaking itself into a global brand (World Intellectual Property Organization 2012). 'Now is a time of great change for Vlisco', the company's then-CEO states in a handout distributed at Vlisco's exhibit at the 2013 Dutch Design Week in Eindhoven, an important moment in Vlisco's public refashioning. 'We are evolving from a factory making fabrics for Africa to a design house. We want to show that with the Vlisco brand our vision is global, we are not only focusing on Africa' (Vlisco 2013). Key to this rebranding process were advertising campaigns featuring the company's signature textiles and communicating its new brand identity. Campaigns included television ads, like the one above, and also oversized billboards in key West- and Central-African cities, as well as online campaigns on the company's website and social media outlets.

A cross-cultural commodity par excellence, Dutch wax cloth is the outcome of encounters between Indonesia, Europe and West Africa at the turn of the twentieth century. The cloth is the product of the mechanization by European textile manufacturers of the Javanese batik printing technique (Nielsen 1979). As it came to be produced specifically for West African markets in the 1890s (Kroese 1976), its aesthetic was adapted by manufacturers to suit these new consumers' tastes through market research (Steiner 1985) and what anthropologist Nina Sylvanus has denoted 'collaborative design' (2016) between European manufacturers and West African distributors and users of the cloth. Existing work on Dutch wax cloth and its batik antecedents has interrogated transformations of the cloth's signification as it moved between Indonesia and Holland (Legêne 2009), and between Europe and West Africa (Nielsen 1979; Steiner 1985; Sylvanus 2016). With Vlisco's latest business strategy, 'the global' enters the fray as the latest 'site' in this commodity's network; it is this movement that the present chapter examines.

Cross-cultural commodities have long offered anthropologists a means of interrogating the makeup of distinct regimes of value and the politics of translating across them (Thomas 1991; Appadurai 1988).[2] We learn from this work that the possibility of a thing's (commodity or otherwise) movement from one stage to another, its possibility of exchange, hinges on the negotiation of its forms and meanings by social actors along the path. A close look at these negotiations reveals not only the 'multiplicities and ambiguities of value [that] inhere in the workings of all commodity networks' (Foster 2006: 290), but also makes visible the configuration of power in the spaces that the commodity traverses. In particular, it illuminates the agency of consumers and of other social actors beyond production.

My premise in this chapter is that as Vlisco sought to reinvent itself, its rebranding into a global luxury brand hinged on the translation of the high-value that Dutch wax cloth has come to hold in West and Central Africa into the high-value of a luxury brand. Another passage in Vlisco's handout at the Dutch Design Week mentioned above posits the company's textiles as luxury items *prior* to their uptake by West and Central African consumers:

> Our heritage is quite unlike any other. Since 1846, when Pieter Fentener van Vlissingen founded the company, our luxury textiles have had a significant influence on the fashion landscape in West and Central Africa. These distinctive designs have become part of the very fabric of life for generations of women.
>
> (Vlisco 2013)

By emphasizing the 'influence' of Vlisco's textiles on West and Central African social life, this statement situates agency squarely in the company's textiles, in effect emphasizing the company's design and technical expertise in explaining the cloth's prominence in this region of the world. But scholars of material culture have shown us that commodities' value is articulated not only in production, but rather in *interactions* between actors all along commodities' trajectory between production and market, through 'trials of value' (Appadurai 1988) or, again, acts of 'qualification' (Callon et al. 2002).

In Lomé, Togo, which was, for much of the twentieth century, the hub for Dutch wax cloth's distribution throughout West and Central Africa, the cloth is known as *tsigan-vɔ*,[3] which translates literally as high-value or high-cost cloth in Mina, Togo's *lingua franca*. I show in what follows how Dutch wax cloth's status as a high-value item in Togo and throughout West and Central Africa more broadly is not only a product of the cloth's material qualities and Vlisco's technical prowess, but also – especially, perhaps – an outcome of the 'consumption work' (Miller 1987; Foster 2007) of Togolese and other West and Central African buyers and users of the cloth, who, through their meaning-making practices since Dutch wax cloth's introduction to West African markets, have invested the cloth with exceptional worth.

What are we to make of the 'global' aspect in Vlisco's rebranding as a 'global luxury'? In the Dutch Design Week handout, the then-creative director equates it with geographical location: 'We are certainly going global. And if you look at that from a business point of view, it means we will be selling products worldwide' (Vlisco 2013). Anthropologist James Ferguson (2006) reminds us, though, that questions of status and rank must be foundational to contemporary conceptualizations of the global; that engaging the globe requires paying close attention to questions of membership and inequality in the world order.

African social actors have had a tenuous relationship to the global, characterized by 'highly selective and spatially encapsulated forms of global connection combined with widespread disconnection and exclusion' (Ferguson 2006: 14). Today, we find ourselves in a moment when Africa's place in the world, and thus its relationship to 'the global', is ostensibly being rearticulated. Under the banner of 'Africa rising', 'The New Africa' or some conceptualizations of Afropolitanism (Selasi 2005), the image (quite literally) of 'Africa' appears to be undergoing a makeover (Nothias 2014; Ogunyankin 2016).[4] Vlisco's advertising images, which render wax cloth in the idiom of high fashion, can be said to be part of this makeover. The images are central to the company's strategy for communicating its new identity as a global luxury brand. And, by virtue of the product it promotes, a textile that is today colloquially referred to as 'African print', they also put forward a vision or version of African globality. What might Vlisco's refashioning from manufacturer of highly valued textiles for Africa into global luxury brand reveal about current articulations of the historically complicated relationship between Africa and 'the global'?

To get at this question, I first discuss how Vlisco's signature product, Dutch wax cloth, has been marketed as high-value cloth, *tsigan*, in Lomé by Togolese sellers, users and tailors of the cloth. I will then examine the logics that guided the company's approach to producing advertising images for brand communications – how Dutch wax cloth was 'qualified' as global luxury in these images. Advertising is a key node in the articulation of the dialectical relationship between consumers and brand: brands depend on consumers' attachment to and investment in the brand to generate surplus value, even as brands produce categories of consumers through marketing practices like market research and advertising (Foster 2007; Arvidsson 2005; Lury 2004). I argue that Vlisco, like all brands, appropriates the consumption work of its longstanding consumers – those who predated the company's rebranding efforts. Its brand communications also render those same consumers and their preferences invisible because they do not match industry standards for the look of 'global luxury'. The effect, I argue, is a reification of the distinction between those who count as 'global' actors and those who do – or can –not. I suggest that this amounts to something like a gentrification of Dutch wax cloth as this marker of Africanness goes 'global'.[5]

Enacting Dutch Wax as High-Value Cloth: Consumption Work in Lomé

'*Tsigan-a, enu gɔme enɔna*'. Uttered with dramatic emphasis by Mme Attigbo, a second-generation Loméan Dutch wax cloth seller in her sixties, these words capture the value that Dutch wax cloth holds for Loméan women today: *tsigan* is something that you keep hidden away, like a treasure.[6] Since its introduction to Lomé's markets in the early twentieth century,[7] Dutch wax cloth has been appropriated by Togolese users into cloth-centred meaning-making practices that predated the cloth's arrival. In Togo, as in much of West Africa, these practices, applied to both locally produced textiles and textiles procured via transcontinental and transoceanic trade networks (Kriger 2009; Riello and Parthasarathi 2011; Picton and Becker 1995), have leveraged cloth not only as dress and adornment, but also in the marking of kinship ties, and in the celebration of important life events, such as births, marriages and funerals, and as a form of currency and wealth – female wealth specifically (see Hansen

2004; Hendrickson 1996; Kriger 2009). Through the consumption work of selling, tailoring, wearing and keeping the cloth, Togolese social actors – largely women – have made Dutch wax into *tsigan-vɔ*: high-value cloth.

Mme Attigbo entered the Dutch wax cloth trade in 1987, joining and eventually taking over her mother's extremely lucrative business. Though, unlike the famed Nanas Benz, the wholesalers who gained control of the extremely lucrative Dutch wax cloth trade in Togo in the 1950s and sustained their control through a matrilineal system of succession, Mme Attigbo and her mother specialized in 'fends': slightly defective Dutch wax cloth prints sold at a discount.[8] Like the Nanas, however, Mme Attigbo and her mother made sizable profits from this trade, distributing the cloth through a network of retailers from both Lomé and from as far afield as Congo and Angola.

The Nanas Benz were key to building up the Dutch wax cloth trade throughout West and Central Africa, and establishing the cloth as a high-value item in the post-independence era (Sylvanus 2016). Indeed, as Mme Attigbo and other sellers I spoke with explained, such was the reach of their influence that buyers from outside of Togo often remarked that 'the nicest Dutch wax cloths are the ones that come from Lomé', even though all of Vlisco's Dutch wax is printed in the same factory in the southern Dutch town of Helmond. The Nanas and sellers like Mme Attigbo and her mother accomplished this not only through their business acumen and their relationship with state power, but also through their own dressed bodies, by wearing the Dutch wax designs they sold as a means of advertising them. When the Nanas Benz wore these designs, they 'enhanced the cloth's semiotic power and currency' through their bodies (Sylvanus 2016: 94).

As was the case during those early days of the cloth's trade, tailoring continues today to be a key technology through which Dutch wax cloth is enacted as *tsigan* in Lomé. A recurring observation – sometimes more of a reproach – from Togolese tailors and wearers of the cloth I encountered throughout my fieldwork was: 'You don't put scissors in *tsigan* any which way'; the implication being that the cloth must be cut, crafted, 'the right way'. Mme Johnson, a tailor who has been working in Lomé for over thirty years, explained that sometimes she goes as far as to veto a customer's plans for the *tsigan* they bring her: 'I'll tell her, "We can't make that with this fabric. This fabric, you shouldn't waste it". You see', Mme Johnson explained to me from the *salon de couture* where she sees her relatively well-heeled clientele, 'our mothers' mindset [*mentalité*] about *Wax Hollandais* is that the cloth must be pampered [*chouchouté*]'.

The special treatment that Dutch wax cloth commands is not just predicated on its high cost – although the cloth certainly is expensive; in 2013, the standard 6-yard length cost approximately 35,000FCFA (or 70USD), which is equal to the Togolese SMIG, the monthly minimum salary (Kokoura 2011). Rather, if Dutch wax cloth should be handled carefully, it is also because of the ways that it functions as a memory object; specifically, as a material manifestation of the relationship between a woman and her mother – or *mothers*. Along with money, spirits and other gifts, *tsigan* is one of the most significant components of the gifts a prospective groom's family offers the bride-to-be (*la dot*, in French, or bridewealth), and the cloth is meant to be passed down from mother to daughter as part of a woman's inheritance. In the words of Mme Johnson, a mother's gift of *tsigan* to her daughter is 'like a transfer of love'. In fact, the deep attachment that Togolese women have cultivated to Dutch wax cloth over the decades since the cloth's introduction is captured in a common appellation for the oldest Dutch wax designs in Lomé: *mya maman-wo bavɔ*, our grandmothers' cloth. This way of naming the cloth ties any Togolese woman – or man, for that matter – to collective mothers, enlisting Dutch wax cloth in the marking of the nation, a process mediated by women's bodies and labour.

As a memory object, then, *tsigan* mediates transgenerational continuity (Bickford 1994), playing a particularly important role in processes of social reproduction. A woman's *tsigan* collection, built over a lifetime through gift-giving, purchasing, bridewealth and inheritance, serves as a cherished repository of memories where printed designs become symbolic of particular relationships and people, creating a wearable photo album of sorts. Similar to jewellery in certain traditions, *tsigan* holds both sentimental and monetary value. It is a form of 'wearable wealth' (Gott 2009), as women keep their *tsigan* collection, not only to commemorate important life events and relationships, but also as an emergency fund that can be sold in times of financial hardship. It is for this reason that the cloth must 'remain hidden' as Mme Attigbo explained – typically in suitcases or metallic trunks, under beds or deep in closets.

For these reasons, Dutch wax cloth tailoring in Lomé is often seen by tailors and wearers as an exercise in either preservation or conspicuous consumption (Veblen 1912), two sides of the same coin. The Loméan tailors I interviewed routinely contrasted Togolese attitudes to the cloth with what they considered the more liberal approach taken by Ivorian tailors, for instance, who 'cut the cloth' freely.[9] In Lomé, however, many tailors still considered the *jupe-pagne* the most appropriate garment to be crafted from *tsigan*. The customary three-piece style (a long skirt, blouse and a piece of fabric to be draped over the shoulder, tied around the hips or used to secure a child to the back) is cut in such a manner that the skirt and blouse can be undone and most of the fabric recuperated. But regardless of whether she is creating a *jupe-pagne* or not, Mme Johnson explained, when clients entrust her with their *tsigan*, she looks for a style that will last, that her clients will be able to continue wearing when fashion trends – and their bodies – change. For that reason, she consciously designs *tsigan* garments to be easily size-adjustable. This is why having *tsigan* sewn into a garment from which the cloth can clearly *not* be recuperated can be a form of conspicuous consumption, a way for the wearer to display her economic power.

Whether crafted into conservative or ostentatious styles, *tsigan* is leveraged by Togolese women in their performances of female respectability (also see Sylvanus 2013). And the enacting of this cloth as a high-value object extends to its care, with specific washing techniques deployed as a means to prolong the cloth's longevity. Per Mme Johnson's instructions (reprised time and again in my conversations with Dutch wax cloth sellers and wearers in Lomé): 'You're supposed to lay it out to air after you wear it. If you got the bottom dirty by walking, then you take some Savon de Marseille,[10] and you gently rub it off. You do the same for the armpits also, or wherever else you might have sweated. And then, you dry it in the shade. But you're not supposed to wash it every day'.

It is through practices like these – selling, tailoring, giving and keeping – the consumption work of African social actors like the Togolese women above, that Dutch wax cloth has been made and continues to be made into, or enacted as, a high-value cloth. It is the high value with which these women have imbued the cloth that forms the basis of the high value Vlisco's leadership alluded to in the company's global aspirations at the time of its rebranding, as in the statement from the CEO that 'we're well-known in Africa, but not in the rest of the world. This is the right time to get our story out there' (Vlisco 2013). What happens to Vlisco's longstanding consumers' labour in the process of getting Dutch wax cloth out to 'the rest of the world'?

Rebranding Vlisco: Dutch Wax Cloth as Global Luxury

The imperative to 'get Vlisco's story out there' grew out of the drastic reshaping of market conditions in West Africa that started in the early 1990s, changes that pushed the company to revisit its business strategy in order to stave off bankruptcy. In the early 1990s, Togo, like much of West Africa, found itself in the midst of economic and political upheaval. Not only had the austerity measures imposed by the World Bank and IMF's infamous structural adjustment plans in the 1980s dealt a hard financial blow to most of the Togolese population, but these effects were cumulated by the devaluation of the CFA franc, the currency used throughout Francophone Africa, by 50 per cent in 1994. The purchasing power of consumers throughout the CFA 'zone' was effectively cut in half overnight (Kalife 2016).

Brand communications were key to Vlisco's re-imagining. More than merely a means of distinguishing producers from one another, brands communicate meaning, values and identities (Lury 2004; Arvidsson 2005; Foster 2005), and advertising, one of the key sites where the specific characteristics of a brand are given visual form, is a critically important component of branding. For Vlisco, the company's advertising images had to recast Dutch wax cloth, widely perceived as specifically African and, for many observers outside of Africa, as a marker of 'tradition', as a high-end commodity desirable to elite customers not only in Africa, but also in the global North, the new target of the brand's 'global' expansion. In other words, these images had to mediate the cloth's translation into a 'global ecumene of world-class consumption' (Mazzarella 2003: 33).

This proved to be a constraining position for the communications staff tasked with producing Vlisco's advertising campaigns, as they found themselves caught between the aesthetic standards of the global luxury industry and those of their established African clientele. For, unlike established luxury brands targeting new markets, who might look to adapt their existing brand communications to new contexts (see Hoffman and Coste-Manière 2013 on Dior and Louis Vuitton Moët Hennessy [LVMH]), Vlisco needed to build its identity as a luxury brand from the ground up. To do so, its challenge would be to figure out how to bridge the dual imperatives of making itself recognizable as global luxury – to reach its aspirational consumers – while satisfying the preferences of its established clientele – because the company needed to retain its existing customer base, even as it sought out new markets.

The approach the company adopted was to apply industry standards for the comm-unication of a luxury brand identity to its advertising images – to things like the choice of model, how the model was styled (dress, hair, makeup) and the staging of images, including the poses the model struck and conventions about smiling (see Edoh 2016, for a more detailed discussion of campaign photoshoots). At times, the strategy has also involved partnering with photographers with international notoriety in the fashion industry. And as a general rule, renowned luxury brands were a key reference for campaigns' creative direction.

These choices could prove to be contentious. In particular, the age and size of models that fit the aesthetic of luxury branding – young and thin – was at odds with what Vlisco's market research revealed as the preferences of the company's core consumers.[11] 'We need more fat ladies on billboards', a senior member of the communications team reported hearing repeatedly, along with concerns that the models were too young, on a recent market research trip to Nigeria during a campaign production meeting in 2013. For the customers she encountered, who represented Vlisco's core consumer demographic, large body size was valued as a sign of wealth and fertility. But 'you can't put the Maggi lady on a billboard and call yourself a luxury brand', the communications team member had explained to me in a later conversation, as she conveyed the ongoing challenge of reconciling the preferences of Vlisco's core and most loyal consumers with the exigencies of the company's new brand identity. A prominent figure in advertisements for Maggi, an international seasonings brand, the 'Maggi lady', in her West African instantiation at least, is typically a matronly figure. Ample-bodied, smiling, motherly, she is generally in naturalistic poses, as opposed to the stylized poses of fashion photography.

The tension between the preferences of Vlisco's core consumers and luxury branding standards manifested also with regards to the dress styles portrayed in campaign images. For a campaign I followed during my fieldwork, for instance, asymmetric, form-fitting garments combining multiple designs, colourways and all three varieties of wax-printed textiles that Vlisco produces were created for the ad campaign. Though these styles were consistent with the collection's concept, which sought to capture an eclectic, slightly wild persona, communications staff grew concerned that they might have strayed too far from acceptable ways of wearing the cloth for many of the company's core consumers in West Africa.

The communications team's approach in the face of these constraints consisted of seeking compromises where possible. Body size was not negotiable, but campaigns could feature a model in her thirties, which, though not 'older' in the ways that core consumers intended, was 'old in model years', as it was put during a campaign production meeting. And the in-house fashion designers who created the styles for the campaigns created two sets of looks – a more conceptual set like the styles above for the global campaign, which would be displayed online and on billboards, and a more conservative set for regional-level communications.

These styles, which included several skirt-and-blouse combinations and less fabric mixing, were meant to more closely reflect actual dress practices in West and Central Africa.

Vlisco's approach to rendering Dutch wax cloth in the idiom of luxury, as defined by advertising industry standards, can be understood as an instance of what Callon et al. conceptualize as 'qualification' (2002), a means of enabling a commodity to move along its trajectory to new markets by satisfying the qualitative or aesthetic exigencies of targeted consumer groups. If successful, this qualification would establish a link between the brand, Vlisco, and new consumers, consumers of 'global luxury', and offer a means of translating the cloth's *tsigan* high-value into the high-value of luxury. But, we might ask, what does this process of qualifying Dutch wax as 'global luxury' do for the relationship between the brand and its longstanding consumers, given that the qualities of 'global luxury' put forth in advertising images are often at odds with the qualities that these consumers value? The 'Love through the ages' advertisement described in the opening of this chapter offers the beginnings of an answer.

Disappearing Acts: African Subjectivities and the Consumer Politics of Global Luxury

'Love through the ages' presents a striking example of how the historical and contemporary consumption work of Vlisco's core consumers is taken up in the brand's creation of surplus value, or profit. Anthropologist Robert Foster has argued that to derive a profit, brands appropriate not only the labour of production workers, but also that of consumers, who, through their consumption work, imbue the brand with meaning (Foster 2005, 2007). This value that consumers produce for the brand – the consumers' 'labor of love' – is then re-appropriated, through mechanisms like consumer research and brand management, into the brand's process of value creation (Foster 2005). 'The premium price that consumers pay for brands [thus] represents a charge levied for access to the meanings, social relations, and affect that consumers themselves have produced' (Foster 2007: 718). As such, 'brands represent the appropriation of the appropriations of branded goods by consumers' (Foster 2007: 718), or differently put, the appropriation of consumers' love labour.

In 'Love through the ages', the value with which West African women have imbued Dutch wax cloth over the past several decades is transposed into the aesthetic of 'global luxury'. It is embodied by a young, thin model wearing a gown cut from iconic Dutch wax cloth designs in the modernist aesthetic of a high-end hotel room, as well as the British-accented English of the voice-over. Dutch wax cloth in the advertisement figures as an object of the female realm, and, more particularly, a form of female wealth; mother and daughters wear the same print as a symbol of their affective bond; the woman's Dutch wax cloth collection is stored in a suitcase, the customary mode of storage of the cloth in West Africa; and the narrative underlines the passing down of Dutch wax cloth from mother to daughter as part of her legacy. The fact that the ad ends with a statement promoting the company's latest innovation (shorter lengths) offers a potent example of how the means by which Dutch wax cloth has been enacted as *tsigan* in Togo, for instance, are leveraged by the brand to derive surplus value.

Consumer love is not only made explicit in the ad, but is in fact the *focus* of the ad and captured in its title. Consumer love also figures in other forms of brand communications for Vlisco, such as its self-definition as a 'love brand' (Schäfer 2014). And, to the extent that it is the company's longstanding customers who, through their appropriation of Dutch wax cloth into meaning-making practices, have made the product's 'originality' and 'authenticity' valuable qualities, the tagline of the company's brand and logo – 'The true, the original' – also reflects the appropriation of Vlisco's longstanding consumers' labour of love for brand value creation.

But even though, as Foster tells us, '[t]he persons of consumers enhance the value of brands' (2005: 11), in the case of Vlisco's communications of its brand identity as global luxury, the consumers whose labour is being appropriated are made invisible. It is indeed the consumption work of these longstanding consumers – women for whom large body size and advanced age are markers of respectability and status – that Vlisco's brand is built on; the images in the 'Love through the ages' advertisement accordingly reflect several aspects of this labour. Yet even as the value with which these women have imbued Dutch wax cloth is appropriated into Vlisco's advertising images like the television spot above, their preferences – namely women who look like them – are absent from the brand's public image. In the case of advertising Dutch wax cloth as global luxury, then, the standard brand appropriation of consumers' labour is coupled with the making invisible of the very consumers whose labour is being appropriated.

The industry standards for luxury, employed by Vlisco's communications team, promote a particular vision of beauty and femininity, one where aspirational female beauty takes the form of youthfulness and a thin body. On the one hand, Vlisco's application of these standards in its brand communications might be seen as a form of the 'shadowing' between Africa and the West that Ferguson describes in *Global Shadows*: the aspiration towards western material realities not as a matter of 'blind copying', but rather as a means of claiming coeval-ness between Africa and the West (2006). But the problem here is that the aesthetic norms on which these standards for luxury are built were constructed with blackness and Africanness as their Other (see Nuttall 2006). Continuing to leverage them in this manner not only reinforces these norms, but may even be read as a form of epistemic violence (Spivak 1988). 'Global luxury', when mobilized as a singular set of norms, as in Vlisco's brand communications, does political work: it reifies the distinction between who counts as a 'global' consumer and who does not.

Conclusions: The Gentrification of Dutch Wax?

Wax cloth is today ubiquitous in the global cultural arena, almost *de rigueur*; as a signifier of African identity in the Afrobeats music videos distributed via YouTube, or in the collections of African fashion designers, or again as the latest trend in major European department stores. This wax craze occurs at a time when African cultural production is being revalued in global markets. While welcome, to the extent that it indicates a favourable resignification of Africa and of its place in the world, this new 'positive' valuation of African cultural production also carries risks, art historian Chika Okeke-Agulu reminds us. Focusing on African modern art, Okeke-Agulu (2017) warns of the 'gentrification' of African cultural production in the age of The New Africa: the very fact that African artists' work is now being recognized and appreciated by global institutions and on global markets threatens to make them (even) less accessible to the overwhelming majority of people in the countries from which the work originates.

Might Vlisco's remaking of Dutch wax cloth as 'global luxury' be considered a form of gentrification of the cloth? Though the cloth is not indigenous to West Africa, it has become a marker of Africanness through the consumption labour of Togolese and other West and Central African women – sellers, wearers, tailors – over the course of decades. As this cloth is taken into new realms and increasingly visible beyond the bodies and lives of these women, who have made it an object of high-value, these very women are skipped over in the new story of Dutch wax. The rebranding of Dutch wax cloth as global luxury highlights lingering concerns with regards to the conditions for African recognition and participation in the global: who gets to be the face of African globality? As the image of 'Africa' is redrawn, who is left out of the picture?

Acknowledgements

I wish to thank the participants who enabled me to carry out the research on which this chapter is based, as well as Mehita Iqani and Simidele Dosekun, Meredith Coleman-Tobias and two anonymous reviewers for their careful reads and insightful comments on earlier drafts of the chapter.

References

Appadurai, Arjun (ed.) (1988), *The Social Life of Things: Commodities in Cultural Perspective*, Cambridge: Cambridge University Press.

Arvidsson, Adam (2005), 'Brands: A critical perspective', *Journal of Consumer Culture*, 5:2, pp. 235–58.

Bickford, Kathleen E. (1994), 'The ABCs of cloth and politics in Côte d'Ivoire', *Africa Today*, 41:2, pp. 5–24.

Callon, Michel, Méadel, Cécile and Rabeharisoa, Vololona (2002), 'The economy of qualities', *Economy and Society*, 31:2, pp. 194–217.

Chalfin, Brenda (2004), *Shea Butter Republic: State Power, Global Markets, and the Making of an Indigenous Commodity*, New York: Routledge.

Edoh, Amah M. (2016), 'Doing Dutch wax cloth: Practice, politics, and "The New Africa"', Ph.D. thesis, Cambridge, MA: Massachusetts Institute of Technology.

Ferguson, James (2006), *Global Shadows: Africa in the Neoliberal World Order*, Durham, NC: Duke University Press.

Foster, Robert J. (2005), 'Commodity futures: Labour, love and value', *Anthropology Today*, 21:4, pp. 8–12.

—— (2006), 'Tracking globalization', in C. Tilley, W. Keane, S. Küchler, M. Rowlands and P. Spyer (eds), *Handbook of Material Culture*, London: Sage, pp. 285–302.

—— (2007), 'The work of the new economy: Consumers, brands, and value creation', *Cultural Anthropology*, 22:4, pp. 707–31.

Gott, Suzanne (2009), 'Asante hightimers and the fashionable display of women's wealth in contemporary Ghana', *Fashion Theory: The Journal of Dress, Body & Culture*, 13:2, pp. 141–76.

Gott, Suzanne, Loughran, Kristyne, Quick, Betsy and Rabine, Leslie (2017), *African-Print Fashion Now! A Story of Taste, Globalization, and Style*, Los Angeles: Fowler Museum at UCLA.

Hansen, Karen T. (2000), *Salaula: The World of Secondhand Clothing and Zambia*, Chicago: University of Chicago Press.

—— (2004), 'The world in dress: Anthropological perspectives on clothing, fashion, and culture', *Annual Review of Anthropology*, 33, pp. 369–92.

Hendrickson, Heidi (1996), *Clothing and Difference: Embodied Identities in Colonial and Post-Colonial Africa*, Durham, NC: Duke University Press.

Hoffmann, Jonas and Coste-Manière, Ivan (2013), *Global Luxury Trends: Innovative Strategies for Emerging Markets*, London: Palgrave Macmillan.

Kalife, Nadim M. (2016), 'La genèse du franc CFA', in K. Nubukpo, M. Ze Belinga, B. Tinel and D. M. Dembele (eds), *Sortir l'Afrique de la servitude monétaire*, Paris: La Dispute.

Kokoura, Germain (2011), 'Le salaire minimum du travailleur togolais relevé à 35.000F CFA', TogoPortail, 20 December, http://www.togoportail.net/2011/12/le-salaire-minimum-du-travailleur-togolais-releve-a-35-000-f-cfa/. Accessed 24 June 2018.

Kriger, Colleen E. (2009), '"Guinea cloth": Production and consumption of cotton textiles in West Africa before and during the Atlantic slave trade', in G. Riello and P. Parthasarathi (eds), *The Spinning World: A Global History of Cotton Textiles, 1200–1850*, Oxford and New York: Oxford University Press, pp. 105–26.

Kroese, W. T. (1976), *The Origin of the Wax Block Prints on the Coast of West Africa*, Leiden: Smit.

Legêne, Susan (2009), 'Dwinegeri multiculturalism and the colonial past (or: The cultural borders of being Dutch)', in B. Kaplan, M. Carlson and L. Cruz (eds), *Boundaries and Their Meanings in the History of the Netherlands*, Leiden: Brill, pp. 223–42.

Lury, Celia (2004), *Brands: The Logos of the Global Economy*, London: Routledge.

Mazzarella, William (2003), '"Very Bombay": Contending with the global in an Indian advertising agency', *Cultural Anthropology*, 18:1, pp. 33–71.

Miller, Daniel (1987), *Material Culture and Mass Consumption*, New York: Basil Blackwell.

Nielsen, Ruth (1979), 'The history and development of wax-printed textiles intended for West Africa and Zaire', in J. M. Cordwell and R. A. Schwarz (eds), *The Fabrics of Culture: The Anthropology of Clothing and Adornment*, Berlin: De Gruyter Mouton, pp. 467–98.

Nothias, Toussaint (2014), '"Rising", "hopeful", "new": Visualizing Africa in the age of globalization', *Visual Communication,* 13:3, pp. 323–39.

Nuttall, Sarah (ed.) (2006), 'Introduction: Rethinking beauty', in *Beautiful Ugly: African and Diaspora Aesthetics,* Durham, NC: Duke University Press.

Ogunyankin, Grace A. (2016), '"These girls' fashion is sick!": *An African City* and the geography of sartorial wordliness', *Feminist Africa,* 21, pp. 37–51.

Okeke-Agulu, Chika (2017), 'Modern African art is being gentrified', *The New York Times,* 20 May, https://nyti.ms/2qFwc0D. Accessed 24 June 2018.

Picton, John and Becker, Rayder (1995), *The Art of African Textiles: Technology, Tradition, and Lurex,* London: Barbican Art Gallery.

Riello, Giorgio and Parthasarathi, Prasannan (2011), *The Spinning World: A Global History of Cotton Textiles, 1200–1850,* Oxford: Oxford University Press.

Schäfer, Maarten (2014), *CBNWS: Around The World in 80 Brands,* New York: CoolBrands.

Schrobsdorff, Waridi (2017), *Mtindo: Style Movers Rebranding Africa,* New York: Rizzoli International Publications.

Selasi, Taiye (2005), 'Bye-bye Babar', *The LIP Magazine,* 3 March, http://thelip.robertsharp.co.uk/?p=76. Accessed 24 June 2018.

Spivak, Gayatri (1988), 'Can the subaltern speak?', in C. Nelson and L. Grossberg (eds), *Marxism and the Interpretation of Culture,* Champaign: University of Illinois Press, pp. 271–313.

Steiner, Christopher B. (1985), 'Another image of Africa: Toward an ethnohistory of European cloth marketed in West Africa, 1873–1960', *Ethnohistory,* 32:2, pp. 91–110.

—— (1994), *African Art in Transit,* Cambridge: Cambridge University Press.

Straight, Bilinda (2002), 'From Samburu heirloom to new age artifact: The cross-cultural consumption of Mporo marriage beads', *American Anthropologist,* 104:1, pp. 7–21.

Sylvanus, Nina (2013), 'Fashionability in colonial and postcolonial Togo', in K. T. Hansen and D. Soyini Madison (eds), *African Dress: Fashion, Agency, Performance,* New York: Bloomsbury, pp. 30–44.

—— (2016), *Patterns in Circulation: Fashioning Prints, Aesthetics, and Women's Economic Power in West Africa,* Chicago: University of Chicago Press.

Thomas, Nicholas (1991), *Entangled Objects: Exchange, Material Culture, and Colonialism in the Pacific,* Cambridge, MA: Harvard University Press.

Toulabor, Comi (2012), 'Les Nana Benz de Lomé', *Afrique contemporaine,* 4, pp. 69–80.

Veblen, Thorstein (1912), *The Theory of the Leisure Class,* New York: MacMillan & Co.

Vlisco (2013), 'Vlisco unfolded', YouTube, 18 October, https://www.youtube.com/watch?v=yfu_jzX1KOU. Accessed 26 November 2017.

—— (2015), 'Love through the ages', YouTube, 17 February, https://youtu.be/ndyLoqxpN_o. Accessed 26 November 2017.

—— (2018), 'Vlisco products', https://www.vlisco.com/world-of-vlisco/design/vlisco-products/. Accessed 26 June 2018.

Weiss, Brad (2003), *Sacred Trees, Bitter Harvests: Globalizing Coffee in Northwest Tanzania,* Portsmouth: Heinemann.

World Intellectual Property Organization (WIPO) (2012), 'The fabled cloth and its IP future', http://www.wipo.int/ipadvantage/en/details.jsp?id=3501. Accessed 24 June 2018.

Notes

1 In addition to Dutch wax, also known as Wax Block, Vlisco produces three other varieties of textiles: Super Wax, Java, and the latest addition, Wax Wax. The three textiles vary primarily in terms of the number of colours used in printing them, and the number of steps in the printing-dyeing process (see Vlisco 2018).

2 See for instance Steiner (1994) on African art; Hansen (2000) on second-hand clothing; Straight (2002) on beads; Weiss (2003) on coffee; and Chalfin (2004) on shea nut.

3 The term *tsigan-vɔ* is a composite of *tsigan* (high-value or high-cost) and *avɔ* (fabric). Dutch wax cloth is known interchangeably as *tsigan* or *tsigan-vɔ* in Lomé; I do the same here.

4 Also see Schrobsdorff (2017) and the 'Africa is the Future' art intervention (http://africaisthefuture.com) as two among plethora of examples of this visual makeover.

5 This chapter is based on ethnographic research conducted over the course of 13 months between 2013 and 2015 in Lomé, Togo, and in Helmond and Amstelveen, Holland. During this time, I observed transactions in tailor shops and Dutch wax cloth selling sites in Lomé, and conducted interviews with Dutch wax cloth sellers and tailors. In Holland, I attended meetings in Vlisco's brand communications and design departments and conducted interviews with staff members in both.

6 The idiomatic phrase '*enugome enɔna*' literally translates as 'it stays/must stay under something'.

7 Wax cloth started being traded in West Africa in the mid-nineteenth century (Kroese 1976; Nielsen 1979). Though the trade was originally centred in Gold Coast present-day Ghana, it moved to neighbouring Togo in the mid-twentieth century. For more on this history, see Sylvanus (2016).

8 For more on the Nanas Benz's story and their significance in the political-economy of colonial and postcolonial Togo, see Nina Sylvanus' ethnography of the Dutch wax trade in Lomé, *Patterns in Circulation* (2016) and Comi Toulabor's 'Les Nanas Benz de Lomé' (2012).

9 For more on wax cloth dress practices in West Africa, see Gott et al. (2017).

10 Savon de Marseille is a gentle soap that, as the name indicates, and like Dutch wax cloth itself, is another appropriated commodity that integrated Togolese markets via colonial-era trade networks.

11 The market study referenced here was an ethnographic study conducted in Ghana, Nigeria and the Democratic Republic of Congo (DRC) in 2011 to understand consumers' wax cloth consumption habits. Over the course of two weeks, a team of four Vlisco staff members conducted focus groups and one-to-one interviews with a total of 50 women and men (primarily women) identified by Vlisco store staff in each location.

Chapter 5

The Playful and Privileged Africanicity of Luxury @AlaraLagos

Simidele Dosekun

Alára is a luxury concept store in Lagos, opened in 2015. Founded and run by Reni Folawiyo, a self-declared design enthusiast – and a member of what is reportedly one of the richest families in Nigeria – the store was purpose designed by the renowned Ghanaian-British architect, David Adjaye, and features clothing, design and art from across Africa and the wider world. In late 2016, the store threw a lavish, cabaret-themed party to launch and promote its status as the first official distributor of Christian Louboutin shoes in West Africa, and to mark the arrival of the exclusive goods. As pictured on Alára's active Instagram page and by guests using hashtags like #LoboutinatAlara and #Alararouge, the many elaborate details of the event included an acrobat descending from the store's high ceiling to the strains of a solo violinist, a champagne bar and candle-lit tables festooned with red flowers and feathers. Red was the colour of the night, being the colour of Alára's branding and likely also a nod to the trademark soles of Louboutin shoes, samples of which were dangled from the ceiling as well as displayed in transparent triangular cases held by female models. Shadowy, cast in dark red hues, the images of these models on Alára's Instagram page are ceremonial in mood. Holding the shoes in almost reverent fashion, dressed in large *aso oke* headwraps out of which single feathers jut, the women look almost as if engaged in some kind of traditionalist ritual, evoking colonial stereotypes of Africans greeting new material commodities, new 'stuff' of whatever stripe, with fetishistic and disproportionate attention.

Read as such, these images, as well as the mere fact that 'Louboutin in Lagos' garnered such celebratory notice and promotion, could suggest the coming of luxury to a place where it does not ordinarily reside, and to people for whom it is not familiar or expected. A visit to Alára or wider browse through the store's Instagram account, @AlaraLagos, belies this kind of reading, however.[1] It reveals instead an Afrocentric aesthetic vision, an 'Africanicity', and a knowing, ironic and playful approach to the construction, staging and consumption of luxury. As Folawiyo explained in an interview with *Vogue*: 'Alára is an expression of myself – my travels, my interests. And it's an expression of this place [Lagos/Nigeria], how we live here' (Singer 2014: n.pag.). These remarks gesture towards the theoretical view of luxury that the chapter takes, namely that luxury is performative. Not an inherent property, luxury is a matter of designation and declaration. Ultimately, it is whatever is cast successfully – whatever seduces, as such. It is for such reasons that critical luxury scholars John Armitage and Joanne Roberts (2016) suggest that, to understand what luxury comprises and means in any given context, we must ask after its 'spirit'. Luxury goods are 'auratic', as Delphine Dion and Eric Arnould (2011) similarly put it. They function, certainly they sell, by inspiring a relative sense of awe and transcendence. The luxury retail store is or needs to be thick with atmosphere, then. There must be something in the air, 'something which flows forth spatially, almost something like a breath or haze' (Böhme 1993: 117). This something is not simply there, freely or organically arising. Atmospheres 'proceed from and are created by things, persons and their constellations' (Böhme cited in Degen et al. 2017: 6). This means that they can be produced, instrumentalized, manipulated and so on, for instance to create a '"buzz" […] to galvanise consumer behaviour' (Hudson 2015: 293). Shaped by and shaping tastes, sensibilities, aspirations and even bodily comportments – variously inclusive and exclusive, fundamentally classed – atmospheres are vectors of power.

This chapter is concerned with the performative content and constellations of luxury at Alára and the atmosphere that ensues. Atmospheres can be gleaned by decoding their constituent elements and signs, and by the more tacit, bodily and synaesthetic processes of experiencing and being moved by these things (Biehl-Missal 2013; Bille et al. 2015). This is because the experience of an atmosphere is one 'in which affects, emotions, sensations and meanings are inextricably mingled' (Edensor 2015: 334). Extended visits in the flesh would be one way to get a sense of the atmosphere at Alára – arguably the most obvious and complete way. However, the chapter is based on a reading and feeling of the store's Instagram account. Images have a presence that is more than merely representational – a presence of their own – and in and through this they generate, have and communicate atmospheres and moods (Biehl-Missal 2013). The impressions that they make are more than visual. To the extent that they are highly staged and rhetorical, for instance depicting luxury items in persuasive combinations that may not necessarily be found on the (also highly staged) shopfloor, they also serve to lend further appearance and atmosphere to that which they depict (Böhme 2003: 72). Images serve as aesthetic marketing devices, in short, and thus, as in this chapter, they can be broached as not simply reflecting or representing the atmosphere of the place in question but contributing to its construction.

It is in this last regard that the digital photo sharing app, Instagram, becomes especially apt for the present purposes. With 600-million-plus users at the time of writing, who are able to post, caption and hashtag their own still and short moving audio-visual content as well as browse through, like and comment upon others' posts, the core logic of Instagram is to give appearance, feel and value – to things, experiences, places, embodied selves, brands and so on – to attract views and thereby promote (e.g. see Carah and Shaul 2016; Marwick 2015). Instagram has become a powerful tool for building brands. It stimulates and capitalizes upon aesthetic and affective labours of 'making look' (Carah and Shaul 2016). A new technology of public intimacy, it comprises a new site and surface for the production, seeing and sensing and circulation of glamour and allure – processes that are critical to the aesthetic and attention economies of contemporary consumer capitalism (Thrift 2008). 'Insta-attention', we could call it, is typically fleeting: a glance before one moves on to the next of a virtually endless stream of content and hyperlinks. The analysis in this chapter is based upon my repeated glancing in this everyday fashion, but also more slowly, deliberately and analytically, through the 400 or so images, with accompanying captions and hashtags posted on @AlaraLagos between the inception of the Instagram account in March 2015 and May 2017. The analysis also draws on published interviews with Reni Folawiyo about her ideas and intentions for Alára, as well as two visits that I made to the store in 2016.

Setting the Promise of Luxury: #LikeABoxOfChocolates

The very first image on @AlaraLagos is a wide angle of a side façade of the building, taken from below and rising up to a dusky blue sky. It shows a thick and level ochre-red surface, etched with deep lines running into repeated geometric patterns, and interrupted haphazardly by square and triangular cutouts. A glass surface behind the cutouts reflects the sky. In a city with over fifteen million inhabitants, and without anything approaching adequate infrastructure for them, where space is at a high premium and the rhythms and textures of daily life anything but smooth, this tactile image conveys a sense of breadth, ease and plenitude, and a quiet and confident drama. Captioned 'Alára is here!', the image announces the store as not only a new site of soaring extravagance in Lagos, but also one centred on a local aesthetic. The patterning of the building's skin and the red, grid-like ornamental metalwork at the front, back and top of the structure reference the geometry of traditional Yoruba motifs (Conway 2014). The cutouts are reminiscent of the expensive Austrian laces that Yoruba and other Nigerian women favour for the most important of social occasions. The much-remarked fact (e.g. see Conway 2014; Singer 2014) that the structure was designed by Adjaye, a global African 'starchitect', only adds to its luxurious *Africanicity*.

Inside, between the solid glass panes that make up the building's front and back walls, is a triple-height space comprising a series of ascending white terrazzo landings connected by short moveable staircases of the same cool material and hue. The landings serve as the store's primary display stage. About halfway up, to the right, is a walled-off space dubbed 'the cage room' for its partial encasing by black metalwork wrought in yet another geometric pattern. At the very top is an outdoor roof area. Momentous in scale, sweeping insistently upward, suffused with both natural and artificial lighting, the main interior space of the store is, at the same time, grounded and warmed by a dark cladding that lines the ceiling and one side wall, as well as by the many colourful items on sale that are dotted artfully around. Its scale is also humanized by its subdivision into landings, which renders it navigable as a series of smaller places. Thus, the interior space of Alára impresses and communicates grandeur, but without coming to feel cold or empty, or forbidding. Indeed, the space beckons, lures in. Looking like stacked Lego pieces, for instance, the squat staircases invite a playful clamber.

An early image of the store's interior posted on its Instagram account is taken from the right-hand side of the ground level, from which position some but not all of the landings and staircases and their items on display can be seen. The caption reads 'Alára's stairway to heaven', which articulates, with both what the image shows and what remains beyond the frame, that more and more delights are to be had as one ascends. A sense of the delightful unknown is repeated in another picture of the interior also taken from below, focused, in this case, on the cage room. Because of the black metalwork and the darkness of the space behind it, the image does not reveal what the room holds, and the contents of the area just outside it are likewise indistinct, a little blurred. But bright ceiling spotlights twinkle down on everything, enchanting, and what does filter through the 'cage' are splashes of colour. Magical things are to be had here, the image winks, they need only be sought. The accompanying text verbalizes this promise: 'You never know what you might find #likeaboxofchocolates'. This phrase and hashtag derive from the well-known movie *Forrest Gump*, where they summarize the eponymous character's optimistic openness to whatever may come.

What comes at Alára, what is found as one mounts the self-declared 'heavenly stairway', is an eclectic yet carefully selected mix of things. Giving an overview of what is in the store, Folawiyo said in an interview: 'there's furniture from Moroso, the Italian brand, but also objects I've picked up in markets in, say, Turkey. We have designers from South Africa making furniture for us, baskets from women in Zimbabwe, scarves from Ethiopia, weaving and leather goods from Nigeria' (Singer 2014: n.pag.). Otherwise put, the stock ranges from 'global' luxury brands, which is to say mostly western ones, such as Valentino, Stella McCartney and Louboutin, to locally celebrated and globally 'rising' African brands like Maki Oh, to little known or new African lines, to craft and artisanal work from the continent and beyond. Suggested by Folawiyo's indicative list is that there is a particular emphasis at Alára on Africa as a site and source of luxury, not just a receptacle for it. In fact, according to a *Wall Street Journal* article, Folawiyo's 'ambitions for Alára go far beyond filling a gap in Lagos' luxury-retail landscape. She hopes to address a deeper issue – the fact that so little of what's made in Africa is considered luxurious in the first place' (Conway 2014: n.pag.). Below I describe and theorize how Africa becomes central to not just the material provenance of luxury at Alára but also to its aesthetic and spirit.

Creating and Curating an African Luxury: #ThisIsWhatWeLove

Dion and Arnould propose that things become luxurious through a series of performative symbolic and material processes that can be understood as a kind of magic. Magic is 'a system for managing the transfer of qualities through similarity and contiguity', or through likeness and contact (Mauss and Hubert [1902] 1933, cited in Dion and Arnould 2011: 504). This, to be clear, is not the magic of rabbit-in-the-hat, magic as cheap trick or bamboozlement. Nor is it magic in the African sense of *juju*. Rather it is a 'secular magic' of allure, seduction, beguilement (Thrift 2008: 9). These are aesthetic properties, practices and states utterly foundational to consumer capitalism. If increasingly needed to distinguish even the most mundane of consumer goods (Bohme 2003), they are indispensable for the constitution and demarcation of 'luxury'. For this, according to Dion and Arnould (2011), the 'charismatic creative director' becomes key.

This is Reni Folawiyo at Alára. The first full image of Folawiyo on the store's Instagram account shows her in a quirkily stylish patchwork coat looking captivated by and in the process of capturing an image of something, out of the shot, said to have 'caught our eye at Sacai', a Japanese luxury brand. A woman dubbed '#mrsF' stands in a semi-darkened room. A pale grey wall behind her is dotted with reflections of small circles of light that look like golden bubbles blowing in the wind. The scene and atmosphere are almost wondrous. A flurry of hashtags locate Folawiyo in Paris, at '#pfw' – Paris Fashion Week, to be more exact. Looking for luxury, and transferring and transmuting it from *her* view into 'ours', are at the heart of Folawiyo's work. As in the two brief quotes from her that I have already cited above, Folawiyo makes clear in interview accounts that the store is an expression of her singular vision, a product of her 'magic touch'. Thus even when she is not physically depicted or explicitly named, we can read the framing and voice of @AlaraLagos as her own. Figuratively and performatively, then, it is Folawiyo who renders also 'wondrous' the turquoise Fulani wedding slippers said to be en route from Agadez, central Niger; who casts as '#localgems' the pendant lines of coloured glass beads pictured at Lekki Market, a somewhat kitschy touristic arts and crafts market located in a working-class neighbourhood of Lagos. Very far from Paris Fashion Week or the Salone del Mobile Milano where a number of the posts by @AlaraLagos also impute Folawiyo's physical presence, the caption for the image of beads from Lekki Market makes the performative claim that, with the right eye, we never know what luxuries might turn up in seemingly unlikely places: '#alaraloves… Impromptu walks through Lekki market… you never know what you'll find #localgems #straightouttalagos #craft'.

The goods at Alára not already widely considered luxurious are granted entry to this exclusive rank in the first place by the store's envisioning and branding of them as such. For the African amongst these things, Ethiopian scarves say, or the glass beads from Lekki Market (if they do indeed end up in the store), this process of becoming luxury by charismatic designation contains an element of what we could call postcolonial re-enchantment; that is, a remembering and recasting (if also sometimes 'upgrading' or 'updating') of their 'native charms'. Two images of artisanal leather handbags on the Instagram page speak to this process of transformation. In the most recent of the two posted images, the handbags, tagged 'bags made in Africa', are staged with a series of other items in the store. A visitor to the Instagram page comments nostalgically and appreciatively: 'Gosh! I used to have loads of those bags when I was a child. My dad used to bring them back from the North (Kano). They stank to high heavens for a few weeks but they were beautiful'. The earlier image showing the same kind of bags confirms what is implicit in this remark: that, however beautiful and special 'now', they were not always regarded at this level of luxury. In this image, the bags are displayed against mouldy green corrugated iron sheets; in other words, they are obviously not at Alára. The accompanying texts reads: 'This is what we love! #comingsoon #alaraloves #artisans #handmadebags #africanluxury #nigeria'. Declared 'loved' by Alára and soon to be loved, the artisanal bags in this image are not yet luxury but on their way there: '#comingsoon'.

As in this example, the physical, conceptual and, on Instagram, visually mediated space of the store contributes to bequeathing (additional) luxury to the goods that cross its various thresholds. With this in mind, we could be more specific and say that what Alára gives or imparts is that which I have already termed luxurious Africanicity. Having been deemed suitable for, and/or of sufficient likeness with, the store, the goods there become not simply luxury but *African* luxury. The fact and space of the store also allow for the lateral transfer of both luxury and Africanicity between the various items and brands in stock. In the shop, as on the Instagram page, the African is intermingled with the western/global, 'certified' already as luxury. Maki Oh is modelled with Marni; peppered at the feet of mannequins dressed in Alessandra Rich are beaded Southern African baskets; cushions from Senegal surround Bottega Veneta bags. Visually and stylistically, the African and the western/global are in some instances indistinguishable. But this is not because the former looks like or mimics the latter, as the ready assumption might be. The resemblance flows *the other way around*: the Valentino bag in what looks like (and could well be) African print, for example;[2] the Stella McCartney in colours and patterns akin to the indigo-dyed Yoruba cloth, *adire*; the Bottega Veneta woven leather men's bag, of which one visitor to the Instagram page asks 'was this made in Lagos?' because, in terms of how it looks – its material, form, style and detailing – it well could be.[3]

This is no coincidence. Folawiyo purposely curates Alára with and for what she refers to, and thereby seeks to promote as, an African – and I would suggest more specifically Lagosian – eye and feel. Referring to the western/global brands that are or are not chosen for the store, she explains: 'I tried to choose based on our aesthetic. I've tended to go for brands that have a lot of work, a lot of colour. It's not about a streamlined look here. I love Jil Sander, but that's not our aesthetic' (Singer 2014: n.pag.). Her curatorial approach to western/global luxury is to bend it to 'our' tastes and needs: it must fit and cater to these, otherwise it will not be admitted. In itself, this makes Alára a critical case study of African luxury to challenge assumptions that Africans will or do simply lap up whatever is western, always already desiring and deeming it superior (e.g. see Iqani, this volume). As to what Alára's 'African aesthetic' comprises, in the same interview Folawiyo describes it as 'expressive', 'embellished' and 'adorned'. To think with her counter-example, where Jil Sander is streamlined, modernist, unfussy and tending to monochromes (black and white especially), Alára's brand of luxury looks like brightness and warmth: embellishments and adornments; beads, lace, embroidery and appliqué, studs, sequins and other rough and complex textures; and the mixing of all the above – that is to say, mixed colours, patterns and textures. The taste is not for the sleek and glossy and immaculate or, alternatively, the shiny and 'bling'. The look and feel are loose, limber, lively and expressive, not tight, controlled, muted or sombre.

The rendering of western/global luxury on what could be read as localized terms also manifests discursively on the store's Instagram account. Two Anya Hindmarch clutch bags with glittery detailing in the shape of a thundery and sunny cloud respectively are described as 'the perfect accessory for the rainy season'. A time of heavy and dramatic downpours, lasting about eight months of the year, rainy season is a defining aspect of Lagos life. A pair of Louboutin shoes 'now in store' are described as 'owambe with a twist'. '*O wa mbe*' is Yoruba for 'it is here', but is also the name given to the large, expensive, virtually open access parties that Nigerians famously throw. We can read the 'twist' to which the caption refers as a play on what is already a Yoruba play on words: the Louboutin shoes whose arrival is being announced (*o wa mbe*, it is here) are precisely what a stylish, moneyed Lagos woman might want to wear to an *owambe* party. Such translating of western/global luxury items and logics by @AlaraLagos – of which there are not many, in any case – must not be read as somehow 'necessary', however – as if the store's audience and clientele cannot comprehend or access the non-African without such mediation. Rather they are humorous and knowing. What is being played at and upon here, and in the store as a whole, is the mobility across and between, and mutual imbrication of, the local and global.

The concept of the 'Afropolitan' might seem to encapsulate the analysis that I am putting forward here. Very briefly, the portmanteau term – Afropolitan for African and cosmopolitan – is thought to have first been coined by the writer Taiye Selasi (2005). Of Nigerian and Ghanaian parentage, raised and schooled across the world, Selasi speaks from her own dizzyingly transnational positionality and subjectivity to define Afropolitans as contemporary 'African emigrants' for whom locales on the continent like Lagos, Nairobi and Johannesburg, *and* 'a G8 city or two (or three)', London, Paris and New York, say, are equally and fluidly home (Selasi 2005: n.pag.). Decidedly privileged, by definition mobile, the Afropolitan subject, and the Afropolitan aesthetic, are urbane, self-reflexive, cool, stylish and insistently hybrid. I initially read Alára as in this vein. But in fact I am of the view that the concept of the Afropolitan is tautologous: cosmopolitanism, or worldliness, is already contained within the category and name of 'African' (Mbembe and Nuttall 2004). I also concur with Grace Musila that this tautology speaks to 'anxieties about the "African" on its own' (2016: 110). These views led me back to a reading of Alára's vision and construction of luxury as 'African', where African precisely can and does include, and signify, being in, of and with the world, too.

Alára's splicing of Africa and the store's 'kind' of African are of the most exclusive rank. If the Afropolitan has been criticized as elite, a position that not every African can occupy materially, aesthetically and ideologically (e.g. see Dabiri 2016), Alára's African is '*super*-elite' (Thurlow and Jaworski 2014, emphasis added). In addition to Folawiyo's personal place at the highest socio-economic strata of Nigerian life, in interviews she names amongst Alára's intended clientele other ultra-wealthy Nigerians, the type who would ordinarily hop on a plane to London to go shopping for luxury.[4] Without reducing her talents and labours at Alára to this, it is indisputable that her spectacular wealth and the global and hyper-stylized mobility this enables are utterly key to her ability to make luxury. In and from the very particular Africa where she and the ideal or intended Alára clientele reside, the whole world is one's stomping ground. The store is this world, come home to Lagos.

Fashionable Fun and Games: #ComeThru

While it is the work of @AlaraLagos to draw and invite in, it does not follow that entry into the physical space of the store is promised or given to all. The Instagram account depicts few customers or other visitors having taken up the invitation, posted on many of the images, to '#comethru'. The exceptions are notably elite, and in all cases stylish: invitees only at the Louboutin night, a number of whom are recognizable as local celebrities and wealthy socialites; sophisticates, sipping champagne and chatting keenly at the art and other pop-up cultural exhibitions staged in the easily reconfigurable space; the global hip-hop star, Yasiin Bey (formerly known as Mos Def) and so on. Atmospheres are created and flow through proximal bodies, human and nonhuman, such that their quantity and quality must be carefully selected and regulated in and for the luxury store, to produce the necessary air of exclusivity. Alára is not a place for crowds, for jostling or sweating or struggling; *that* Lagos, which, to be sure, is the empirically and materially predominant, is elsewhere, beyond the store's walls. Also tending to be out of the visual frame are the labouring bodies – Folawiyo being the exception – that necessarily populate the store and render it possible. While this is a logic fundamental to capitalist consumer culture, at @AlaraLagos, labour is further invisibilized, and moreover (re)commodified, by its aestheticization.

Crispin Thurlow and Adam Jaworski (2014) identify the aestheticization of workers and the work produced by their hands as one of the visual and material strategies in the representation and production of luxury spaces, experiences and atmospheres. They conceive of the labour that produces luxury as 'visible–invisible'. Visible–invisible labour is an oxymoronic outcome of the simultaneous and contradictory constitution of luxury by perfection, craft, customized service and the like, by labour intensivity, at the same time as leisure, calm, space and discretion, or the absence of labour and stress. The sight and sound of the hard working bodies upon which luxury depends do not a luxurious experience make, hence it is common that techniques in the representation and branding of this experience include the 'blurring, decentring, disembedding, desaturation and the metonymic reduction' of these bodies (Thurlow and Jaworski 2014).

At @AlaraLagos, it is *parts* of bodies of models – professional or not is unclear – used repeatedly in the space of the store to stage and model, and in this dabble and frolic with the goods on offer. Disembodied feet are pictured walking against the same grey wall in Valentino and Sophia Webster for example, while an anonymous hand lightly suspends a shiny blue Louboutin shoe in front of a multicoloured canvas. In a two-second video, a female body, dressed in designer wear from its unseen head down, sits on a high stool and leisurely dangles its feet. That, per Instagram's design, the video runs on auto-loop amplifies its message by iterating its playful randomness: bedecked in Marni sandals, the feet dangle on and on and on. Another micro-splice of video captures the mist escaping from a perfume bottle as a hennaed hand depresses the nozzle. What, from the henna, looks like the same hand boasts a set of rings as it grips one of the rods on a stylized foosball table that is, itself, all the more an amusing surprise for being re-purposed from the colourful wooden fishing boats that dot the West African coast.

The mood is similarly jokey and ironic when the luxury goods are staged on their own. A pair of chunky Nicholas Kirkwood shoes are hooked on to the side of an unidentifiable piece of furniture also made from old fishing boats, one foot cocked at a spry angle. Perched on and amongst the branches of a plant, one mirrored lens reflecting the surrounding foliage, is a pair of sunglasses. So improbably placed, the glasses look like part of a treasure hunt. A clutch bag embellished with large semi-precious stones that could be mistaken for rock candy is described, in another example of double-punning, as 'hand candy'. 'I'll have a clutch on the rocks, please', continues the punning in reference to an image of two other clutches laid out on a bed of white pebbles. In a number of cases, as with the foosball table, or the sandals beaded in the image of Frida Kahlo's iconic face, or the designer sunglasses in the shape of an open, red-lipped mouth, peep of teeth and tongue included, the fun and jokes start with the luxury goods themselves.

At Alára, luxury, including even the work of producing, staging and selling it, is anything but a solemn or reverent affair. Things are not taken too seriously – the highly expensive and exclusive things for sale, that is. Indeed, these things are treated like toys, props for play.

Conclusion

Premised on a theoretical view of luxury as performative, including as a diffuse quality of feeling that arises from objects, places and people, and their ordering and interacting, this chapter has offered a reading of the content and atmosphere of luxury through @AlaraLagos. The chapter argues that Alára's highly curated brand of luxury looks and feels like fashionable fun and games, and this centres around a certain African aesthetic, taste and self-reflexivity that quite casually and knowingly includes and incorporates goods and brands from elsewhere. Spectacular (and stratospherically expensive) though they are, I would argue that it is not so much the fact and design of the store, or the things for sale there, that comprise its ultimate luxury: rather, it is the spirit of play, the mood of magic; the stylized carefreeness, dabbling and frolicking on display on Instagram; the staging of adventure and new or re-enchanted delights; the mixing and mashing of the African and the not. For the hyper-privileged few who can take up the store's invitation to drop by and partake, and, presumably, for the many more whose participation is limited to browsing @AlaraLagos and sometimes posting enthusiastic and desirous comments about what they are seeing and feeling, the store offers itself up as a playground for the fashioning of luxurious African – African and/as global – living.

Play is a highly political matter. Who gets to play, where, how and with what and whom are questions about both productive and reproductive labour, leisure and its material and moral dialectics, time and of course sheer means in the basic yet quite brute sense of money, 'cash'. But play is political also because it is dispositional, a matter of both mental and bodily attitude and self-perception. It is simultaneously and recursively a product, performance and sign of one's imagined, lived and felt place and priority in the order of things. As produced, represented and promised by @AlaraLagos, its place and priority is at the very top, at the very front, entitled to and getting, *affording*, in all senses of the word, the very best. This, too, is and must be understood as a mode of African 'being-in-the-world' (Mbembe and Nuttall 2004: 347). It demands further attention and critique, as, amongst other things, a complex site and instantiation of a series of interlinked gross inequalities, from the very local to the global. But given the stubborn insistence with which representations of Africa are expected to in one way or another 'bear testimony to Africa's [putative] difference constituted [...] by its slum life and chronic poverty' (Nuttall and Mbembe 2005: 194), it becomes another form of critique to surface that, for some Africans, insouciant play and privilege, both at home and abroad, are in fact a way of life.

Acknowledgements

Yewande Omotoso (who, quite conveniently for the purposes of this chapter, is both an architect and writer) helped me understand and find the language to describe some of the detailing of the Alára building.

References

Armitage, John and Roberts, Joanne (eds) (2016a), 'Critical luxury studies: defining a field', in *Critical Luxury Studies: Art, Design, Media*, Edinburgh: Edinburgh University Press, pp. 1–21.
—— (2016b), 'The spirit of luxury', *Cultural Politics*, 12, pp. 1–22.
Biehl-Missal, Brigitte (2013), 'The atmosphere of the image: An aesthetic concept for visual analysis', *Consumption Markets & Culture*, 16:4, pp. 356–67.
Biehl-Missal, Brigitte and Saren, Michael (2012), 'Atmospheres of seduction: A critique of aesthetic marketing practices', *Journal of Macromarketing*, 32:2, pp. 168–80.
Bille, Mikkel, Bjerregaard, Peter and Sørensen, Tim (2015), 'Staging atmospheres: Materiality, culture, and the texture of the in-between', *Emotion, Space & Society*, 15, pp. 31–38.
Böhme, Gernot (1993), 'Atmosphere as the fundamental concept of a new aesthetics', *Thesis Eleven*, 36, pp. 113–26.
—— (2003), 'Contribution to the critique of the aesthetic economy', *Thesis Eleven*, 73, pp. 71–82.
Carah, Nicholas and Shaul, Michelle (2016), 'Brands and Instagram: Point, tap, swipe, glance', *Mobile Media & Communication*, 4:1, pp. 69–84.
Conway, Megan (2014), 'Redefining African Luxury in Lagos, Nigeria', *The Wall Street Journal*, 29 May, https://www.wsj.com/articles/redefining-african-luxury-in-lagos-nigeria-1401375313. Accessed 4 November 2016.
Dabiri, Emma (2016), 'Why I am (still) not an Afropolitan', *Journal of African Cultural Studies*, 28:1, pp. 104–08.
Daly, Catherine M., Eicher, Joanne and Erekosima, Tonye (1986), 'Male and female artistry in Kalabari dress', *African Arts*, 19:3, pp. 48–83.

Degen, Monica, Melhuish, Clare and Rose, Gillian (2017), 'Producing place atmospheres digitally: Architecture, digital visualisation practices and the experience economy', *Journal of Consumer Culture*, 17:1, pp. 3–24.

Dion, Delphine and Arnould, Eric (2011), 'Retail luxury strategy: Assembling charisma through art and magic', *Journal of Retailing*, 87:4, pp. 502–20.

Featherstone, Michael (2014), 'Luxury, consumer culture and sumptuary dynamics', *Luxury: History, Culture, Consumption*, 1:1, pp. 47–69.

Hudson, Chris (2015), 'ION Orchard: Atmosphere and consumption in Singapore', *Visual Communication*, 14:3, pp. 289–308.

Marwick, Alice (2015), 'Instafame: Luxury selfies in the attention economy', *Public Culture*, 27:1, pp. 137–60.

Mbembe, Achille and Nuttall, Sarah (2004), 'Writing the world from an African metropolis', *Public Culture*, 16:3, pp. 347–72.

Musila, Grace (2016), 'Part-time Africans, Europolitans and "Africa lite"', *Journal of African Cultural Studies*, 28:1, pp. 109–13.

Nuttall, Sarah and Mbembe, Achille (2005), 'A blasé attitude: A response to Micheal Watts', *Public Culture*, 17:1, pp. 193–201.

Rocamora, Agnes (2016), 'Online luxury: Geographies of production and consumption and the Louis Vuitton website', in J. Armitage and J. Roberts (eds), *Critical Luxury Studies: Art, Design, Media*, Edinburgh: Edinburgh University Press, pp. 199–220.

Selasi, Taiye (2005), 'Bye-bye Babar', *The LIP Magazine*, 3 March, http://thelip.robertsharp.co.uk/?p=76. Accessed 4 November 2016.

Singer, Maya (2014), 'Lagos rising', *Vogue*, 7 November, https://www.vogue.com/article/lagos-style-print-magazine. Accessed 4 November 2016.

Sylvanus, Nina (2007), 'The fabric of Africanity: Tracing the global threads of authenticity', *Anthropological Theory*, 7:2, pp. 201–16.

Thrift, Nigel (2008), 'The material practices of glamour', *Journal of Cultural Economy*, 1:1, pp. 9–23.

Thurlow, Crispin and Jaworski, Adam (2012), 'Elite mobilities: The semiotic landscapes of luxury and privilege', *Social Semiotics*, 22:4, pp. 487–516.

—— (2014), 'Visible-invisible: The social semiotics of labour in luxury tourism', in T. Birchnell and J. Caletrío (eds), *Elite Mobilities*, Abingdon: Routledge, pp. 176–93.

Notes

1 At the time of writing, all images are available at https://www.instagram.com/alaralagos/?hl=en.

2 The fact that 'African print' itself has a foreign or non-indigenous, and colonial, provenance is telling and useful for what is at the crux of my argument here: namely that Africanness or Africanicity is performative. Although first originated from Javanese batiks by way of Europe, African print is African because it has *become* so. For more on this see, for example, Nina Sylvanus (2007), and the chapter by Amah Edoh in this collection.

3   Interestingly enough, and perhaps telling, is that in the time since I first drafted this chapter and included the link to this comment, the comment has been taken down and the Instagram account with which it was posted has been disabled. However, Alára's response to the comment is still up. It reads: '@prncesse_lkyi Hello. No it's not [made in Lagos]. Bottega is an Italian brand and it's produced in Italy'.

4   Folawiyo says in her *Vogue* interview, for example, that the store is '*for*' a woman like Nana Otedola, who is the wife of Femi Otedola, still a stratospherically wealthy Nigerian, although in 2016 he did not make the annual Forbes index of African billionaires because, due to falling oil prices and the linked collapse of the Naira, his estimated wealth had reportedly 'plunged' from US$1.8 billion to US$500 million.

Chapter 6

Fields of Marigold: Makers and Wearers of Luxury African Beaded Necklaces

Pamila Gupta

It is a community of women that includes both makers and wearers.

(Joni Brenner 2013)

Introduction

This chapter focuses on the delicate material and affective ties that bind (mostly) female makers and wearers of Marigold beaded necklaces, an initiative (based on a pre-existing cooperative) started up by South Africa-based artist Joni Brenner in 2010 in Bulawayo (Zimbabwe) and sold exclusively in Johannesburg.[1] I became fascinated with them, once I started seeing them showcased by their wearers at certain fashionable events (academic events, book launches, art openings) in and around Johannesburg. I then travelled with Brenner to Bulawayo in 2014 to visit this cooperative, and meet their makers, those women whose labour these beautiful necklaces are dependent on.[2] It is an initiative that I am very much committed to, just as much as I fell in love with the materiality of the beads themselves. The project is a return to craft; it is also a type of transnational labour and 'African investment in style' as one wearer described it. Mine is a dual-sited ethnography, where I look to the fields of production (Bulawayo) and consumption (Johannesburg) in order to suggest that these beaded necklaces have much to say not only about (African) craft, but also its role as an emerging luxury form tied to aesthetic politics in Africa today.

There is currently a 'rapid expansion in writing about craft' that Glenn Adamson's edited book, *The Craft Reader* attests to (2010: 1). If we define craft in simple but open-ended terms, according to Adamson, it is 'the application of skill and material-based knowledge to relatively small-scale production' (2010: 2). Richard Sennett reminds us that craft engages certain kinds of techniques that should be seen as 'cultural' rather than as 'mindless procedure[s]' and 'involves dimensions of skill, commitment and judgement in a particular way' (2008: 8–9). Adamson makes a compelling argument for craft, stating that 'it is not a way of thinking outside of modernity, but a modern way of thinking otherwise' (2010: 5). It is a term 'established and defined through difference' (2010: 5), that is practised less in opposition to globalization; rather it is integral to new forms of globalization (2010: 272). Thus, while the Marigold bead project reflects this larger trend of the return to 'artisanal labour' (yet another way to define the 'discourse of craft' according to Adamson 2010: 5), it also reminds us of Africa's role as a serious player in neoliberal global markets, including that of craft. It is an area that is still under-represented and under-researched as James Ferguson confirms in his book, *Global Shadows: Africa in the Neoliberal World Order* (2006). As anthropologists, we must take specific African settings as subjects for analysis, and undertake more ethnographic research to detail specific African markets, including a profile of its producers and consumers, as Sara Berry has done in her work on Nigerian motor mechanics (2010) and Patrick R. McNaughton has explored for a group of Mande blacksmiths in West Africa (2010). Lastly, we must attend to the textures, feel and aesthetics of these handmade goods in particular settings and as tied to practices of craft-making across and beyond Africa. David Doris' work on repurposed Nigerian textiles (sheets and pillowcases) made from recycled cloth ('leader sheeting' that is designated as trash after its use for test printing in the United States) full of Disney animated characters such as Winnie the Pooh and Mickey Mouse (2010) is one such example.

Craft is also at the centre of new forms of value being assigned to luxury-making, a point made by Mike Featherstone in a recent collection entitled *Critical Luxury Studies: Art, Design, Media* edited by John Armitage and Joanne Roberts (2016). He writes:

> A central aspect of luxury is value. Luxuries proclaim value: they suggest things that can readily be valued above others. Luxuries embody the promise of special things: not merely things of quality, scarcity and wonder that are beautifully made, but also eventful and sensory fulfilling experiences. Indeed, some luxury goods are deliberately made to be noticed: to embody authority and announce their experiential dimension. It is this power of luxuries to offer more, to hold out the promise of a process of familiarisation which unfolds new aesthetic and sensory dimensions.
>
> (2016: 108)

As well, the findings of a recent *What is Luxury* exhibit that took place at the Victoria & Albert museum in London in 2015 (Banks 2015) confirm that a return to individually made, time and person invested, carefully made items is where luxury is now located. Ms Jana Scholze, one of the co-curators of the exhibit, suggests that 'contemporary craft is poised to fill something that has been lost in the boom of the luxury industry' (Banks 2015). She continues: 'Craft in luxury is about making something that is so unique it can only be made one time, and perhaps, even more, appreciating the passion and endless obsession of these makers' (Banks 2015). Herein ideas of 'expertise, innovation, preciousness, and exclusivity' play a defining role in craft's resurgence as a new luxury (Banks 2015), traits that Marigold makers and wearers identify with and that are very much tied to their success as an 'it' item in Johannesburg today. In three subsequent ethnographic sections, I will suggest that the way that Brenner has carefully styled (or 'crafted') the Marigolds beads initiative is also a timely one; it very much reflects a larger global trend where a return to craft is at the centre of new value forms of luxury-making, and is rooted in African identity-making.

Bulawayo: Craft or Slow Beading

See the shambling gait of the unemployed,
the vacant stare of the dispossessed;
the plastic bags by breezes buoyed
or, when evening settles, at rest.
Hear the cry of hornbills lost in yards
Of rubble and rags, to split the ears
Of those who stand and watch; and the guards
unguarded, hammering, hammering.
Smell the blood and mucous, ashes damp;
breath the birds turned children clamouring,
children clamouring. A tyrant's stamp:
a boot, a fist, a fourteen pounder:
come and witness our city flounder.

('Sonnet with One Unstated Line', Eppel 2014)

There is an indelible quality in Zimbabwean poet John Eppel's sonnet that spoke to me after my visit to Bulayawo (KoNtuthu ziyanthunqu, in SiNdebele, a 'place of smoky fires') in September 2014 with Zimbabwean-born, Johannesburg-based artist Joni Brenner, as witness to a city floundering.[3] If we think of Eppel the poet as a 'weaver' (Bringhurst 1992: 25), creating his own tapestry out of words and images in order to evoke a sense of place, then perhaps his poem gave me solace akin to the way this cooperative of female weavers gave me hope amidst the despair and impoverishment I witnessed on this first visit. I travelled to Bulawayo with Brenner in order to gain a sense of the women who create these beautiful necklaces on a daily basis in order to support themselves and their families, which very often includes young children being raised by a single female parent. I wanted to think and write about the Marigold beads but from both a behind the scenes production line and a high-end consumer market. I was interested in craft and design on a small scale and their worth as material objects, consumer goods and increasingly luxury items. I came away with a sense of pride in being able to document an initiative directed by Brenner that fully employs fourteen women on a regular basis and provides them with a steady income in this forlorn city.[4] It is a rare creative workplace when one considers the pressures of this cooperative to sustain itself in the face of high unemployment rates under the iron grip of the interminable Mugabe, who resigned under political pressure in November 2017. Brenner has suggested on one occasion that against the backdrop of the devastation of Zimbabwe in this political moment, the Marigold cooperative and its current buoyancy is perhaps all the more interesting.[5]

We arrive by car to a quiet, nondescript street in Pelandaba, on the outskirts of Bulayawo. It is an un assuming place where a group of modestly mannered (and dressed) women spend their day hand-looming beads. We enter a sparse but spanking clean brightly painted green three-room brick building. They greet Brenner with warmth and trust, whereas they are more cautious towards me, understandably for I am new to their world. They appear shy even as they seemingly enjoy each other's company. In the period of time spent in the workshop, I engage with the women, and see clearly that each one contributes something valuable and specific, and that every beader has her own style of working, with a leaning towards particular designs and colour combinations. I watch Jestinah Nyoni's adept hands as she studies a hand-drawn master design, carefully picks first the thread and then the bead colour. I see her string a few beads onto a needle before weaving it across, the misshapen beads quietly snipped away at the end. I hear the 'sonic' whirring of the gathering of the beads in a plastic plate as the women are poised to put them onto a needle, a sound first described to me by Brenner in Johannesburg in January 2013 when I was introduced to the project. These women loop their needles back around and continue to weave this same pattern over the next five hours. They break for tea and talk before returning to their seats at the various tables; they constantly touch their handiwork to make sure the tension is right otherwise the necklaces will not lay flat; a crinkle in the fold serves as a telltale sign that they are not correctly beaded.

As Sennett writes: 'every good craftsman conducts a dialogue between concrete practices and thinking: this dialogue evolves into sustaining habits, and these habits establish a rhythm between problem solving and problem finding' (2008: 9). This group of trained beaders, craftswomen in every sense of the word, is very much amused by all my questions, especially when I try my own hand at it and see how difficult it is. I learn by practice and observation how highly skilled they are – theirs is an 'intimate connection between hand and head' (Sennett 2008: 9) – to be able to perform this kind of delicate handiwork that transforms a single bead and its one dimensionality into a multidimensional, playful, tangible and beautiful strand of beads. I see a glimmer of the complexities of their intimate lives and livelihoods from the series of life biographies that Brenner and I jointly conduct with them over the space of one day; their sense of security and pride in their work shines through.[6] We are given a tour of the stockroom where 'mother beader' Siphiwe Dube – it was she who had come up with the hopeful name Marigold for the cooperative – proudly shows us the ordered shelves and stacks of beads, in clear plastic bags, all neatly organized.

Brenner had initially relied on Chinese seed beads found in Bulawayo, but as their availability in bulk quantities diminished, she turned to other sources, particularly once it became clear that the project was to develop and continue. She then began sourcing small glass seed beads from Japan and the Czech Republic from various importers across the globe (Vancouver, New York and Cape Town) and sending them to the cooperative.[7]

I learn from Brenner that there has been very little growth or innovation across the craft industry more generally in Bulawayo. I see this lack of drive and creativity very clearly at the other waning craft centres we visit on our tour of Bulawayo in 2014. Brenner is trying (and I think succeeding) to do something different. Previously these trained beaders had been told what to make with basic how-to instructions; Brenner's approach to the cooperative is a different one. The beaders choose the colour combinations (of both bead and thread), while it is she who suggests changing design patterns, always with room for improvisation and suggestions from the beaders themselves. It is a smooth and rhythmic production process where collaboration and trust between Brenner and the beaders, and amongst the beaders, are key elements. There are three tiers of beaders – those who have been beading for 10 to 20 years, those who have been at the cooperative for one to three years, and finally a new crop of young women who are being trained in the art of beadwork.[8] I watch Concilia Mukarobwa, a beader who has been an employee of Marigold for two years, choose a combination of green thread with light blue matte beads. They are curating beads – in separating them by colour, shape and quantity, each woman is making aesthetic design choices for each and every necklace. It is a place where 'unplanned error is transmuted into wilful design' following Doris (2010: 275). It is interesting to think about 'how much one can do with one form' and 'how much you can stretch it', a point made by Brenner in an earlier conversation that I dwell on now.[9]

At the same time, I see a thriving community of mothers and daughters, many of the older women training the younger ones, taking them on as an apprentice working in a guild. Dzidzais Hwende (whose name means 'I learn') tells me that the cooperative is a home for them, a place where they share the everyday details of their lives. It is Sibongile Gotami, a beader in training, who does the cooking for them, her 4-year-old son Takukwa ('blessing') playing on the floor nearby. I watch Teresa Nkomo, an experienced beader who specializes in closing the necklaces once they are done, carefully and seamlessly attach the two ends. This one will soon be put in a plastic bag and sent with a runner to Brenner's home in Johannesburg in a few weeks' time.[10] I see in this ethnographic moment how much the initiative reflects new forms of transnational materials and labour, as well as South Africa's continuing informal economic ties with neighbouring Zimbabwe in the face of its severe economic and political problems.[11] By the end of our three-day visit, I have an appreciation of 'the[ir] sense of pride in work' as craftswomen (Sennett 2008: 9), at the centre of this innovative project.

The Marigold beads project is a quiet return to craft, imbued with a respect for handmade local goods, valuation in the bespoke. The female beaders incorporate ideas of patience, practice and repetition in each and every necklace they produce, for as Brenner reminds me, beading can only take place at the pace of the body, and the width of the span of a beader's hand.[12] I like to think of the production side of the initiative as a slow beads movement, akin to the slow foods, slow cities, slow schooling and slow reading movements that are taking place the world over (Cilliers 2006), in much the same way that a return to individual crafted items is a response to speed of the production, consumption and anonymity of previously defined luxury goods. These practices of slowness operate against unreflective speed at all costs; rather, they advocate a forward-looking approach that perhaps allows us to cope with a complex world better, as Cilliers has argued (2006). It is these same values – ones of gradual learning of a set of knowledge skills and a commitment to a slow crafted practice – that produce a range of necklaces of astonishing skill and variety, and is at the centre of their appeal for a certain kind of Marigold wearer, to whom I now turn.

Johannesburg: Marianne Fassler Style

We'll walk in fields of gold
We'll walk in fields of gold

('Fields of Gold', Sting 1993)

Wearing a single strand of Marigold beads evokes ideas of a Mobius strip, a rosary and string fingers games (such as the cat's cradle) that we all played as children. The necklaces are mathematical and continuous, meditative and compel tactility. The sensuality of these beads lies in the fact that they are passed through the hands, and worn on the body (De Witte 2013: 2). You see other women checking out your beads as you walk past, looking at how the combination of strands that you have put together (or rather curated) changes colour, complexity and sheen in relation to each other and the incoming light. No one strand looks alike for each is a hand-made original – it takes one such female bead maker one to three days of work to hand-loom one strand, depending on its length, thickness and intricacy of design.[13] How many can you really (and realistically) afford to buy at the latest Saturday Joburg pop-up as you drink a glass of chilled white wine and hold one up to the light?[14] It is a moment of style forming in its inchoateness, it is enthralling to watch, to take part in. In this second ethnographic part of the chapter, I want to locate luxury as coming from Africa and set the scene for the consumers of Marigold beaders, one that very much contrasts with the scene of the producers based in Bulawayo that I offered up in a previous section.

I sip my glass of chilled white wine and finger strand after strand of beads, all carefully laid out and colour coordinated on tables, so as to offer the buyer a range of options, and to prompt and suggest the multiple possibilities at play. I don't know which one to choose, as there are too many that I desire. I watch as a woman at the other end of the room looks at herself in a full-length mirror and tries on several necklaces. I spot one I like that she has; I look for its duplicate in front of me. I fail to find it. I move onto another table, a sea of reds and purples. It is November 2012 and I am at my very first Marigold 'pop-up shop'. Here I want to offer up the possibility to think about a pop-up as another form of an informal market, as akin to a craft fair, but located indoor. I imbibe the buzz of luxury in the air – for me it is the din of women laughing and the sound of champagne bottles popping open and the luxuriousness of the shopping that is taking place. That is, I read luxury in this ethnographic moment as much a sensory category as a material one that includes not only touch and sight, but also smell, taste and hearing combined. I feel overwhelmed by the sea of strands in front of me, but I still manage to buy three necklaces, ones that I fall in love with (for their colour and design) but can't explain why; I decide to depart before I reach the point where they all start to look the same and I don't know which ones I want anymore. As I am leaving, I realize that they are the perfect gift item for my friends overseas. I go back inside and purchase a green and brown combination one for Rachel, and a turquoise blue one for Miriam. I feel assured knowing that I can stop by Kim Sacks Gallery[15] located nearby in the Rosebank suburb of Johannesburg if I need to buy more of them as gifts before my planned trip to New York.

By the time of my third pop-up shop experience, this time at Brenner's home in September 2014, I am a seasoned Marigold wearer.[16] That this event took place two weeks after my fieldwork visit to Bulawayo with Brenner makes me more attuned to think about the ties (of materiality and affect) that bind the no longer anonymous female makers to these Joburg female wearers in front of me. I see some familiar faces, just as I see some familiar designs from past pop-up events. I also see new faces, new Marigold designs. I reflect for a moment on their widespread appeal amongst a group of Johannesburg women; both Brenner and I have noted that their popularity resides amongst a racially diverse group that is very much part of certain art and academic circles in Johannesburg, women very much like myself and Brenner who both desire them aesthetically whilst appreciating the history of their making.[17] Perhaps their popularity also lies in the fact that the beads encompass a variety of different looks and can be worn in different ways, doubled at the neck or hanging straight, or even bandolier-style across the shoulders, the latter often the choice of the small number of men who wear them. And that the range of colours and textures is luminous, going from 'rustic to refined, from Bauhaus to Gatsby' as Brenner noted at this pop-up (2014).[18]

However, it is not only their beauty that lies at the heart of their appeal. Rather, I would argue that it is very much about the thoughtfulness that went into both conceiving and making them, that is their style is embodied in the very fabric of their substance – the materials (threading, beads), labour and craftsmanship that went into their production is highly visible on their surfaces and I argue is key to their appeal, and that makes their *making* at the centre of their wearing, a form of slow beading consumption that matches that of their production. It is something I hear often at the multiple pop-ups that I attend, as one woman after another asks the same questions that prompted me to find about how and where they were made, and to desire them even more as a result. It is the infectious way in which Brenner tells the story of their making, including their ever-changing packaging which now includes a Marigold insert that features images of the makers in Bulawayo, and more recently, a link to the newly formed website.[19] As I wander throughout the city of Johannesburg on my daily routines, I am always looking to see who is wearing them, and how (in combination with what clothes, colours, etc.) and at what kinds of events (art openings, walking down the street, at restaurants). I always see something new, some sort of combination that is unexpected, and which makes me feel that the necklaces bind us together as a community of like-minded Marigold wearers across the city.

In April 2014, the Marigold beaded necklaces were featured on the runway models for South African fashion designer Marianne Fassler's winter collection for Mercedes Benz Joburg Fashion Week in Sandton.[20] I attended this event with Brenner, and witnessed Fassler's showstopper that featured garments fashioned from South African and Lesotho blankets transformed into quirky winter coats and shawls, accompanied by Marigold beaded necklaces draped in abundance around the models' necks. I understand why Marianne Fassler, who is a quirky Joburg-based fashion designer, chose these hand-crafted pieces; she saw exactly what I saw in them, in that they were the perfect accessory, one that has a distinct look on each individual wearer and that reasserts one's location on the African continent. On Fassler's runway, the models strutted their stuff, exuding glamour, seductiveness and of course luxury. Here I want to suggest that wearing or rather swaying around with one or more strands of Marigold beads (and here I imagine Sting's line from his song 'Fields of Gold' that I opened this section with playing in the background), on or off the runway, holds considerable potential, following Simidele Dosekun, to explore 'who we are, and who we can and indeed should be' (2016: 5) as African women.

Surfaces, Bodies and Identity-Making

In this last section, I want to explore and experiment with Sarah Nuttall's recent work on rethinking surfaces (Nuttall 2013) as offering a set of tools for an alternative reading of the Marigold initiative as constitutive of African identity-making and experiences. In other words, can we think about the play across surfaces that these beaded strands or threaded beads invoke for their makers and wearers? Nuttall's writings might allow a reading of the (slowness) of production and consumption, and desire for Marigold necklaces less in terms of an investment in material things as a way to perform identity (wealth or class), but more as a means to unfix and reconstruct a notion of self through things.

These beaded accessories embody a range of values embedded in their surface: time, labour, skill, creativity and innovation – significantly, these are the same traits that define craft at the centre of luxury-making – alongside a dazzling array of colour combinations and designs, tactility, rhythm, continuity and possibility. All of these qualities are there in the material surface, and thinking about the necklaces in these multiple ways invites engagement with Nuttall's notion that the particular surface of things is a site where fixed or conventional meanings can begin to be 'unmade' (like race, class and gender), where attention to the material surface is a way of knowing more, to 'seeing' and recognizing depth and complexity, where the undoing of entrenched ideas is generally 'generative' and 'recompositional' (Nuttall 2013: 17). Recognizing complexity through surface a form of play here is a way of moving beyond the flattening, or rather overdetermined, equation of beadwork with African heritage as style (De Witte 2013) towards a rather more specific sense of what is happening with the Marigold necklaces at a certain time and in a particular place, and that is at the centre of their appeal as carefully crafted luxury items.

Here I want to briefly discuss my own experiences of wearing the beads, as well as my ethnographic observations of Brenner herself, wearing them at a variety of occasions and events, both locally and abroad. I myself am a frequent and fond wearer of them for a range of occasions. I store my stock in a much-loved tin that houses them nicely, and keep them tied up in bundles of three, as Brenner has instructed. I often throw on a single necklace on my way out the door, for work or play. As a practised wearer, I am comfortable experimenting with different colours and combinations (of differing lengths and widths, skinnys alongside fat ones) to complement my outfit for the day. Sometimes, I double them up or even triple them up, or wear a single one doubled around my neck. I like the feel and weight of them on me and often finger them throughout the day, turning and twisting them to the light. When I receive compliments for my beads, I am pleased. The Marigold necklaces frequently attend workshops and conferences with me, both locally and abroad; they embody signifiers of elegance, confidence and thoughtfulness, and my rootedness in Johannesburg. They feel like 'me' in terms of an awareness and openness to gender, race, class and sexuality markers that I want to represent to others. I make a style statement when I choose to wear more than three of them around my neck. Recently, I took a stash of newly acquired necklaces (alongside some tried and tested older ones) with me for a two-month fellowship in Stellenbosch (April–May 2018) and wore them on a daily basis; I enjoyed creating new colour combinations as I laid them on my bed before getting dressed. They were a huge hit amongst the other female fellows who had come from a range of countries, and asked the same questions of history and culture of these beautifully crafted luxury items; the circle of makers and wearers continues.

Whenever I meet Brenner for lunch or coffee, she is wearing her Marigolds, always with a set of different ones that I have not yet seen beautifully wrapped around her neck. On such occasions, I want to touch them, feel the way they look and hear about how this latest design experiment came about. She tells me that in fact, some mornings, she picks a random combination of necklaces. I start to think that it doesn't matter which ones you put together; the play of surfaces (of skin, beads and sheen) works its charm regardless.

Perhaps if we play with the idea of surface, and with the complex interplay of these complex strands, their embodied surfaces touching and adorning one's own embodied surface or rather skin (so multiple surfaces operating together as a form of adornment), we can somehow get closer to their intangible and elusive appeal for an ever-increasing 'community of women' (to return to Brenner's words[21]) and which includes both makers and wearers. Is it these links that each woman in Bulawayo quietly affirms for herself as she handlooms a strand of beads? In the very same moment, is that what each wearer in Johannesburg is buying into when she passes her Marigold beads from her hands around her neck, and onto her body? Perhaps it is an assertion of one's Africanness (regardless of the colour of one's skin surface), her 'sartorial worldliness' (Grace Adeniyi Ogunyankin quoted in Dosekun 2016: 4) but in a way that is re-composed, re-purposed, re-imagined or 're-thought' in a more generative and powerful manner (Doris 2010: 277). Possibly, this allows for a reanimation of the body as an active form of 'untribing' (Hamilton and Leibhammer 2016) within a vocabulary that is less dependent upon reified notions of race, gender or class (Nuttall 2013: 433) than the past has made room for in producing and consuming African beads. Is there somewhere in the material surface of these necklaces a wide open field (to evoke Sting and his song 'Fields of Gold' once again, and to which my chapter title pays tribute to) that allows one such wearer to express her feeling that the Marigold beaded necklaces have changed the way that she dresses now, and that putting them on in the morning is her one coveted creative act each day?

Conclusion: The Colour of Butterflies

Bulawayo, only fifty years old, has nothing to offer but surprise.

(Vera 1998: 6)

The slow, the artisanal and the personal are where the value lies in these beautiful luxury items that are akin to ribbons of silk, and that reflect a rainbow of colours – a range close to those of butterflies – a direct reference to Yvonne Vera's powerful novel *Butterfly Burning* set in Bulawayo, only here I move away from the idea of their burning to focus on their colours instead, to end on a note of hope rather than despair in this specific transnational African setting. As Brenner has noted, these necklaces provide an 'opportunity to play with colour'[22] for the community of women involved, not only for the makers but equally for Marigold wearers. The Marigold bead cooperative project is one that empowers, albeit in different ways, both the producers and consumers of the necklaces. In other words, to make or buy the Marigold necklaces is to enter a personalized slow world of craft as luxury, design and personal interaction following Susan Terrio whose fine-tuned ethnographic work on artisanal chocolate making in contemporary France shows the potential of tracing the threads that connect producers to consumers (2010: 259). It is to enter a 'charmed circle' according to Isabel Hofmeyr who offered up this apt description during a conversation on the topic of the Marigold necklaces,[23] one that allows its wearers to temporarily step out of the abstractions of capitalism where one is accordingly embedded in the impersonal relations of the market, and the commodity chain of anonymous purchases. Instead, Marigold beaded necklaces have the potential to relativize our relationship to our things (much like beloved books) that we as individuals living and labouring in an increasingly fast-paced world resist seeing or treating as ordinary commodities that are easily disposable and/or replaceable. Is that part of their appeal as part of a larger return to slow motion lifestyle choices, including hand-crafted luxury items even as they are produced and consumed in a very real capitalist world system, that links South Africa and Zimbabwe? Do these crafted luxury necklaces return us to a time when 'dignity lay in silence and beauty in subtlety' following Kamaladevi Chattopadhyay (2010: 198)?

I would also like to propose that we think of Marigold beaded necklaces as 'gifts' following Marcel Mauss ([1925] 1966). That many wearers, including myself, consistently suggest that they are the perfect gift item for close friends (in both South Africa and globally) suggests that these hand-loomed necklaces are animated by qualities of reciprocity, trust and relatedness between makers and wearers, gift givers and recipients. Here a poignant ethnographic moment comes to mind, that of watching the Marianne Fassler video with the female beaders of the cooperative in Pelandaba in September 2014, and seeing the looks of pride on many individual faces as they focused on the content of the fashion show – identifying certain Marigold necklaces worn by the models, commenting on their craftsmanship, who had made which one, as well as on the dizzying array of colours and combinations on display, etc. I saw a group of women enjoying each other's company, laughing, smiling and taking pride in and seeing the fruits of their labour.

My case study showcases the Marigold beaded necklaces from the perspective of both its makers and wearers, one that is made possible by a multi-sited ethnography in Bulawayo and Johannesburg. I wanted to look at the community of women who produce and consume these beautiful necklaces as a way to deepen our understanding of them, and highlight both aspects as defining features. I showcase a case of craft as a newly valued form of luxury-making on the African continent, and use Nuttall's writings on surfaces to think about the appeal of these hand-loomed beaded necklaces as a distinct form of African identity-making and experience. Lastly, I have attempted to reverse the trend of thinking about what luxury is from a globalized western neoliberal narrative; instead, I chose a case study that is produced *by* Africans *for* African consumption, one that reflects and connects labour to aesthetic politics in Southern Africa.

Acknowledgements

I would like to thank Joni Brenner for introducing me to the beautiful world of makers and wearers of Marigold beaded necklaces.

References

Adamson, Glenn (ed.) (2010), 'Introduction', in *The Craft Reader*, New York: Berg Press, pp. 1–5.

Banks, Libby (2015), 'Defining luxury for a modern era', *The New York Times*, 26 March, https://www.nytimes.com/2015/03/27/fashion/in-craftsmanship-defining-luxury-for-a-modern-era.html/. Accessed 22 November 2016.

Berry, Sara (2010), 'From peasant to artisan: Motor mechanics in a Nigerian town', in G. Adamson (ed.), *The Craft Reader*, New York: Berg Press, pp. 263–71.

Brenner, Joni (2013, 2014, 2016), personal communication, Johannesburg, South Africa.

—— (2014), personal communication, fieldwork trip, September, Bulawayo, Zimbabwe.

Brenner, Joni and Burroughs, Elizabeth (2017), *Making Marigold: Beaders of Bulawayo*, Johannesburg: Palimpsest.

Bringhurst, Robert (1992), *The Elements of Typographic Style*, Vancouver: Hartley & Marks.

Chattopadhyay, Kamaladevi (2010), 'Indian handicrafts', in G. Adamson (ed.), *The Craft Reader*, New York: Berg Press, pp. 192–98.

Cilliers, Paul (2006), 'On the importance of a certain slowness', *E: CO*, 8:3, pp. 105–12.

De Witte, Marlene (2013), 'Wearing beads: Ambiguous heritage on the surfaces of the body', *Heritage, Performance and the Everyday Conference, HUMA*, University of Cape Town, Cape Town, 23–25 January.

Doris, David (2010), 'Destiny world: Textile casualties in Southern Nigeria', in G. Adamson (ed.), *The Craft Reader*, New York: Berg Press, pp. 272–86.

Dosekun, Simidele (2016), 'The politics of fashion and beauty in Africa', *Feminist Africa*, 21:2, pp. 1–6.

Eppel, John (2014), 'Sonnet with One Unstated Line', http://johneppel.co.za/. Accessed 24 July 2014.

Featherstone, Mike (2016), 'The object and art of luxury consumption', in J. Armitage and J. Roberts (eds), *Critical Luxury Studies: Art, Design, Media*, Edinburgh: Edinburgh University Press, pp. 108–28.

Ferguson, James (2006), *Global Shadows: Africa in the Neoliberal World Order*, Durham, NC: Duke University Press.

Hamilton, Carolyn and Leibhammer, Nesser (eds) (2016), *Tribing and Untribing the Archive: Identity and the Material Record in Southern KwaZulu-Natal in the Late Independent and Colonial Periods*, vol. 1, Durban: University of KwaZulu-Natal Press.

Hofmeyr, Isabel (2013), personal communication, September, Johannesburg, South Africa.

Mauss, Marcel ([1925] 1966), *The Gift: Forms and Functions of Exchange in Archaic Societies*, London: Cohen & West.

McNaughton, Patrick R. (2010), 'The Mande blacksmiths: Knowledge, power, and art in West Africa', in G. Adamson (ed.), *The Craft Reader*, New York: Berg Press, pp. 372–78.

Nuttall, Sarah (2013), 'Wound, surface, skin', *Cultural Studies*, 27:3, pp. 418–37.

Sennett, Richard (2008), *The Craftsman*, New Haven, CT: Yale University Press.

Simone, AbdouMaliq (2004), 'People as infrastructure: Intersecting fragments in Johannesburg', *Public Culture*, 16:3, pp. 407–29.

Sting (1993), 'Fields of gold', *Ten Summoner's Tales*, London: A&M.

Terrio, Susan (2010), 'Crafting Grand Cru chocolates in contemporary France', in G. Adamson (ed.), *The Craft Reader*, New York: Berg Press, pp. 253–62.

Vera, Yvonne (1998), *Butterfly Burning*, New York: Farrar, Straus & Giroux.

Notes

1 Brenner took a pre-existing cooperative started up in 1992 by Zimbabwean beaders Siphiwe Dube, Teresa Nkomo and Sifiso Mathe who had attended government training workshops in Bulawayo in the early 1990s on how to run and manage cooperatives. Brenner then commissioned them to do the beadwork for her necklaces.

2 This was a joint fieldtrip to Bulawayo with Joni Brenner, 3–6 September 2014. I thank Joni for her generosity in opening up the Marigold initiative to me; and her candid conversations with me on the never-ending topic of the beads!

3 After gaining independence from British colonial rule in 1980, newly independent Zimbabwe (formerly Rhodesia) developed under the leadership of Robert Mugabe who turned from a much-respected freedom fighter into a corrupt dictator who rigged elections in his favour and sanctioned violence and corruption over a 37-year period (first as prime minister [1980–87] and then as president [1987–2017] of Zimbabwe). A severe economic crisis in the late 1990s was followed by Mugabe's sanctioning of the violent seizure of white farmlands by black Zimbabweans, which led to the exodus of many of its white citizens. He continued to rule the country with an iron fist that led to impoverishment, high rates of unemployment and wide spread homelessness and rapidly increasing inflation rates. During this period of the 2000s, many black Zimbabweans fled to neighbouring countries such as South Africa and have sustained the economy back in Harare by way of informal

markets and the smuggling of goods and money across the border. Mugabe, at the ripe old age of 93 (and with his young wife Grace having political aspirations of her own to take over after his death), was finally forced to resign on 18 November 2017 in a coup by his own ZANU-PF Party members (https://www.aljazeera.com/news/2017/11/rise-fall-zimbabwes-robert-mugabe-171119144029554.html. Accessed 8 June 2018).

4 Once bustling with plenty of work and over twenty members during the 1990s and early 2000s, the cooperative had ground almost to a halt at the point of Brenner's involvement with it in 2012. Over the three-and-a-half years of their collaboration, the cooperative grew to employ fourteen members. At the time of my visit in September 2014, the members of the cooperative were Nothando Bhebhe, Simagele Dube, Siphiwe Dube, Lydia Gama, Sibongile Gotami, Dzidzais Hwende, Thokozile Maseko, Sifiso Mathe, Edas Msuku, Concilia Mukarobwa, Lethukuthula Ncube-Ndou, Teresa Nkomo, Jestinah Nyoni and Princess Shumbaimwe.

5 Personal communication, 26 November 2014.

6 On our second day in Bulawayo – 7 September 2014 – Brenner and I sat in the stockroom with each of the women and recorded their life biographies, including how each came to work for the cooperative and the length of her employment with Marigold.

7 Personal communication, 10 January 2013.

8 Missing is a middle tier of beaders between four and nine years, which, in turn, reflects its waning and the reinvigoration of the cooperative once Joni started commissioning them for her necklaces, and the demand for more trained beaders in the recent past.

9 Personal communication, 10 January 2013.

10 'Runners' refers informally to small privately operated businesses that transport and deliver goods across distant spaces, in this case weekly between Bulawayo and Johannesburg. More generally, runners are a commonplace form of infrastructure that many informal markets the world over are reliant on, and that use people to cross goods more easily over national borders. See AbdouMaliq Simone's much-cited and controversial piece on people as infrastructure (2004). Brenner relies on a runner named Innocent who is an important thread in this project that enables beads, designs and occasional rejects to be delivered to Marigold, and the new and repaired necklaces and samples to be delivered back in Johannesburg via nondescript plastic bags, similar to the ones found all over Bulawayo, which John Appel makes reference to in his sonnet (2012). Personal communication, 26 November 2014.

11 Talk about inflation and lack of goods, and the ways in which they cross borders.

12 Personal communication, 15 November 2016.

13 They come in a range of widths from 'skinny' to 'normal' to 'wide' and a range of lengths that include 'singles' and 'doubles'.

14 In the same way that the necklaces come in a range of colours, lengths, thicknesses and designs, their prices range from R300 to R400 for a single normal width necklace to up to R2,500 for a double in length necklace or a thicker single one. In the five years that I have been a buyer of Marigold, the prices have also gone up; a necklace valued at R300 in 2014 was sold in 2018 for R450.

15 Brenner sells approximately 200 marigold necklaces a month (this includes the Kim Sacks Gallery in Johannesburg, which is a small, well-established gallery-cum-art space run by

Sacks herself and a friend of Brenner's, as well as the San Francisco MOMA shop where Brenner also has a personal connection to the owner). Other shops often approach her to sell them, but she purposely wants to keep this craft project small-scale, not turn it into an 'abstraction, that is mass produced'. Personal communication, 10 January 2013.

16 Thus far, I have visited three Marigold pop-up shops (November 2012, December 2012 and September 2014). The pop-ups are generally announced by e-invite or by word of mouth through certain academic and art circles in Johannesburg. In more recent times, Brenner sells them more informally to smaller gatherings, timed often with the arrival of new stock or a visitor from out of town who somehow is connected to someone who knows her.

17 My intention is to show that these traits cannot be separated out as their appeal relies on their twining together. More generally, this group of mostly female middle-class consumers is educated, associated with Wits University and/or the art scene and reflect the racial diversity of Johannesburg.

18 Brenner used the term 'different personalities' to describe the necklaces. Personal communication, 29 November 2014.

19 Brenner is a savvy entrepreneur who creatively comes up with new ways to showcase the necklaces. She increasingly relies on the *making* of the necklaces as part of the appeal for the *wearing* of them. See her evolving website: https://www.marigoldbeads.com (accessed 6 June 2018). Brenner recently published a book on the Marigold beads, the launch for which I attended on 13 December 2017 at her home in Johannesburg. Written by Joni Brenner and Elizabeth Burroughs, and with photographs by Liz Whitter, *Making Marigold: Beaders of Bulawayo* includes glossy photograph inserts of the necklaces and detailed information on the makers of the necklaces. The inside jacket blurb includes a prompt that states: 'looking slowly and repeatedly is to experience the world of Marigold, where many collectors of the beads already belong'.

20 Marianne Fassler is a Johannesburg-based fashion designer whose design company is named Leopard Frock. She works out of her home in the suburb of Saxonwold and has been designing clothes for over 30 years and uses South Africa (and the larger African continent) as a source of inspiration for her Afro-chick collections. See her website: http://leopardfrock. co.za/ (accessed 7 June 2018).

21 Personal communication, 10 January 2013.

22 Personal communication, 10 January 2013.

23 Personal communication, 10 January 2013.

Section 3

Ambiguous Luxury Spaces

Chapter 7

Luminance and the Moralization of Black Women's Luxury Consumption in South Africa

Ndapwa Alweendo and Simidele Dosekun

The Luminance boutique, opened in 2013 in the ultra-exclusive Hyde Park Corner mall in Johannesburg, aims to provide those women who can afford it the opportunity to 'live life beautifully' by partaking of a 'world class shopping experience with an African appeal' (Luminance Online 2015a). On its website, Luminance also describes itself as an 'accessible luxury and contemporary fashion and lifestyle department store for consumers who covet world-class quality and beauty' (Luminance Online 2015a). To walk into Luminance is indeed to partake in the finest of luxury retail, to indulge and to pamper oneself, from the store's plush carpets and gently perfumed air, to its glistening displays of the loftiest brands of western fashion. The brainchild of black South African businesswoman and media mogul Khanyi Dhlomo, the store's opening echoed contemporary narratives of black economic empowerment in South Africa, which proclaim that post-apartheid South Africa has become a space in which black excellence is both recognized and rewarded, and in which black mobility is possible. Luminance was framed as a space in and through which black women especially were entering into what, in South Africa, was previously a white world of both luxury consumption and luxury retail. It was reported at the time that Dhlomo and her mother were the majority shareholders in the business, while the minority stake was shared between private investors, staff and the black rural women employed to produce some of the merchandise (Pillay 2013). Majority ownership has since been transferred to Dr Judy Dlamini, one of South Africa's most successful black businesswomen (City Press 2014).

Luminance's opening did not go unremarked upon in South African popular and media discourse. Some saw the endowment granted to the boutique by the National Empowerment Fund (NEF) as an unfair diversion of government funds from the many South Africans economically disenfranchised in ways that Dhlomo, an already successful entrepreneur, was not (City Press 2013a). Other critiques ranged from disapproval of what many considered the store's exorbitant prices, to outright scepticism about the transformative potential of a space that could be accessed by so few South African women, regardless of colour (Pillay 2013). This said nothing of the criticism directed towards the NEF itself for funding a project that, at face value, appeared to do little in the way of improving black empowerment (City Press 2013b). In fact, it was the intense media scrutiny of Dhlomo – an elite black woman in a still racially divided and sexist society – that piqued the research from which this chapter derives, which sought to explore what Luminance represents and possibly effects in the post-apartheid context (Alweendo 2016). This chapter examines the meanings and politics of the exclusive boutique as a space for a new kind of black woman in South Africa to live out new ideas of cosmopolitan lifestyle and luxury. The chapter is based on in-depth, semi-structured interviews with seven black women in Johannesburg aged between 21 and 36, three of whom were regular customers at Luminance, and four of whom had shopped there once. It also draws on newspaper coverage of the boutique, published remarks by its owners and the store's website.

The chapter argues that Luminance represents an 'arrival' for black South African women, more specifically an arrival at consumerist and seemingly carefree self-making via what is branded the finest in global luxury. The store marks a stark departure from not only the severe burdens placed upon black women by apartheid, but from continued, implicit expectations and demands for them to assume a gendered responsibility for the general upliftment of the black community. Nthabiseng Motsemme notes that, caught between the double oppression of racism and patriarchy, some black women in South Africa choose 'to assume consciously supportive and secondary roles that do not challenge black men's power' (2002: 649). As such, the spaces in which black women's participation is deemed most acceptable and welcome are predominantly private, communal and domestic. For women in patriarchal societies, their value is directly connected to how well they 'adhere to the expectations of domesticity' (Gqola 2013: 57).

By contrast, the heuristic figure that we call 'the Luminance woman', that is, the type of black woman for whom shopping at the store is not only desirable but feasible, is an increasingly individualist subject. We understand and approach 'figures' as material and semiotic, thoroughly historicized and contested, social types (e.g. see Gqola 2016; Tyler 2008). They emerge in particular sociopolitical contexts. The Luminance woman emerges and circulates within, and contributes to, dominant neoliberal narratives of what individual hard work and determination can deliver in the 'new South Africa'. Indeed, she is a type of 'new South Africa woman', which Pumla Gqola conceptualizes as a highly corporatized and glamourized figure of feminine agency and freedom, and an embodiment of 'women's empowerment, but not necessarily feminism' (2016: 123). Simidele Dosekun (2015) elsewhere makes a case for thinking of this kind of class-privileged, new African feminine subject as 'postfeminist', in the sense of seemingly being beyond or 'post' the need for feminism as politics. Keenly attuned to the limitations of the Luminance woman's brand of empowerment, but also recognizing that she disrupts historical forms and sites of racist exclusion and elitism in South Africa, the chapter draws on Melissa Harris-Perry (2011) to propose a critical view of Luminance as a 'crooked room', a structurally unequal and imbalanced space in which black women attempt to stand.

Bringing the 'World-Class' Home

Luxury is a complex concept to pin down because it is by definition relative. At a literal level, luxury refers to that which is non-essential, to something desired rather than truly needed.

However, part of what has made the luxury goods industry so successful has been its ability to transform the desired into perceived need (Kovesi 2015). Luxury consumption is also about assigning symbolic meaning to goods, rendering them not only symbols of wealth and status but also signifiers of the wearer's personality and taste, and of her ability to access a world of exclusivity and superior craftsmanship (Shipman 2004; Heine 2010; Featherstone 2014; Wierzba 2015). At Luminance, luxury means the most well-known and well-regarded European and, to a lesser extent, American brands. Accordingly, luxury derives almost exclusively from the metropoles most associated with 'high fashion': Paris, Milan, London, New York and so on. As Agnès Rocamora explains, for example, 'in the realm of fashion, France and, in particular, "Paris" are highly loaded signs, synonymous with fashionability, elegance [...] and the "good taste" which grants one the sense of distinction on which luxury thrives' (2016: 208).

That the Luminance woman is well acquainted with places like Paris came up repeatedly in the interviews. Painting a descriptive picture of this woman, Palesa[1] ventured:

> she's somebody who's very crazy about travel, crazy about experiencing new things, and who, who's seen a bit of the world, you know, and who's probably seen a bit, or a lot of the world. So you can't lie to her about what you're giving to her [i.e. in Luminance], she's seen it in Milan, she's seen it, in, in, Paris, she's seen it in New York and she just wants it here too at home, you know...

Lerato echoed the notion that the reason why the Luminance woman could 'assess the value of the brand' was because she was 'well-travelled'. According to Dhlomo herself, it was her own global travel and exposure that led her to found the store in the first place, perceiving, from abroad, a gap in the South African marketplace:

> It's a venture I've been thinking about for at least ten years, it started when I was living in Paris as Head of South African Tourism. And really from just walking around and taking in the retail experiences, the brands, the labels, how people shop, it dawned on me that none of that really existed in South Africa.

> (SABC 3 Top Billing 2013)

African brands are in short supply in Luminance, by contrast. Stoned Cherrie, a brand that claims to represent the latest and best in South African fashion, was originally in the line-up of suitably high-quality local lines to be stocked at Luminance, if with the caveat that it would 'take time' for a set of exclusive designs to be made available (Pillay 2013). Three years later, while a smattering of South African designers have made the cut, the brand remains absent on the boutique's roster of designers (Luminance Online 2015a). Stoned Cherrie, whose look 'is often described as distinctively "African"' (Vincent 2007: 82), is just one of many high-fashion South African labels that have emerged in the post-apartheid era to cater to a new generation of black South Africans determined to unapologetically (re-)embrace their blackness and Africanicity, and to style themselves as simultaneously local and global (e.g. Motsemme 2003; Nuttall 2004; Vincent 2007). Nthabiseng Motsemme describes them as seeking 'to liberate black female bodies from their histories of oppression to a stylised freedom' (2003: 57). Yet despite the way black South African elites have chosen to embrace such brands, comments made by Luminance's new owner, Judy Dlamini, continue to reinforce an imagined distinction between the ultimate calibre of the foreign versus homegrown:

> This year has seen Luminance embrace and welcome on board talented local designers ... Sitting alongside international heavyweights, our local designers have still proved to be a favourite amongst clients in remaining true to their aesthetic and roots.
>
> (Luminance Online 2015b)

The implication of Dlamini's remarks praising local designers for 'still' being favourites, and able to hold their own against the global heavyweights is that the former would be outclassed ordinarily. Luminance positions itself as a cut above what it constructs as *South African* luxury, or *local* standards. 'Truest' and also 'global' luxury thus remains western and imported. This strategy of putative ultra-distinction would appear to be successful. One participant described the store appreciatively as 'the first of it's [sic] kind, of that calibre [...]. In terms of the boutique, I've never seen anything like that before *in this country*' (emphasis added).

Buying Our Way In

Consumption practices have been long fraught with meaning for black South Africans. Historically, part of the mechanism of apartheid was the economic disenfranchisement of black people, as the political system distributed wealth, and therefore the sheer material ability to consume, along strict colour lines. Black consumption was also limited by the apartheid state delimiting and aggressively policing black people's movements, as well as by racist entry and service policies in retail arenas. For instance, department stores in downtown Johannesburg were long reserved for white customers only (Kenny 2015). Deborah Posel (2010) argues that regulating black consumption, and distinguishing it from white consumption, was not incidental to the apartheid project but at its heart. The very 'making of the racial order was, in part, a way of regulating people's aspirations, interests and powers as consumers. The desire and power to consume was racialised, at the same time as it was fundamental in the very making of race' (Posel 2010: 160).

It follows that consumption was an important mode of black resistance to apartheid, including as a way and means for black women and men to continue to find pleasure and exercise agency in their everyday lives (e.g. see Thomas 2006; Johnson 2009; Ferreira 2011; also Madikizela-Mandela 1985). Despite the heavy hand of the apartheid state apparatus, black women were active players in the spheres of fashion and beauty, and neighbourhoods like Sophiatown, in Johannesburg – before its destruction by the state in the late 1950s – were hubs of black creativity and enterprise. Black South Africans also actively breached the consumer and other spaces denied to them. In her autobiographical writings, Winnie Madikizela-Mandela (1985), a prominent figure in the anti-apartheid struggle, describes with relish the times when she deliberately entered and disrupted the normative proceedings in shops and other retail arenas in which her race marked her as not belonging (also see Iqani 2015a). Given these histories, as well as the fact that South Africa emerged from apartheid isolationism in the early 1990s into a heightened neoliberal consumerist economic order, it is no surprise that consumption has become an important arena of post-apartheid black self-making and self-representation, and aspiration (Posel 2010; Iqani 2017; Nuttall 2004; Odiahmbo 2008). Consumption has become imbricated with 'freedom' and 'citizenship'. At a material level, the rise in black consumption is also due to the growth in the black middle and elite classes occasioned by post-apartheid political-economic policy.

It is in light of these histories that Luminance represents what we are calling 'an arrival' for the black women who can afford to shop there. In popular parlance and as we use it here, 'to arrive' is to attain a distinguished and desirable rank or status. It is to reach some promised land finally, and to be recognized and heralded as belonging there. All this means that to arrive is also, evidently, to depart or leave behind some other lesser place or 'level'. For the Luminance woman, the store represents an arrival of the highest order because it is an utterly exclusive space and also purports to adhere to the most rarefied of standards (supposedly rare in South Africa). It represents arrival at not only the privileged socio-economic status required to shop in such a place but also at the level of cosmopolitan discernment to even know how to do so, such as heard earlier in the chapter from interview participants. Thus the Luminance woman has arrived at financial and cultural capital. Arguably, these translate into a certain psychological and embodied 'confidence capital' too. The Luminance woman walks into the store with confidence. She knows that she belongs and is welcome, unlike a black middle-class woman like Madikizela-Mandela in the apartheid days, say, whose mere presence disrupted, notwithstanding the fact that she had money to spend. Indeed, the store is now *hers*. Luminance belongs literally to an elite black woman, and remarks by Dhlomo suggest that this was the demographic for whom she founded the store in the first place. As Dhlomo proclaimed, in what can be read as an explicit invitation for black women to now boldly enter the world of luxury, black women have 'got to start going into unexpected places' (Pillay 2013).

And yet, in South Africa, when it comes to consumption, lifestyle and other material concerns, black arrival, or what some might still deem 'unexpected' black presence, is highly contested and moralized. Mehita Iqani argues that in the global south middle-class consumption (much less luxury consumption) tends to be moralized 'precisely because of the extremes of social inequalities that are [visibly] present' (2016: 32). Black South African consumption is further moralized by being cast as 'new', a product of 'new money' and 'new values' (Iqani 2017). Terms like 'new money' or 'nouveau riche' are derisive, being associated commonly with values and practices such as 'excessive consumption', ostentation and 'bad taste' (Bourdieu 1984; see also Smit, this volume). These values and practices are readily racialized. In terms of 'new values', the counter-reference in the South African context is to the old ideals of the anti-apartheid liberation struggle, and of the African National Congress (ANC), the ruling party since 1994 and home of the erstwhile freedom fighters. If the old values centred on communal black advancement and social and economic justice, or in fact socialism, new, elite black consumption then comes to be seen in some quarters as a 'selling out' (Iqani 2017).

Grappling with the many criticisms levelled at Luminance, which are both indirectly and directly also criticisms of the Luminance woman for participating in the store's values, interview participants ruminated: 'Why shouldn't we have nice things? Why can't we indulge every once in a while without feeling guilty?' These rhetorical questions are as much about the past, referencing how far the Luminance woman had come, as about the present, rejecting notions that black women's luxury consumption is necessarily selfish and frivolous, especially because the larger black community is still mired in poverty. Lerato reasoned:

> Even in a society like ours that's so polarised and with inequalities, there are people with cash to spend somewhere […]. People still have a right to choose, and just because they're rich, doesn't mean they must go and pour all their money [i.e. philanthropically] in Soweto or in the Eastern Cape.

As we continue to elaborate in the following section, participants were of the view that black women who could afford to shop at Luminance had, in multiple senses of the term, *earned* it. Not only did the Luminance woman earn an independent income that she was therefore at liberty to spend, she had paid her dues historically. Having long suffered oppression and exclusion, having had few avenues to enter the formal economy, she was now free. As Amanda put it:

> It was really important [for Luminance to] have a black face. Black people, especially black women don't want to be known as nurses and social workers anymore. I mean, we have proper career goals and it also just shows that you can have a business in fashion. You can run a fashion business in the country, and not just be a designer or be an intern at a runway show.

The woman who shopped at Luminance represented a step, or several steps, forward for black women who had grown up seeing their mothers, aunts and grandmothers denied access not only to luxury but to the kind of jobs that would allow them to even dream of it. Her arrival was therefore also at the right to self-prioritize, or what Lerato termed 'the right to choose' in the quote above. According to Palesa, the Luminance woman was an individualist subject: 'somebody who likes distinction, she likes standing out from the crowd […] she's not just any individual, she's an extraordinary and an exceptional individual, you know?' Now individually empowered (Dosekun, forthcoming), now individually exceptional, she did not owe any apologies for this.

Don't Burn It Down, Strive to Also Stand

Reflecting on the fact that shopping at Luminance is neither materially possible nor designed for everyone, interview participants reasoned that this was just in the order of things. Lerato reflected: 'As much [as my] instinct would be to change the prices so everyone can afford [Luminance], then it kills what the brand is for, right?' In the words of another participant: 'I think that they didn't create a brand that was for everybody, that was for every, for [just] anyone, which was intentional'. The women were referring here to the 'logic of exclusion that fuels luxury', without which the luxury brand or space fails to have meaning or distinction, and is therefore no longer luxury (Rocamora 2016: 216). In this line of thinking, the fact that Luminance was not for everyone and the Luminance woman, not an 'everywoman', served instead to render both *aspirational*. The store became a space to which the currently excluded would also want to arrive, and the Luminance woman stood as an exhortation to other black women to strive hard like she had or did, so that they could one day get to where she was:

> If the rest of us can't afford it, you mustn't be angry and wanna burn the shop down [*laughs*]. We must work harder [...] I guess when you shop there you'll feel like, 'I have arrived' type of thing so I guess it will motivate you to [think] 'why can't I shop there'.

Nandi's above remarks gestured towards the spectre of popular black anger and disenchantment about the continued inequalities of the post-apartheid socio-economic and institutional landscape. In recent years, this has manifested increasingly in mass protest, and has begun to implicate the black ruling class (e.g. see Alexander 2010; Gibson 2017). Nandi's use of rhetorics of 'aspiration' and 'self-motivation' served to depoliticize this anger, however, and to propose that a better or more fruitful direction of black energies was to 'work harder'. The solution to structural exclusion became not collective movement or redress, but individual and internalized effort.

Participants also rejected suggestions, including by Luminance itself, that the existence and success of the boutique would or could actively empower currently disempowered black women. Lerato stated: 'In my view and in my mind, again, I know [Luminance is] not about woman empowerment, it's about high-end fashion. And there's a place for it anywhere'. Nthabiseng spoke on this theme at some length:

> I struggled to draw the connections between how that business and that, that strategy [Dhlomo] said at the time was going to empower or change a black woman's life who's sitting in Soweto and can't even shop in that shop. So when I broke through and went through all of it, and filtered it to make sense for myself, I came to the conclusion that it is a *business*, at the end of the day.
>
> (personal interview, original emphasis)

Luminance did not have to empower under-privileged women, or even claim or intend to, to be justifiable or legitimate. While the boutique's origin story included a certain pride that it created a platform for less privileged black entrepreneurs, it was not obliged to have a higher and communal black purpose. It was a business, profit-driven 'at the end of the day', and there was room for this in South Africa. Hence, as Nthabiseng went on to say about the business owner: 'She has to make money. And who is she gonna take care of? The women who walk *in*: with the card, with the money. Now, when we're doing that, don't tell me that's now bringing change or transformation to women. It's a business transaction like any other'. Via care and attention to her moneyed customers, the black businesswoman's ultimate care, attention and responsibility were to her bottom line, *not post-apartheid transformation*.

Continuing an individualist and celebratory framing of the Luminance woman, the foregoing remarks by Lerato and Nthabiseng could be critiqued for seeming to evade any notion that the new black South African woman has even corporate social responsibilities, much less more substantive or radical ones. The Luminance woman is an exemplary neoliberal subject, interpellated and swayed by 'rational entrepreneurial action, conducted according to a calculus of utility, benefit, or satisfaction against a micro-economic grid of scarcity, supply and demand, and moral value-neutrality' (Brown 2003: n.pag.). Yet the picture becomes more complicated if we consider, alternately, that what the research participants were rejecting was that black South African women have a particular responsibility, a black feminine one, to empower and uplift others around them. Black women themselves were rejecting what would amount to yet another intersectional burden placed upon black women, yet another 'boulder' for them to push against, to cite Nomboniso Gasa's (2007: 150) metaphor for the continuous struggle in which black women engaged under apartheid and during the political transition not just for themselves but for the nation as a whole. We can revisit in this vein the earlier-cited plaint: 'Why can't we also have nice things?' Rather than hear this question as selfish, materialistic or grasping, we can consider that what it was asking was: 'why can't *someone else* make the requisite sacrifices? why must it still be *us*?'

While far from transformative, falling as it does squarely within the ideological and moral bounds of neoliberal consumer capitalism, for black women in South Africa to assert an unapologetic, individualist right to not only consume but in the case of Luminance also trade in and profit from luxury *is* political. The slant or skew of both South Africa's past and present renders it so. Melissa Harris-Perry suggests in reference to the ways in which black women in America are forced to contort themselves in order to negotiate their place in society that their struggle is akin to attempting to 'stand up straight in a crooked room' (2011: 29). As Harris-Perry (2011) formulates it, the crooked room refers to the world of dehumanizing and distorting stereotypes that black women face, to which they must constantly rise and respond. We find it productive to borrow and extend Harris-Perry's (2011) conceptual metaphor, however, to think of Luminance as a kind of crooked room itself for black South African women. Luminance is a crooked room in the sense that it is founded upon several compounded layers of structural inequality and imbalance: the elitism of the sheer concepts and practices of luxury consumption and branding; the boutique's insistent sourcing and importing of the so-called best in sophistication, glamour and style from the West; its ownership and business structures that, while now black and female at the top, are still corporate and accumulative, and likely exploitative at base. Some of the exclusive brands to be found in the store are alleged to engage in exploitative labour practices in their global south factories, for instance (e.g. see Rocamora 2016).

Thinking of Luminance as a crooked room is also productive to understand, and to make allowance for, what such a space tends to do. Citing experimental studies in the field of cognitive psychology, Harris-Perry (2011) notes the finding that, when placed in rooms and around objects that are quite literally crooked, people reorient themselves to, or get their bearings from, these things. In other words, people come to 'figure out which way is up' (Harris-Perry 2011: 29) in relation to their surroundings, and in this way may end up unwittingly positioning themselves aslant, too. If elite black women in South Africa today are invested in luxury consumption, if they desire and find pleasure in high and exclusive style, and furthermore ardently defend their right to, it is because this is the predominant way of the world into which they have arrived as now-materially privileged subjects. This is how they come to stand in the crooked room in which they are positioned and interpellated. Our point here is not to denude black women of agency, as if they cannot help themselves. Much like the interview participants cited in the chapter, our aim is rather to reject *moralized* judgements of black women's luxury consumption in South Africa. Designed to keep black women in their – our – 'proper place', these judgements are racist and/or sexist, and disciplinary, and so must be resisted and critiqued.

Conclusion

In South Africa and beyond, in societies that perceive themselves as increasingly inclusive and tolerant, black women's practices and representations of self remain subject to particular gendered and racialized scrutiny, and moralized judgement. Amongst many other factors, the heightened scrutiny of what black women get up to and prioritize is due to the fact that they are not seen as individualized subjects, as women who might think of themselves only or first. Rather black women tend to be fixed in communal and relational terms and frames, as subjects who have particular matriarchal and/or filial responsibilities toward their communities; subjects who should be dutiful, then. Their responsibilities are to not only represent but uplift; to pass on whatever 'empowerment' they may have gained themselves; to sacrifice and put their needs as well as *wants* second to those of others. At the same time, as this chapter has also shown, black consumption, both women's and men's, is a fraught and highly politicized terrain in post-apartheid South Africa, implicating struggles over taste, both national and global belonging and citizenship, and putative racial authenticity.

It is in these intersecting, deeply historicized contexts that a hyper-elite, luxury boutique like Luminance becomes a complex, even charged space to read from a black and African feminist perspective. While some might simply celebrate the existence of the space and its black female clientele as representing the break down or surmounting of long-entrenched intersectional barriers, we would suggest that this is not enough. Even for black South African women, long-denied access, luxury consumption does not add up to radical or transformative politics, and neither do the neoliberal visions and constructs of 'empowerment' – black economic empowerment and women's empowerment – that have dominated official discourse and development programming in the country since 1994. By conceptualizing Luminance in terms of arrival, we have sought in this chapter to critically if briefly reflect upon how it is that elite black South African women have got to where they are, and where and how exactly this place is. Moralizing their luxury consumption, we argue, constitutes not only a continued symbolic and ideological violence against black women. It also diverts critical focus from the structural and cultural conditions that invite their luxurious and luminous practices of self in the first place, and that continue to make unjust the spaces in which they are invited to enter and stand crooked.

References

Alexander, Peter (2010), 'Rebellion of the poor: South Africa's service delivery protests – A preliminary analysis', *Review of African Political Economy*, 37:123, pp. 25–40.

Alweendo, Ndapwa (2016), 'New spaces and old stories: The Luminance woman, black womanhood and the illusion of the "new" South Africa', unpublished master's thesis, Rhodes University, Grahamstown.

Brown, Wendy (2003), 'Neo-liberalism and the end of liberal democracy', *Theory & Event*, 7:1, n.pag.

Burger, Ronelle, Louw, Megan, de Oliveria Pegado, Brigitte and van der Berg, Servaas (2015), 'Understanding consumption patterns of the established and emerging South African black middle class', *Development Southern Africa*, 32:1, pp. 41–56.

City Press (2013a), 'Hyde Park's state-funded luxury', News24, https://www.news24.com/Archives/City-Press/Hyde-Parks-state-funded-luxury-20150430. Accessed 16 November 2018.

—— (2013b), 'Black industrialists do not own "spaza shops and KFCs"', News24, https://www.news24.com/Archives/City-Press/Hyde-Parks-state-funded-luxury-20150430. Accessed 16 November 2018.

—— (2014), 'Luminance is free', News24, https://www.news24.com/Archives/City-Press/Luminance-is-free-20150429. Accessed 16 November 2018.

Dosekun, Simidele (2015), 'For western girls only? Postfeminism as transnational culture', *Feminist Media Studies*, 15:6, pp. 960–75.

—— (2020), *Fashioning Postfeminism: Spectacular Femininity and Transnational Culture in Nigeria*, Champaign, IL: University of Illinois Press.

Edwards, Iain (1988), 'Shebeen queens: Illicit liquor and the social structure of drinking dens in Cato Manor', *Agenda: Empowering Women for Gender Equity*, 3, pp. 75–97.

Featherstone, Mike (2014), 'Luxury, consumer culture and sumptuary dynamics', *Luxury*, 1:1, pp. 47–69.

Ferreira, Nicolette (2011), 'Grace and the townships housewife: Excavating black South African women's magazines from the 1960s', *Agenda Empowering Women for Gender Equity*, 25:4, pp. 59–68.

Gasa, Nomboniso (ed.) (2007), *Women in South African History: Basus'iimbokodo, Bawel'imilambo (They Remove Boulders and Cross Rivers)*, Cape Town: HRSC Press.

Gibson, Nigel C. (2017), 'The specter of Fanon: The student movements and the rationality of revolt in South Africa', *Social Identities: Journal for the Study of Race, Nation & Culture*, 23:5, pp. 579–99.

Goetz, Anne Marie and Hassim, Shireen (eds) (2003), *No Shortcuts to Power: African Women in Politics and Policy Making*, London: Zed Books.

Gqola, Pumla (2013), *A Renegade Called Simphiwe*, Johannesburg: MF Books Joburg.

—— (2016), 'A peculiar place for a feminist? The New South African Woman, *True Love Magazine* and Lebo (gang) Mashile', *Safundi*, 17:2, pp. 119–36.

Harris-Perry, Melissa (2011), *Sister Citizen: Shame, Stereotypes, and Black Women in America*, New Haven, CT: Yale University Press.

Hassim, Shireen (2004), 'Nationalism, feminism and autonomy: The ANC in exile and the question of women', *Journal of Southern African Studies*, 30:3, pp. 433–56.

—— (2006), *Women's Organizations and Democracy in South Africa: Contesting Authority*, Madison, WI: University of Wisconsin Press.

Heine, Klaus (2010), 'The personality of luxury fashion brands', *Journal of Global Fashion Marketing*, 1:3, pp. 154–63.

hooks, bell (2000), *Where We Stand: Class Matters*, London: Routledge.

Hunter, Mark (2010), *Love in the Time of AIDS: Inequality, Gender, and Rights in South Africa*, Scottsville: University of KwaZulu-Natal Press.

Iqani, Mehita (2015a), '"The consummate material girl?": The contested consumption of Winnie Madikizela-Mandela in early post-apartheid media representations', *Feminist Media Studies*, 15:5, pp. 779–93.

—— (2015b), 'Agency and affordability: Being black and "middle class" in South Africa in 1989', *Critical Arts*, 29:2, pp. 26–145.

—— (2017), 'A new class for a new South Africa? The discursive construction of the "black middle class" in post-apartheid media', *Journal of Consumer Culture*, 17:1, pp. 105–21.

Johnson, Rachel (2009), '"The girl about town": Discussions of modernity and female youth in *Drum* magazine, 1951–1970', *Social Dynamics*, 35:1, pp. 36–50.

Kenny, Bridget (2015), 'Servicing a racial regime: Gender, race, and the public space of department stores in Baltimore, Maryland, and Johannesburg, South Africa, 1940–1970', in M. Bay and A. Fabian (eds), *Race and Retail: Consumption Across the Color Line*, New Brunswick, NJ: Rutgers University Press, pp. 99–119.

Kovesi, Catherine (2015), 'What is luxury? The rebirth of a concept in the early modern world', *Luxury*, 2:1, pp. 25–40.

Luminance Online (2015a), 'Home: Live life beautifully', Luminance, http://luminanceonline.com/. Accessed 16 November 2018.

—— (2015b), 'Magazine: Luminance magazine third edition 2015', Luminance, https://luminanceonline.com/magazine/index/read/id/6/. Accessed 16 November 2018.

Madikizela-Mandela, Winnie (1985), *Part of My Soul Went with Him*, New York: Norton.

Motsemme, Nthabiseng (2002), 'Gendered experiences of blackness in post-apartheid', *Social Identities: Journal for the Study of Race, Nation & Culture*, 8:4, pp. 647–73.

—— (2003), 'Distinguishing beauty, creating distinctions: The politics and poetics of dress among young Black women', *Agenda: Empowering Women for Gender Equality*, 17:57, pp. 12–19.

Ngidi, S. (1997), 'Akhona! Women investing in women', *Agenda: Empowering Women for Gender Equality*, 35, pp. 58–60.

Nuttall, Sarah (2004), 'Stylizing the self: The Y Generation in Rosebank, Johannesburg', *Public Culture*, 16:3, pp. 430–52.

Odhiambo, Tom (2008), 'The black female body as a "consumer and a consumable" in current *Drum* and *True Love* magazines in South Africa', *African Studies*, 67:1, pp. 71–80.

Pillay, Verashni (2013), 'Khanyi Dhlomo: More heat than Luminance', *The Mail & Guardian*, 2 August, http://mg.co.za/article/2013-08-02-00-the-crucifixion-of-khanyi-dhlomo. Accessed 4 November 2016.

Posel, Deborah (2010), 'Races to consume: Revisiting South Africa's history of race, consumption and the struggle for freedom', *Ethnic & Racial Studies*, 33:2, pp. 157–75.

Rocamora, Agnes (2016), 'Online luxury: Geographies of production and consumption and the Louis Vuitton website', in J. Armitage and J. Roberts (eds), *Critical Luxury Studies: Art, Design, Media*, Edinburgh: Edinburgh University Press, pp. 199–220.

SABC 3 Top Billing (2013), 'Khanyi Dhlomo's Luminance Launch (full insert)', YouTube, 3 August, https://www.youtube.com/watch?v=RKa3iugyBTE. Accessed 16 November 2018.

Shipman, Alan (2004), 'Lauding the leisure class: Symbolic content and conspicuous consumption', *Review of Social Economy*, 62:3, pp. 277–89.

Thomas, Lynn (2006), 'The modern girl and racial respectability in 1930s South Africa', *The Journal of African History*, 47:3, pp. 461–90.

Tyler, Imogen (2008), ' "Chav mum chav scum": Class disgust in contemporary Britain', *Feminist Media Studies*, 8:1, pp. 17–34.

Verhoef, Grietjie (2001), 'Informal financial service institutions for survival: African women and Stokvels in urban South Africa, 1930–1988', *Enterprise & Society*, 2:2, pp. 259–96.

Vincent, Louise (2007), 'Steve Biko and Stoned Cherrie: Refashioning the body politic in democratic South Africa', *African Sociological Review*, 11:2, pp. 80–93.

Wierzba, Leanna (2015), 'What is luxury? Curating connections between the hand-crafted and global industry', *Luxury*, 2:1, pp. 9–23.

Note

1   All participants are referred to by pseudonyms in the chapter.

Chapter 8

The Politics of Repair: Talatona and Luxury Urbanism in Luanda, Angola

Claudia Gastrow

Eu queria morar em Talatona, eu queria morar em Talatona, eu queria morar emTalatona, o meu sonho é morar em Talatona.

('Eu Queria Morar em Talatona', MCK 2012)

Introduction

It was poetry night at King's Club, a nightclub in the up-market neighbourhood of Vila Alice. Due to its pool tables and dedication to live music, it was a favoured venue for those Luandans with some disposable income who were seeking a reprieve from the commercial Brazilian and US pop hits streaming from the speakers at the beachfront area of the Ilha, or the loud bass of one of the city's other favoured evening haunts, Elinga. It offered more alternative possibilities, occasionally hosting talks on African history and identity, and regular open mic nights for the city's aspiring poets. The success of the evening relied on nervous newbies proffering their words to a supportive crowd and a smattering of regulars who would perform to shouts of approval. On this evening, though, the emcee was having problems getting regulars to come on stage. Turning to a woman in the audience, who, from the familiar way he addressed her, seemed to be a regular, he asked her to come up and share some of her poetry. She declined, laughing. He then began to get the audience involved, explaining that she was a great poet and whipping up support for her. She still, however, refused to bow to the pressure. Eventually, trying to jokingly persuade her, he looked at her across the audience and, lowering his voice, whispered into the mic, 'I'm cement, you're sand. Let's mix and make a house'. The crowd roared with laughter. The house, after all, amongst its many meanings, is strongly associated with matrimony and reproduction in Luanda. In fact, the Portuguese word house (*casa*) is a homonym of marry (*casar*), leading to headlines in newspapers, especially during the housing shortages of the 1980s and 1990s, regularly being titled 'Quem casa quer casa' (Who marries, wants a house). The reference to sand and cement indexed the most common means of accessing housing in Luanda, especially amongst the urban poor: autoconstruction (*autoconstrução*).[1] Across the city, and especially as one edges towards the periphery, roadside vendors peddling crushed rock, trucks of sand and bags of cement indicate the 'quiet encroachment' (Bayat 2000) of the contemporary world's most insistent city-builders.

In Luanda, the gradual construction of a cement-block house is a long-term process through which people establish urban belonging (Gastrow 2017). Builders make a material claim to place and in the process signal to others their intention to make a life in the city. Families, businesses and friendships multiply in these homes that constantly emerge on the urban periphery. It is from these deeply entrenched understandings of social reproduction that the emcee drew when he asked the female poet to create a house with him. With such a good line, it seemed the only answer she could give was 'yes'. However, she smiled and called back 'sure, but only if it is a three story in Talatona!' The crowd roared even more with approval, and the emcee jumped back, his eyes wide open as if recovering from shock. There were few responses that could have better stumped the emcee's statement. Talatona, home to oil executives, gated communities and Luanda's most well known mall, *Belas Shopping*, is widely identified as a zone of the elite. In a city where the majority of the population lives in *musseques* ('slum' areas largely made up of decaying colonial social housing or autoconstructed cement-block homes), the manicured lawns, spacious residences and infrastructural services of Talatona's *condomínios* (gated communities) are indications of luxurious consumption and sensual experience. The woman was suggesting that unless the emcee was extremely wealthy, his chances of making a *casa* with her were limited. With such a brilliant response, the emcee pleaded poverty, admitted defeat and eventually managed to convince someone else to take the stage.

The comedic exchange however, while a jovial one, trod into the murky realms of economic segregation and political power in Luanda. Houses enable a parsing of emic notions of belonging and status as they are 'both concrete embodiments and imaginary representations of people's relations to their conditions of existence [...] they channel personal experience into a public idiom, architecture' (Holston 1991: 456). Luanda was no exception to this. If I passed a particularly luxurious home or building, and asked who owned it or lived there, I was given the response '*um chefe*' (a boss). Talatona's houses then, like the houses of the wealthy anywhere in the world, are objects of conspicuous consumption, performing economic power through their materiality. However, to make a claim to Talatona is not only about wealth, but status and power. The division between Talatona and the *musseques* is not simply understood as one of affluence, but one of modernity and development. Although usually translated as 'slum', *musseque* has a far more substantive meaning, used to refer to almost any area that deviates from shared norms of desirable urbanism (Gastrow 2017). In this model, normative urbanism, represented by what Angolans refer to as *cidade* (historically used to describe the colonial city centre, but which more generally indexes areas of formality), represents modernity. As the perceived antithesis of the *cidade*, the *musseques* become the location not just of poverty but of backwardness (Roque 2012). To demand a house in Talatona then, as the female poet had, is a demand not simply to wealth, but a status defined by normative imaginations of modernity and urbanism.

In Angola, however, where economic power and social status are almost inevitably linked to political power, these spaces of perceived formality and modernity, as well as the houses that define them, act as a critical assemblage of suspect financial relations, processes of urban displacement and political connection. Suspicions of these homes have only grown over the past two decades as Luanda has undergone a rapid process of urban redevelopment, which has involved the destruction of multiple *musseques* and the forced displacement of their residents (Gastrow 2014). *Musseque* houses, while mocked by the wealthy as poor quality, also constitute their own system of political belonging and aspiration, as construction signals one means through which those marginalized from state power try to instantiate claims to urban belonging, a right to place in the city. Their destruction undoes the political claims that have congealed in them, upsetting existing patterns of negotiation with the MPLA and means of performing urban citizenship, which focused on the construction of the house (Gastrow 2017). The rise of Talatona's condominiums parallel to the destruction of *musseques* means that luxury houses catalyse critiques of the current political system even as they congeal lifestyles that many Luandans aspire towards.

Talatona's houses, however, act as more than sites of critique. In their material and political contingency, they show luxury to be a representation that relies on constant repair to maintain its fragile performance and legitimacy. Talatona's houses draw attention to the fraught relationship between the successful performance of luxury and the socio-economic systems underpinning the wealth that enables it. In Angola, luxury cannot outrun the deep socio-economic inequalities and resulting material processes and affective orientations of its larger context. Materially, Talatona's houses are as embedded in the 'aesthetics of repair' (De Boeck and Plissart 2005: 228), the constant patching and improvisation required to sustain social and material relations of life in many African cities, as the *musseques* are. Politically, their existence generates suspicions regarding the legitimacy of the wealth underpinning their emergence. As a result, Talatona's *condomínios* are rendered materially and politically fragile, their appearance of luxury constantly threatened with moments of slippage.

Drawing on ethnographic fieldwork in the form of interviews, everyday observations and media analyses,[2] the rest of the chapter explores the question of maintenance in relation to Talatona's luxury *condomínios*. In order to do this, the chapter first provides a brief history of Talatona from its conception as part of the Luanda Sul Project to its rise as one of the symbols of Angola's petro-capitalism. Following this, I briefly examine the material conditions of life in these 'luxury' homes to highlight the work that is central to maintaining them. I show how their political significance emerges more from public imaginations of the good life that is assumed to exist behind their walls, than the actual living conditions within the *condomínios*. Finally, I examine Luandans' perceptions of the *condomínios* to unpick how beliefs about the illicit underpinnings of wealth and power are read into and through the walls of Talatona. Rapidly multiplying across the southern stretches of the city over the past two decades, the *condomínios* have become symbols of a 'capitalism gone viral' (Soares de Oliveira 2015: 160). This proliferation has occurred on the ruins of *musseques* demolished to make way for the wealthy. The *condomínios* therefore highlight the production of political belonging as a financial question. Their very bricks and mortar congeal processes of illegitimate accumulation and brutal exclusion. For Luandans, then, the condominiums, while very much a lifestyle that many would like to replicate, are equally evidence that citizenship is more determined by money than by legal status, in a country where as a victim of housing demolitions once explained to me, 'everything is business'.

Talatona and the Rise of the *Condomínio*

The word 'Talatona' inspires imaginations of comfort and luxury amongst many Luandans. The area was born in the mid-1990s as part of the Luanda Sul Project. Responding to the desperate need for housing and infrastructure, the project proposed the development of land to the south of Luanda's existing boundaries. With Angola only having officially abandoned socialism in 1991, Luanda Sul was conceived of and presented as the first market-driven response to the city's housing problem (Cardoso 2015). The vehicle for this development was the Urban Development Company (EDURB),[3] founded as a public–private partnership in 1996 between the Luanda provincial government's company of EPRO-URBE[4] and Brazilian firm Prado Valladares to manage and oversee the Luanda Sul Project. Although EDURB controlled the project and sales, Luanda-Sul was meant to be completely 'auto-financed', with the money for the project being generated through land and real-estate speculation. Land that had been ceded to the Luanda provincial government by the Angolan state would be developed with basic infrastructures by Brazilian multinational Odebrecht (Cardoso 2015).[5] The land would then be sold to real-estate developers, the profits of which would in turn be used to cover the costs of having installed the infrastructure, as well as the building of low-cost housing. With its seeming abandonment of state intervention, the project won international awards for its market-orientated solution to housing.

The success of Luanda Sul hinged off Angola's petrodollars and elite buy-in. The project foresaw the development of three areas – Talatona for the wealthy, Novos Bairros for directed site-and-service construction, and Projecto Morar, a rehousing zone for people to be forcibly displaced by planned urban development initiatives.[6] The project's financial security depended on the profits that were projected to accrue from the sale of land in Talatona for housing development. If investors would not build in Talatona, the project itself could not get off the ground. Angola's oil economy, however, answered the call. The first company to announce, in 1994, that it would purchase land in Talatona for real-estate development was Sonangol, Angola's national oil company (Anon. 1994). The then governor of Luanda, Justinho Fernandes, publicly encouraged other companies to follow Sonangol's example in order to turn the 'dream' of Luanda Sul into a reality. Other oil companies followed suit, promising to rent or purchase housing in Talatona for their employees (Jenkins et al. 2002).

The *condomínio* quickly became the defining architectural and planning feature of Talatona. 'Gated' architecture already had some local origins in the form of housing for *cooperantes*[7] during the socialist period and United Nations staff compounds (Rodrigues 2009).[8] However, the first official *condomínio* is usually identified as the Vila do Gamek, built by Odebrecht in 1986 to house its employees. The *condomínios* really boomed, however, following the end of Angola's civil war in 2002. The end of the war coincided with a surge in the international price of the country's primary source of revenue – oil. The oil bonanza ushered in what Schubert (2015) refers to as a 'culture of immediatism', an environment in which conspicuous consumption and the desire for quick wealth came to permeate everyday interactions and aspirations. Luxury cars, imported food and designer handbags were the manna of the city's oil rich. In Luanda, which has consistently trumped New York, Tokyo and others for the dubious honour of the most expensive city in the world for expatriates (BBC 2017), Talatona became one of the most expensive places to live. In 2013, the average price per metre squared in Talatona for housing was estimated at about US$7000 (Zenki 2013). The area is now home to dozens of upscale *condomínios*, an international school, a business park and a conference centre. Many residents enjoy access to swimming pools, communal leisure areas and the assumed security of a boomed entrance. The city's first major American-style mall is located there, replete with cinemas and a food court.

Talatona has been central in the spread of imaginations of a consumerist and sensually lush 'good life'.[9] With names such as Monte Belo (Beautiful Heights) and Dolce Vita (Sweet Life), advertisements for the buildings emphasize their exclusive features and aspirational lifestyle as part of the world of luxury that they are meant to embody. They promise to lift a person out of the everyday difficulties of urban life, in the process becoming objects of desire. Such dreams of escapism were expressed in everyday actions. A friend of mine who worked as a driver for an NGO once recounted to me how, at a wedding he had attended, the bride and groom, who were not of wealthy means, had spent much of the time after the ceremony driving through Talatona trying to negotiate with the guards of various condominiums to let them take their wedding photos inside. This was a testament not only to the shortage of desirable public space in the city, but to how desire became sequestered behind the walls reserved for only a few. However, the reality of what lay behind the walls often differed from what observers projected on to them. The next section examines this discrepancy to highlight the fantasies that lay at the fulcrum of the politics of luxury in Luanda.

Luxury as Maintenance?

Talatona's *condomínios* are objects of aspiration. Lives are imagined as potentially transformed through inhabiting them. Angolan political hip-hop artist MCK's 2012 track, 'Eu Queria Morar em Talatona' ('I Wish to Live in Talatona'), with which this chapter opens, captures these sentiments. The song is a play on Brazilian musician Gabriel's trenchant critique of socio-economic inequality in Brazil 'O Resto do Mundo' ('The Rest of the World'), whose chorus is a repetition of the lines 'Eu queria morar numa favela, o meu sonho é morar numa favela' ('I wish to live in a favela, my dream is to live in a favela'). In this track, the narrator is so destitute that even life in a favela seems desirable. MCK flips this desire, voicing the prayers of a young man from one of Luanda's *musseques*, who seeks deliverance from his circumstances by wishing to live in Talatona. Imagining a life of ease characterized by public lighting, children's playgrounds, crystal glasses, hot tubs and indoor plumbing, the narrator comments 'Eu não sou Gabriel, eu não quero favela, cresci na miséria', to farto dela' ('I'm not Gabriel, I don't want the favela, I grew up in misery, I'm sick of it').

MCK's track is not only a comment on inequality and consumerism, but also indicates the gap between public representations of elite urbanism that Talatona conjures, and the realities of what luxury means in Luanda. The questionable nature of luxury is most noticeable in the ongoing infrastructural challenges that the *condomínios* face. In 2016, I visited a house in the Condomínio Cajú in Talatona, one of Sonangol's flagship condominiums. From the view outside the walls, it met all imaginations of exclusivity. A peak through the booms suggested a lavish communal area and securitized access. My friend who was driving had to leave his identity card at the entrance. However, as we travelled through the complex, its luxuriousness became increasingly suspect. While some private gardens in front of homes were well tended, the shared areas were largely desiccated green spaces. A disused, weed-ridden children's playground stuck out as a poor experiment in performing US-style suburbia. Even the houses seemed less grand than they had appeared in Sonangol's glossy in-house magazine, *Saber Viver* (*Know How to Live*) for its former employee-housing cooperative, the Cooperativo Cajueira.

After having a drink with some residents of the complex, my friend and I left to pay a visit to an acquaintance of his, promising to return later as we had been invited for dinner. Within the hour, however, the owner called and told us not to bother. The area's electricity had cut and the condominium's generators were not working. The luxurious condominium in one of the most elite areas of the city was sitting in darkness. In an equally awkward situation, in Monte Belo, the condominium complex in Talatona where oil giant Chevron houses many of its foreign employees, residents were instructed to only use bottled water for cooking and brushing teeth (Marques de Morais 2012). The water of the US$250 million dollar complex, it turned out, was being trucked in untreated by tankers, the same ones that serviced many of the 'slum' areas on the periphery of the city. Unable to count on the water grid or even the building's own purification systems, Monte Belo's wealthy residents were dealing with the uneasy contradictions of what 'luxury' meant in Luanda.

Talatona's condominiums powerfully illustrate that luxury is situationally constituted (Armitage and Roberts 2016). In many other parts of the world, Talatona's houses and apartments would have been middle- or upper-middle-class accommodation. However, in a context in which the majority of the population has little to no access to reliably constructed buildings, regular water, electricity or sanitation connections, access to these, which in much of the global North would be classed 'necessities', becomes glossed as a luxury. It is this particularity that highlights the question of repair as lying at the heart luxury. Even when Talatona's residents were meant to have access to infrastructural pleasures, it was not clear that they were guaranteed access in the ways in which the appearance of the houses might have led those accustomed to an easy match between surface and depth to assume. In contrast to descriptions of gated communities in Equatorial Guinea (Appel 2012) or Brazil (Caldeira 2001), even with extensive effort, Talatona's *condomínios* did not manage an entirely successful sense of separation from the city around them.

The point, however, is not that Talatona is 'not' luxurious. In comparison to the conditions of the rest of Luanda, it is. It is significantly more comfortable to live in the Condomínio Cajú or Monte Belo than in a cement-block home with no sanitation in Cazenga.[10] While there are infrastructural problems in Talatona, they are less frequent and more easily resolved by access to improvised back-ups such as generators and water-tanks. Rather than treating Talatona's luxury as a fake or surface, it is perhaps more useful to locate the condominiums as extreme examples of the fact that the images and objects within which shared imaginations of luxury are rooted have to be constantly repaired. If they are not, the dysfunctional socio-economic realities upon which such lifestyles are built might threaten to undo their successful performance of luxury. For, ultimately it is the image of luxury that the general public engages with, not the everyday work of maintaining it.

The desires and disappointments of Talatona's luxury are predominantly produced by its walls. Most Luandans will never step foot inside a condominium in Talatona, and, like MCK's young man praying to live there, can only project their fantasies of what life inside these spaces is like onto them. However, the mystery of these walls, the lack of knowledge of what lies behind them and the suspicions that they catalyse when intersecting with existing political frustrations means that luxury housing becomes a flashpoint for critiques of the wealth that underlies it and by association the ruling elite. The luxury house, as the next section shows, is one of the objects through which imaginations of the workings of political-economic power in Luanda, is constituted.

Disreputable Housing

'Who would spend two million dollars on a shoddily constructed house in the middle of nowhere?' Luis, a Portuguese architect working in Angola asked. His question was posed in relation to the fact that so many of Talatona's houses stood empty. Despite the supposed oil miracle of post-conflict Angola, the dark windows and silent yards indicated that the wealth was not enough to provide a Talatona life for everyone. For Luis, the answer to his question and the reason for the empty *condomínios* lay in the financial networks underpinning their construction. He believed that the houses were products of money laundering, somewhere for people to stash their wealth.[11] Houses were not necessarily there to be sold, but to be stored. An administrator at a property management company reiterated similar beliefs to me in discussing the difficulties of officially registering properties in Luanda. He believed the difficulty was created on purpose. If a property was not registered, the government could not tax it. A lack of registration also meant that there was no way of confirming who owned what or how many properties. 'People organize themselves through disorganization', he explained.[12] For Luis and the administrator, Talatona's houses stood at the centre of rumours and suspicions of illicit wealth, nepotism and corruption. They were material instances of what John and Jean Comaroff (1999: 293) have referred to as 'occult economies', the emergence of suspicions that in the age of neoliberalism, fabulous wealth is being reaped by the powerful in clandestine and inaccessible ways so that 'the majority are kept poor by the mystical machinations of the few'.

While conspicuous consumption has long been recognized as a public performance of economic status, in Luanda, and arguably in much of Africa, luxury consumption is not just an index of economic, but of political power (Bayart 1993; Mbembe 2001). In Angola, beginning in the 1980s, a parallel system of petrodollars became the backbone of the ruling MPLA's[13] patronage system, with those nearest to the levers of power able to access extensive financial resources (Soares de Oliveira 2015). This patronage network tends to peter out as relations of proximity weaken (Messiant 1992; Martins 2016), meaning that the poor and politically unconnected are left tussling for the left-over scraps. Housing is often indicative of where people lie in this political-economic assemblage of influence and favours. The ultimate sign of this is the high price tags of Talatona's homes, which place them beyond the reach of even those who earn a good salary. The question then becomes who could actually afford a house in Talatona and how it was that they came to afford it. An advertising executive, who had largely given up on his dream of purchasing in Talatona, explained to me that the houses were for a *classe rica* (rich class).[14] He would need at least a $6,000 a month salary to even hope to purchase a small apartment in the area.

For many Angolans, condominiums came to symbolize this corrupt socio-economic system and its political consequences in which the rich are often presumed to have come by their fortunes through personal connections to key people in the state. The difficulty of discerning the distinction between public and private interests was evident in a discussion I had with two housing activists, who were trying to explain the imbrication of state, personal interests and housing construction since the end of the war. They explained that during the war, many Angolans had moved to Luanda to flee the fighting. At this point, the state was unable to, as Gaspar commented, 'guide people to build in an urbanized manner'. The mass relocation to Luanda due to fighting meant that after the end of the war, Luanda became the focus of landgrabs as the state and developers began to demolish neighbourhoods to make way for new projects. As Bernardo explained, the poor were being forced out for the wealthy: 'They now build *condomínios* in the areas where they removed people'. I asked if Talatona was one of these areas and he responded in the affirmative: 'In Talatona, like in other neighbourhoods like in Honga, Benfica, and Samba. What happened in these areas didn't benefit the victims. The victims were removed from there, some were put more than forty kilometres away, in the site a condominium was built'. It was not only the violence and exclusion of these removals that aroused their anger, however, but, the fact that they believed politicians or political elites were using these policies to enrich themselves:

Bernardo: The majority of the anonymous rich in Angola are leaders [*dirigentes*] [...]. These are the rich, they are the anonymous rich because they never appear here and say [...] here is a rich person. We know that maybe the thing comes [...] from an order that someone gives. *Nada*. This condominium that is being, like in the case of Talatona, Sonangol's condominium, its constitution is anonymous. It's anonymous.

Gaspar: No one knows who the owner is. No one knows who is behind it.

Bernardo: No one knows the owner. No one knows the owner.

Gaspar: But, it is a state project.

Author: The condominiums are state projects?

Bernardo: For private purposes.

Gaspar: They use state money to build, afterwards someone else manages the property.[15]

The claims they make are difficult to confirm; however, the notable media reports of the corrupt business dealing of Angola's elite lend strong credibility to these beliefs.[16] What is significant, however, is that, in the political world they evoke, Talatona's *condomínios* are the physical instantiation of corruption.

What these accounts suggest is that similar to the material undermining of luxury due to the urban conditions of Luanda, the political-economy of inequality and predation means that even as luxury is strongly desired, its legitimacy is constantly tarnished by the material conditions of its making. The consequences of the *condomínios* as objects of accumulation can, in many people's understanding, be devastating. It is not simply that the *condomínios* produce new patterns of urban socio-economic segregation (see Rodrigues 2009), but, equally as important, as the activists' comments above hinted at, the *condomínios* and their owners are the beneficiaries of the 'creative destruction' that has characterized urban development in Luanda for the past two decades.

Beginning in the late 1990s and into the present, at least 200,000 residents of Luanda's *musseque* areas have been forcibly removed to make way for urban redevelopment projects,[17] many of which have taken the form of condominiums (Gastrow 2014; Amnesty International 2003; Human Rights Watch 2007). Luanda Sul, was, in fact, one of the earliest developments to begin engaging in sustained demolitions (Capai and Viana 2016). At the same velocity at which Luandans have watched the images of luxury villas that circulate in newspapers and billboards physically materialize, they have seen poor people's houses torn down. *Condomínios* can therefore also be read as violent embodiments of displacement, indicative for many of the consumerism and greed that now mediate quotidian and state–citizen relationships. During an interview with a woman who had suffered multiple demolitions of her home in southern Luanda, I asked her why she thought there were so many demolitions taking place. Her response indicated the strong associations drawn between the displacement of the poor and the emplacement of luxury in the form of *condomínios*:

Because the government, they prefer to build condominiums, lots of condominiums, they are for people who have the means to buy a house for $200,000 or $300,000. And, because it is providing an income, this is the thing, it is a business which is creating money, so they prefer the lower level [*camada mais baixa*], that is, the lower level who are the monkeys [*macacos*], should be in the bush, and those that have the possibility to be in the city [*cidade*] stay there. This is their business, condominiums, condominiums, it's only this that we are seeing.

Her comment spoke not simply to a collusion between government and the wealthy, but the very remaking of government into a business. In this world, it was *o governo* that followed profit at the expense of its citizens. Talatona's *condomínios* came under critique then as objects where people assumed the privatization of the state congealed. They were out of reach and built on questionable financial foundations. As *condomínios* mushroomed, the claims to urban inclusions and rights, materialized in the *musseque* home, were undone through demolition. Luxury housing, as much as it was desired, became deeply imbued with a moralizing account of accumulation and the effects of this on the political system and citizenship in Luanda. Its legitimacy was constantly being tarnished, the possibilities for repair waning each time that desire swung to frustration.

Conclusion

Ultimately, the repairs needed to maintain the performance of luxury are imbricated in the political-economic conditions that blemish its public image. Until the highly unequal socio-economic conditions of Luanda are resolved, Talatona's *condomínios* will always be in need of material and reputational repair. In Angola, and perhaps any other context of extreme socio-economic inequality, luxury will always be caught in a balancing act of illegitimacy and desire. As Coronil (1997: 178) has highlighted for the case of Venezuela, luxury consumption is means of gaining 'public recognition' by groups that have historically been excluded. Consumption indexes hierarchy, achievement and belonging both internationally and domestically (Coronil 1997), as such, perhaps especially in contexts of notable inequality, luxury is particular desired as a symbol of inclusion and status. But, in such contexts it is also constantly under question.

The urban material limitations created by the oil economy and suspected corruption constantly threaten to undo the objects and representations in which luxury in Angola is anchored. Houses run on generators and have to have water trucked in. Similarly, the actual status of Talatona's *condomínios* is constantly questioned as many suspect a network of elites and parallel governance to lie behind their construction. Although contemporary scholars have generally tried to move away from moralizing consumption practices both amongst the poor and the wealthy (Miller 1988; Iqani 2015; Armitage and Roberts 2016), as many of my interlocutors' comments suggest, ordinary people who interact with luxury goods bring their own judgements with them. Luis, the administrator, and the activists believed Talatona's luxury *condomínios* to be material manifestations of illicit profits, a means of laundering money and distributing wealth amongst friends and family. International organizations such as USAID have voiced similar concerns (USAID 2010). However, simultaneously, condominiums are also objects of aspiration, with people projecting imaginations of the 'good life' onto their walls. Talatona's *condomínios* have become contradictory sites of both the desire to be included in, but equally of the repulsion of, the political status quo. If repair, maintenance and patching have become one of the hallmarks of African urban life (De Boeck and Plissart 2005; Trovolla and Trovolla 2015) then the life of the wealthy in Angola is no exception to this. Talatona's *condomínios* are constantly in need of reputational repair, in addition to their physical maintenance. A point of view from the African continent then highlights luxury as a constant process of repair and fabrication, something teetering on the edge of unmaking rather than easily performing its status.

References

Amnesty International (2003), *Angola: Mass Forced Evictions in Luanda – A Call for a Human Rights-Based Housing Policy*, AI Index, 12 June, https://www.amnesty.org/en/documents/afr12/007/2003/en/. Accessed 5 December 2017.

Anon. (1994), 'GPL concede terreno à Sonangol', *Jornal de Angola*, 1 December, p. 5.

Appel, Hannah (2012), 'Walls and white elephants: Oil extraction, responsibility, and infrastructural violence in Equatorial Guinea', *Ethnos*, 13:4, pp. 439–65.

Armitage, John and Roberts, Joanne (2016), 'The spirit of luxury', *Cultural Politics*, 12:1, pp. 1–22.

Bayat, Asif (2000), 'From "dangerous classes" to "quiet rebels": Politics of the urban subaltern in the Global South', *International Sociology*, 15:3, pp. 533–57.

Bayart, Jean-François (1993), *The State in Africa: The Politics of the Belly*, London and New York: Longman.

BBC (2017), 'Angolan city "most expensive city for expats"', BBC News, 21 June, http://www.bbc.com/news/business-40346559. Accessed 21 June 2017.

Caldeira, Teresa (2001), *City of Walls: Crime, Segregation and Citizenship in São Paulo*, Chicago and London: University of Chicago Press.

Capai, Eliza and Viana, Natalie (2016), 'Descontruindo Luanda Sul', *Pública*, 7 March, n.pag.

Cardoso, Ricardo V. (2015), 'The crude revolution: Land markets, planning forms, and the making of a New Luanda', Ph.D. thesis, Berkeley, CA: University of California.

Carsten, Janet and Hugh-Jones, Stephen (1995), 'Introduction', in J. Carsten and S. Hugh-Jones (eds), *About the House: Levi-Strauss and Beyond*, Cambridge, MA: Cambridge University Press, pp. 1–46.

Comaroff, Jean and Comaroff, John L. (1999), 'Occult economies and the violence of abstraction: Notes from the South African postcolony', *American Ethnologist*, 26:2, pp. 279–303.

Coronil, Fernando (1997), *The Magical State: Nature, Money and Modernity in Venezuela*, Chicago and London: University of Chicago Press.

De Boeck, Filip and Plissart, Marie-Françoise (2005), *Kinshasa: Tales of an Invisible City*, Leuven: Leuven University Press.

Eisenhammer, Stephen and White, Lawrence (2018), 'Frozen $500 million in Angolan fraud probe came from central bank account with Standard Chartered', *Reuters*, 28 March, https://www.reuters.com/article/us-angola-corruption/frozen-500-million-in-angolan-fraud-probe-came-from-central-bank-account-with-standard-chartered-idUSKBN1H425S. Accessed 28 March 2018.

Gastrow, Claudia (2014), 'Vamos Construir: Revendications Foncières Et Géographie Du Pouvoir À Luanda, Angola', *Politique Africaine*, 139, pp. 49–72.

—— (2017), 'Cement citizens: Housing, demolition and political belonging in Luanda, Angola', *Citizenship Studies*, 21:2, pp. 224–239.

Hatzky, Christine (2015), *Cubans in Angola: South-South Cooperation and Transfer of Knowledge, 1976–1991*, Madison, WI: University of Wisconsin Press.

Holston, James (1991), 'Autoconstruction in working-class Brazil', *Cultural Anthropology*, 6:4, pp. 447–65.

Human Rights Watch (2007), *They Pushed Down the Houses*, Vol. 19.7 (A), New York: Human Rights Watch.

Iqani, Mehita (2015), *Consumption, Media and the Global South: Aspiration Contested*, New York: Palgrave MacMillan.

Jasanoff, Sheila (2015), 'Future imperfect: Science, technology and imaginations of modernity', in S. Jasanoff and S.-H. Kim (eds), *Dreamscapes of Modernity: Socialtechnical Imaginaries and the Fabrication of Power*, Chicago: University of Chicago Press, pp. 1–33.

Jenkins, Paul, Robson, Paul and Cain, Allan (2002), 'City profile: Luanda', *Cities*, 19:2, pp. 139–150.

Marques de Morais, Rafael (2012), 'Water for Chevron and a lesson for the government', *MakaAngola*, 18 December, https://www.makaangola.org/2012/12/water-for-chevron-and-a-lesson-for-the-government/. Accessed 31 July 2017.

Martins, Vasco (2016), 'Politics of power and hierarchies of citizenship in Angola', *Citizenship Studies*, 21, pp. 1–16.

Mbembe, Achille (2001), *On the Postcolony*, Chicago and London: University of Chicago Press.

Messiant, Christine (1992), 'Social and political background to the "democratisation" and peace process in Angola', *Seminar Democratization in Angola*, Leiden, 18 September, pp. 13–41.

Miller, Daniel (1988), 'Appropriating the state on a council estate', *Man*, 23:2, pp. 353–72.

Rodrigues, Christina U. (2009), 'Angolan cities: Urban (re)segregation?', in P. Nugent (ed.), *African Cities: Competing Claims on Urban Spaces*, Leiden: Brill, pp. 37–54.

Roque, Sandra (2012), 'Cidade and Bairro: Classification, constitution, and experience of urban space in Angola', *Social Dynamics*, 37:3, pp. 332–48.

Schubert, Jon (2015), 'A culture of immediatism: Co-optation and complicity in post-war Angola', *Ethnos*, 83:1, pp. 1–19.

Soares de Oliveira, Ricardo (2015), *Magnificent and Beggar Land: Angola since the Civil War*, London: Hurst.

Trovolla, Eric and Trovolla, Ulrika (2015), 'Infrastructure as a divination tool: Whispers from the grids in a Nigerian city', *City*, 19:2–3, pp. 332–43.

USAID (2010), *Review of Real Estate Financing in Angola with Recommended Actions for the BNA to meet New Challenges*, Luanda: USAID.

Zenki Real Estate (2013), 'ZRE report: Angola property market 2013', https://zenkirealestate.com/en/report/zreport-angola-property-market-2013-2/. Accessed 5 December 2017.

Notes

1 The word 'autoconstruction' is a direct translation from the Portuguese word for self-building: *autoconstrução*. It has increasingly been taken up by scholars working on unofficial city-building as both an emic term for the Lusophone world and a more succinct term to describe processes of self-building.

2 The bulk of research for this chapter took place in Luanda between March 2011 and September 2012. It was supplemented by shorter annual fieldwork periods between 2013 and 2017.

3 *Empresa de Desenvolvimento Urbano.*

4 *Empresa Provincial de Participações em Programas de Urbanizações.*

5 Odebrecht is a major Brazilian construction conglomerate. It entered Angola in the early 1980s when it brokered the deal for the construction of the Capanda Hydroelectric Dam. Since then it has cemented its presence in the country through close relationships to the Angolan state. In the post-conflict period it has received various high-profile contracts, such as the rehabilitation of Luanda's roads and the construction of 'social housing'. For a more detailed account of Odebrecht's involvement in Angola, see Cardoso (2015).

6 The housing was designated for people who were to be removed from areas of the city centre earmarked for the construction of a new political-administration centre. In practice, some of these households were not removed or only removed years later, while individuals living in other parts of the city found themselves displaced more rapidly once the war ended. Demolition and rehousing landed up becoming far more complex means of managing urban space and exercising political power in Luanda than was perhaps initially conceived when Projecto Morar was constructed. See Gastrow (2014) for a more extensive account of these processes.

7 'Cooperantes' is a term used to describe foreigners who came to work for the Angolan state under the auspices of international socialist solidarity during the socialist period.

8 See Hatzky (2015) for an account of the residential separation of Cuban workers from Angolans.

9 I use the words 'imaginations' or 'imaginaries' in the plural to indicate that rather than political or other kinds of groups being characterized by monolithic shared narratives about what constitutes reality, 'multiple imaginaries can coexist within a society in tension or in a productive dialectical relationship' (Jasanoff 2015: 4).

10 A municipality in the city characterized by a mixture of self-built housing and poorly serviced colonial-era construction. Formal infrastructure in this municipality is extremely sparse.

11 Interview with Luis, Luanda, 20 April 2011.

12 Interview with Imogestim, Luanda, 3 May 2012.

13 Popular Movement for the Liberation of Angola.

14 Interview with Diogo, Talatona, 18 August 2011.

15 Interview with SOS Habitat, Maianga, 5 May 2011.

16 For examples of reporting on elite corruption, see the work of Rafael Marques de Morais and others at makaangola.org as well as more recent reporting regarding former President

José Eduardo dos Santos' son's involvement in the attempted diversion of 500 million dollars (Eisenhammer and White 2018).

17 This number was derived from a conversation with a representative of Odebrecht, and represents only the number of people that they estimated they have actually rehoused. This does not include those who lost their homes and were not rehoused, or those who might have been removed and rehoused to housing projects not constructed by Odebrecht. Unfortunately, this is the only reasonably reliable number that I came across regarding removals and I therefore use it as my benchmark.

Chapter 9

Welcome to the Jungle: Tropical Modernism, Decadence and Gardening in Africa

Jonathan Cane

When Mobutu Sese Seko summoned renowned South African landscaper Patrick Watson to his ostentatious rooms in the Republic of Bophuthatswana's luxury resort, the Palace of the Lost City, he was, it turns out, being far too optimistic about how much time he had left to build more of his obscene tropical gardens. When Watson arrived at the Lost City (all of which he had landscaped, including the rest of the Sun City resort) he was dressed, as usual, unassumingly in scruffy chinos and a dusty white shirt. Mobutu's protocol officers insisted he was in no state to meet the Zairean dictator but was eventually, after the customary period of being kept waiting, ushered in. There, he was asked via a translator for two things: gardens even larger and more dramatic than the jungles he gestured to from the palace windows, and roses. The first, Watson explained, was possible but the second was not. Money and political power could buy one a tropical jungle of about any size but it could not make roses grow on the equator. The roses that Mobutu obstinately planted were dead soon after that meeting, as was Mobutu in 1997, deposed and exiled in Morocco. In 2015, Watson would be flown to the neighbouring Republic of Congo to receive a similar commission from president Denis Sassou Nguesso for a landscape garden deep in the rainforest, bigger and better than the jungles of the Lost City.

Landscapes of Luxury in the South

When gardening in Africa is studied at all, which it seldom is, the intellectual focus is generally on small-scale, subsistence and vernacular landscaping, or questions of cheap black labour. Consider the Comaroffs' powerful colonial critique of nineteenth-century missionary influence on Basotho gardening in *Of Revelation and Revolution II,* which shows how household gardening and labour were fundamentally transformed by civilizing discourses (1997). Recent, fine-grained studies of rural landscaping (McHale et al. 2013) and township gardening (Coetzee et al. 2007), as well as critiques of oppressive domestic garden labour systems (Cane 2012), show a botanical context that is shot through with aspiration and racial disease. Apart from this, postcolonial scholarship has been concerned with global-scale plant transfers and the role of (often imperial) botanical gardens in the geography of colonial power. For instance, we know quite a lot – dates, names, prices – about the obsession with pineapples in elite eighteenth-century Europe. We know that the first pineapple grown in France by royal gardener Jean-Baptiste La Quintinie in 1642 was for Louis XIV (Wimmler 2017) and that European pineapples would have cost around $3000 in today's terms to grow (Beauman 2006). They were so expensive and difficult to raise that they were rarely eaten; instead, pineapples were left to decompose, their sweet rancid smell perfuming the homes of the rich and royal. This scholarly work offers interesting insights into luxury consumption in Europe, but it also importantly shows how the fashion for certain kinds of fruit was directly linked to plantation slavery in the Caribbean. This postcolonial eco-critique is fundamental for our understanding of luxury consumption and its connection to exploitation in the colonies.

What we don't know, however, is much about luxury consumption and gardening in Africa. We have little sense about how Africa has featured as the recipient of colonial transfers, save for weeds (prickly pear, black wattle) and crops (maize, cassava/manioc, plantains). How have African elites and landscape professionals adopted and adapted plants and gardening fashions from the West? What were the African responses, for instance, to herbaceous borders, to fashions in bedding out, to indigenous grasses, to topiary, to ornamental farming and heirloom vegetables?

In my own research, I have been occupied with addressing an area of neglect by describing how the lawn has been received, adapted, rejected and reused in South Africa. What that research shows is that the lawn's civilizing force and aspirational appeal transcends its British colonial origins. The tactile softness, preternatural greenness, perfect flatness and desired coolness of a well-kept lawn make it a sought-after landscape. And because lawn maintenance (water, labour, fertilizer) is very expensive, having a lawn at all, never mind a large sprawling one, is a sign of wealth.

In order to offer a contribution to the study of luxury in Africa, this chapter presents analyses of three large-scale gardening projects in post-independence Africa. First, it presents a collection of landscapes commissioned by Mobutu Sese Seko, whose flamboyant and aesthetic demagoguery in what was then Zaire resulted in dramatic, decadent and obscene state gardens in Gbadolite, Nsele and Kinshasa, which are now, since his deposition, in various states of ruin and reuse. Second, its analyses the man-made jungles surrounding the Palace of the Lost City at Sun City, the ostentatious resort and casino built in what was then the South African 'homeland' of Bophuthatswana. Designed as a ready-made ruin, this faux tropical forest was conceived of as the lost and then rediscovered kingdom of a rich and mythical African tribe. Last, it offers a description of a twenty-first-century garden, newly laid out for president Denis Sassou Nguesso, in his ancestral hometown of Oyo, far into the Congolese rainforests. Carved out of the equatorial forest, this is a landscape garden of lawns, tree-lined avenues, bold colour-blocked geometric forms and lakes filled with water lilies.

The sites under investigation were selected as examples of postcolonial placemaking that articulate varied forms of 'authentic' African organic sensibility. In different ways, each site and its relationship to the men involved offer the opportunity to theorize the articulation and aestheticization of power. In the sections that follow I offer a theoretical framework for the purposes of analysis; I present a description of the gardens in question drawing on existing scholarly literature, a number of (mainly) low-resolution images of the gardens gleaned from blogs, as well as landscaper's plans, artists' and journalists' photographs, marketing strategies, interviews and newly available internal documents; finally, I offer analysis and argumentation.

Landscape Theory and the Concept of Tropicality

In order to provide a theoretical framing for the chapter, I will recommend two subtending concepts. The first is a theoretical manoeuvre by W. J. T. Mitchell from the influential volume he edited, *Landscape and Power* (1994), which has subsequently been refined and extended by feminist landscape scholar Jill Casid (2005, 2011). Their landscape-as-verb thesis breaks away from the historically entrenched idea that landscapes are views that can be possessed in favour of the provocative idea that they are unfinished and unfinishable processes. The second conceptual knot relates to the problem of 'tropicality'. As a theoretical lens, tropicality is concerned with the critique of constructed or discursive representations of the 'tropical world'. Like the concept of orientalism, tropicality challenges the ways in which western explorers and botanists have imagined and produced a coherent location – hot, romantic, fertile, uncivilized and uncivilizable, dangerous, vegetal – exemplified in the idea of the 'jungle'.

The landscape idea is a contested notion that in recent times has experienced something of a second life as a critical tool for thinking about human–nonhuman relationships. In the 1980s, Marxist art historians rightly pointed out the visual bias or ocular-centricity of the landscape, as 'a way of seeing' that orientated the land towards a rational, masculine, imperial eye (Cosgrove 1984; Pratt 2007). In addition, they pointed out the tendency for landscape to conceal labour (Casid 2011: 111). The seductive revision that Mitchell et al. offered with the landscape-as-verb thesis was to move us past the notion that landscapes *represent* power but that they are rather one part of the operation of power. Landscapes are not 'nouns' that can be owned or possessed; they are 'verbs' – unfinished processes of materialization, inconclusive attempts at fixing a permanent vision of nature and solidifying human–nonhuman relations. The intellectual question that follows, then, is not so much: what do landscapes mean? but rather: what do landscapes do and how? As the cases in this chapter will show, the notion of landscape-as-process is useful for at least two reasons: first, because a landscape is never finished – in a literal sense it must continue to grow, it needs water and fertilizer, it needs expertise, energy and labour – it points to and emphasizes the continued exercise of power or lack thereof. And second, because the landscape is never fully successful – neither humans (owner, landscape architect, contractors, gardeners, guards) nor nonhumans (weather, soil, cuttings, transplants) are able to definitively and unambiguously exercise power over the garden – it opens a space of ambiguity.

Gardens can be, and often are, read as attempts to organize, move, rearrange – that is to say – control nature. While the belief that gardens are (primarily) concerned with domination has some truth, it is also reductive. It misses out on the ways in which human actors engage in sophisticated, nuanced and ambiguous relationships with the natural, which wouldn't easily fit under the notion of 'control' or 'domination'; relations that look rather more like flirtation than coercion. It also neglects the subtle and at other times blatant ways in which nature acts on humans, attempts to organize humans, to dominate humans, to seduce humans (a fear that many humans hold and that is evident in the literature) and relies on an untenable distinction between the two seemingly opposite domains of the human and nonhuman. The polarization of nature on the one hand and civilization on the other is, when pushed to the extremes, hard to uphold.

An essential aspect of the tropical, according to the critique of tropicality, is its ambivalence. On the one hand, the tropics are romantic, abundant and fertile, positively exuberant; on the other, they are pestilential, primitive, diseased, violent and the cause of 'intemperate' conduct. The discourse attributes an incredible power to nature (the climate, vegetation, the organic) over the human. It dwarfs the human scale. Natives are figured as childlike and feminized, unable to advance or civilize. White colonizers are figured as civilized and active but (generally) unable to definitively establish civilization due to the overwhelming effect of geography. The myth was that of 'tropical exuberance: that the tropics encapsulated tremendous biological productivity which, when harnessed to the temperate work ethic, would yield unprecedented bounty. "Luxurious" was the de rigueur adjective' (Sutter 2014: 188).

This 'moral discourse of climate', articulated in publications like *Civilization and Climate* (Huntington 1915), made the argument for settler colonialism but also embodied pessimism about its successfulness. The jungle threatens to enfold and consume the human scale, in a manner that is simultaneously desired and dreaded, and in a way that was always already going to happen. Joseph Conrad famously evokes this in a *Heart of Darkness,* where he describes the Congolese forest as a

> great wall of vegetation, an exuberant and entangled mass of trunks, branches, leaves, boughs, festoons, motionless in the moonlight […] like a rioting invasion of soundless life, a rolling wave of plants, piled up, crested, ready to topple over the creek, to sweep every little man of us out of his little existence.
>
> ([1902] 2005: 31)

This sentiment is echoed by surrealists André Breton and André Masson in their essay 'Creole Dialogue'.

> The forest envelops us: we knew the forest and her spells before we arrived. Do you remember a drawing […] called 'Vegetal Delirium'? That delirium is here, we can touch and participate in it. We are one of those layered trees that holds a miniature marsh in the hollows of its branches, with all its parasitic vegetation grafted onto its central trunk: rising, falling, active, passive, and rigged out from top to bottom with star-flowered lianas. […] It is inevitable that [surrealist landscapes] should find a resolution in those lands where nature has not been tamed at all.
>
> (Breton and Masson, in Creed 2013: 157)

The duality of the tropical forest as both exuberance and horror, its potential to overwhelm and absorb the human and the human scale, its complexity, and the challenge it presents to human attempts at creation and control make it a unique space for examining consumption. That is to say, the jungle as a site of attempts at luxury presents an opportunity to examine the limitations of human ability; the competing desires for, on the one hand, being overwhelmed, subsumed, overawed, enfolded and on the other exercising control over the biological; and the unavoidable logic of decadence and ruination.

Lost Cities and Vegetal Delirium

By the time Mobutu met with Watson at Sun City to plan a new jungle landscape, he had already commissioned and executed a number of outrageous and extravagant gardens in what was then Zaire. The strangest might be the presidential site at Nsele, east of Kinshasa

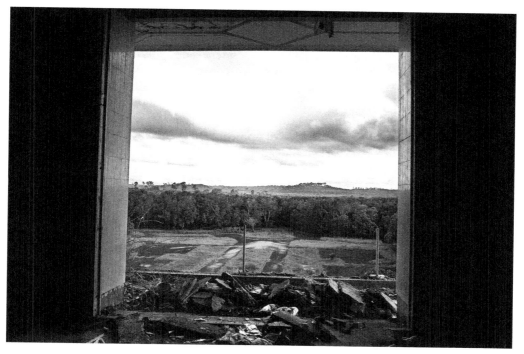

Figure 1: Guy Tillim. The remains of Mobutu Sese Seko's palace at Gbadolite. *Leopold and Mobutu Series 8.* Left panel. Mobutu began work here among his kin in the 1970s, and in later years retreated to this residence for long periods. He built an international airport nearby, and would receive foreign dignitaries and heads of state in the palace's grand reception rooms. It was his last place of residence in the Congo before he fled to Morocco in 1997, September 2003. Diptych. Archival pigment ink on cotton rag paper. © Guy Tillim. Courtesy of Stevenson, Cape Town and Johannesburg.

along the Congo River Basin. With the help of Taiwanese architects, the area was transformed into an 'oriental fantasy' with a large central pagoda, *jiashan* rock gardens, ponds, winding paths, footbridges, gates, courtyards and pavilions. Even stranger were the French formal gardens and pineapple fields that linked these Chinese gardens to the rest of the park. Writing about Nsele, anthropologist Filip De Boeck suggests that this location was 'the stage where the madly decadent and hedonistic side of the Mobutist regime, with its theatrical but corrupt magnanimity and all its grandiose dreams, displayed itself most fully' (de Boeck and Baloji 2016: 229). It was also in this oriental fantasy park, quite surprisingly, that Mobutu laid out the political doctrine of *recours à l'authenticité* in the 1967 'Nsele Manifesto'. It is bizarre that an ideological and aesthetic programme of discovering 'authentic' Congolese culture would be articulated in an oriental garden theme park. However, *recours à l'authenticité* was torn, as Johan Lagae argues, between competing desires for 'authenticity', the rejection of colonial logics, the demonstration of state power and the imperative to keep up (catch up) with international modernization and aesthetic modernisms (Lagae and De Raedt 2014). And, it should be mentioned, personal vanity, authoritarianism and even eccentricity.

The oriental gardens are today a deranged ruin of empty ponds, overgrown flora and crumbling dragon-encrusted infrastructure. Possibly better known, and also now ruined, are the landscapes of Mobutu's rural Gbadolite residence, once derisively called 'Versailles in the Jungle', which in contrast are much more self-consciously modern. This is evident, for instance, in the aquamarine, pink and terracotta pools that artist Guy Tillim photographed for his series *Leopold and Mobutu* (2003). The expressionist curvilinear pools on split levels with rim flow details are contained by grid-like paving in squares with rectilinear detailing, reminiscent of the tropical modernism of someone like Pancho Guedes. Overgrown, swamped with brackish water, cracked and faded, the gardens appear to have been 'reclaimed by the jungle'. It is essential to be reflexive regarding the language and imaging of ruination. There is a sedimented and sentimental language, for instance, of forlorn lions, weeds and buildings being reclaimed by the jungle, which is matched by a visual fetishization, in photography especially, in the form of what is often called 'ruin porn'. Nevertheless, the reality of these failures and their discursive qualities need to be addressed.

The ready-made ruins of the Lost City are instructive because the resort's jungles were designed, constructed and propagated, at great cost and effort, as ruins in the first instance. Built during the *fin de siècle* of apartheid, the Lost City was a shrewd business decision by casino magnate Sol Kerzner who saw the possibilities and threats of the disintegrating Bantustan system that had made Sun City a profitable escape for wealthy (mainly white) South Africans from the legal and moral strictures of apartheid. The Republic of Bophuthatswana, as it was known until 1994, provided a location for, amongst other things, limited racial mixing and imagining a kind of Africanness outside of South Africa characterized by romance, exuberance, extravagance and consumption. Leisure activities banned at the time in South Africa, like gambling and topless revue shows, were naturalized by, amongst other things, the cultivation of exotic natural environments like

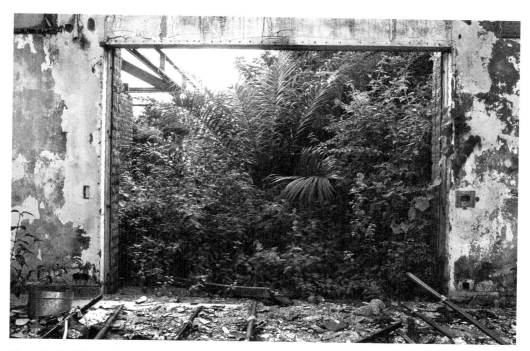

Figure 2: Guy Tillim. The remains of Mobutu Sese Seko's palace at Gbadolite. *Leopold and Mobutu Series 8.* Right panel. September 2003. Diptych. Archival pigment ink on cotton rag paper. © Guy Tillim. Courtesy of Stevenson, Cape Town and Johannesburg.

preternaturally green golf greens, deserts, aviaries and tropical jungles. These immersive landscapes of consumption were implicitly political for Bophuthatswana's president Lucas Mangope, for Kerzner and also for Watson and his contractors. Incredible budgets allowed these men to move earth, form lakes, transplant fully grown trees, import exotic species, develop computer programs to scientifically manage cultivation, establish nurseries, purchase rare plants, propagate hundreds of thousands of plants from cuttings, train and hire hundreds of gardeners. In the Lost City alone, 440 gardeners planted over 1.6 million plants, including 60,000 lilies, 7000 exotic orchids, 300 species of palm and 6000 fully grown trees at a cost of R25 million in 1992 (*The Lost City* c.1993). Internal sub-contractor documents describe plans for '[w]ildly manicured forests, Lush Green lawns and trees, Pockets of Disney Standard [*sic*]. Interesting Plants [...] definitely NOT the plants that originate in Europe and are found in the formal gardens and suburban gardens in the larger cities in South Africa' (Kirkby 2013).

A promotional video from the time shows Watson (seemingly) personally specifying the position of each plant, including wading into the lakes (*The Lost City* c.1993). He is infamous for this kind of eccentric pedantism. Powerful and wealthy patrons have sought his ambitious plans (most of which consist of a single simple sketch, or not even), his audacious sense of what is possible and the scope of his botanical knowledge. Internal documents describe Watson as 'an artist, genius and philosopher [...] shy, difficult, uncompromising and sometimes arrogant' (Kirkby 2013). Having worked on some of the biggest landscaping projects in contemporary Africa – South Africa, Seychelles, Mozambique, Mauritius, Republic of Congo – Watson's oeuvre has been essentially overlooked by historians partly because his design processes leave very little archival data, partly because African gardens don't attract serious attention, but also potentially because of the nature of some of his more disreputable clients and commissions.

Watson's plan for the landscape garden of Congolese President Sassou Nguesso is an abstract composition of bold colours and organic shapes laid onto a sharp graphic axis, a hybrid of French formality and modernist tropicalism. The design, evocative of the tropical modernism of his contemporary, Brazilian landscaper Roberto Burle Marx, is a response to the jungle as both an idea and the material constraint of the project. Watson told me in interviews that Sassou Nguesso had asked him for a wild garden, a Lost City jungle landscape for his family home in Oyo. Watson's response was that Oyo was already a jungle and so the logical intervention would be to add structure and order. It was essential for Watson that the garden require as little skilled maintenance and upkeep as possible; the financial and managerial burden of future upkeep meant thinking through the design in light of the presumed tendency to ruin.

Tall royal palms and coloured flowering trees (red 'Flamboyant', *Delonix regia*, pink *Cassia javanica*, orange *Spathodea campanulata* and yellow *Cassia fistula*) form the avenues that structure the garden. The straight tree-lined avenues are the most 'classical' landscape interventions in the park and as they mature will offer grand walks, frame the users' views of the garden and encourage a particular ambulatory experience of the park, producing the effect of arrival and departure. They function both as a symbol of power and also as the phenomenological experience of being ushered; reminiscent of the iconic imperial palm walkway in Rio de Janeiro's Botanical Garden and the grand entrances to slave plantations. These *allées* connect the abbreviated golf course with the newly built modernist-style pavilion, forming vectors that perforate the jungle walls enclosing the garden. The main pavilion is fronted by an extensive and precise square of lawn that is bounded by huge rectangular flowerbeds of red Cannas. The red flowers foreground the view of a lake and a newly planted oil palm forest. Massive organic-shaped beds of yellow and orange flowers flank the pavilion and pair with two lakes filled with water lilies. The massing of single plant varieties in dense blocks, a modernist form of classical bedding out, is often attributed to Burle Marx. Nancy Stepan argues that he used this technique in Brazil in unexpected ways to produce clusters of dissimilar plants that were antithetical to the tropical jungle aesthetic (2002: 222–33). The indigenous ombrophile forest edging the parklands is cut through with serpentine wooden walkways that lead to viewpoints and small pavilions. Locally occurring orchids have been harvested from deep in the woodlands and are now embroidered into the fabric of the jungle wall.

The Promises and Pleasures of Ruination

If we think of gardening only as domination we miss the point that it is also, axiomatically, a very optimistic practice: planting implies a belief in the possibility of a future, of imagining growth and flourishing (politically and financially). In addition, while it might seem easy and self-satisfying to imagine Mobutu, Sassou Nguesso, Mangope or Kerzner as gardeners with a venal desire to dominate everything, including nature in the form of shrubbery, orchids and fountains, it is important – whatever we may think of them ethically – to acknowledge the genuine flair, passion for plants and style that these men appear to demonstrate in their domination of territory. So, while the stately public garden can be a metaphor of dominion on a micro scale it is not only that; gardens are not principally metaphors, they are messy, muddy, tricky, beautiful, living and dying, useless, delightful, expensive processes in and of themselves. Casid calls this muddiness the promise of ruination: 'if ruin means theorizations based in embodied, sensate encounters with landscape that involve mucking around in the pleasures, difficulties, shame, and desires of the differences within and without' (2011: 99). Gardening, then, isn't only an attempt to control nature, and ruin isn't only a failure at domination of nature but also a range of pleasurable, difficult and shameful effects.

The landscaping of the Lost City is self-consciously occupied with the luxurious and marketable aspects of ruination. Indeed, internal documents show that the gardens 'were envisaged [as] a part of the marketing campaign for the Resort' (Kirkby 2013). The artificial ruin is not at all a modern phenomenon. Mock ruins, also called follies or *fabriques*, were a weird feature of many grand French and English gardens in the eighteenth century. Chinese pagodas, Roman temples, rustic mills, grottos and towers were purposely built as ornamental ruins that, serving no practical propose, provided theatrical self-indulgence, pleasure and appealed to the faded grandeur of the aristocracy. These *fabriques* often emulated ruins depicted in classical paintings and displayed the artistic sophistication of their owners. Picturesque ruins, like those of the Lost City, were highly constructed, carefully considered and artfully managed. 'Designer ruination' also requires professional maintenance, as Sun City found out in the late 1990s when mismanagement by garden contractors caused the jungle ruins to fall into dis-ruin (Kirkby 2013). Neglected gardens are not (necessarily) ruined gardens; it is possible to fail at ruination. Deterioration and decay, when managed aesthetically, suggest the passage of time, a narrative in which nature has triumphed over artifice. The branding narrative of the Lost City – a mythical African kingdom 'lost to the jungle', 'consumed by the jungle' (Sun International Official Website 2017) – is based on the supposed power of the jungle, the wilderness, to overwhelm African civilization.

Mobutu's landscape gardens, it appears, have been consumed by the tropical jungle in just this way. Aerial photographs of Gbadolite suggest a post-apocalyptic scene: modernist structures stripped bare and the sharp edges of the compound's abstract geometry now softened by the feathering of foliage. In the left panel of the diptych *Leopold and Mobutu Series 8* (Figure 1), Tillim frames the forest through apertures in the wall, holes that at one point might have been large windows or French doors festooned with gold damask and leopard print drapery. In the left-hand panel, the photographer's exposure results in a landscape viewed from the darkened interior such that the gardens seem survey-able and knowable in a rational manner. This composition, drawing on classical landscape art traditions, offers a location for reflection and for the consideration of nature, outside. The right-hand panel (Figure 2) is quite different. Because this room presumably lost its roof to looting and decay, there is no distinction between the 'interior' and 'exterior' exposures. The jungle in this photograph is a wall and in its centre is a palm tree.

The jungle discourse of rioting invasion can be contrasted with much more banal kinds of dilapidation. For example, in Kinshasa, Mobutu's Presidential Gardens at Mont Ngaliema, designed as grand French formal public gardens with promontories overlooking the rapids at Kinsuka, are now, as Ruth Sacks has documented, in a parlous condition. Sacks describes the decline of Mobutu's 'controlled greenery': 'the lower lawns have given way to natural eruptions of soil and creepers, and the open ground that was once used as an open-air theatre and the zoo lawns are now used to grow maize for the underpaid military guard' (2017: 302). In V.S. Naipaul's novel *A Bend in the River* (1979) we find a similar description: 'The big lawns and gardens had returned to bush; the streets had disappeared; vines and creepers had grown over broken, bleached walls'. The lawn, when it falls into ruin, has little of the romance or drama of the jungle: no swirling baroque wall of tendrils and vines, only a scruffy, brown, uneven surface.

Golf courses are exponentially more difficult to manage than 'normal' lawns and this fact was a major consideration when Watson planned the president's Oyo landscape. He recounted to me how he managed to convince Sassou Nguesso to jettison his plans for an 18-hole golf course in favour of a single hole and astroturf putting green. Watson presupposed that there would likely be neglect and mismanagement and so he put his design emphasis on the low-maintenance tree-lined avenues and blocks of colourful foliage. Part of the lawn's appeal when on a grand scale is this challenge that it presents; the success of a large-scale lawn can be taken as evidence of the owner's excess capacity for organized labour and (his) commitment to future care.

Thus, while ruined lawns lack the picturesque qualities of the wild jungle, a well-kept, flat, green lawn serves as an aesthetic counterpoint to the tropicality embodied in, for instance, the palm tree. The palm, Braithwaite suggests, symbolizes 'the interesting and relaxing tropics. It is also a symbol of jungle, the antithesis of lawn' (1993: 8). Stepan agrees: the palm functions as *the* sign of the tropics, 'less a botanical species than an imaginative submersion in hot places' (2002: 19). The palm tree is also instructive in advancing a critique of tropicality because of the palm's extensive transplantation between colonies and European metropoles, its movements between colonies, and its connection to plantation slavery and its deployment for the explicit expression of territorial power by demarcating property ownership. While it is taken-for-granted as a native, natural and naturally occurring plant, in most instances, this is not the case at all. For instance, the palm *allée* of *Roystonea regia* in Egypt's Aswan Botanical Garden, like in Oyo, is made up of Cuban royal palms, native to the Caribbean and Latin America.

The palm avenue typology came to embody 'the image of monarchical power, the idea of nobility, distinction and class', because of the palm's elegant proportions that, for observers of the time, evoked classical architecture and classical ruins (D'Elboux 2013: 148). In Europe, palms were grown in greenhouses, adorned the façades of palaces and circulated in popular botanical publications as prints and illustrations (Casid 2005: 55). Derek Walcott argues that these 'proper' palms have a 'civilizing decency', growing as if in a botanical garden, 'as if the sky were a glass ceiling under which a colonized vegetation is arranged for quiet walks and carriage rides' (1992).

The 'civilizing decency' of the cultivated palm signals an ambiguous quality at work in the jungle discourse – the jungle cannot simply be reduced to wilderness. The richness of the tropical forest as a complex signifier is never more apparent than in the Brazilian example of the modern gardens of Burle Marx. In his work, Brazil's most famous landscaper articulated a radical form of tropicality called Lusotropicalism, a problematic and influential postcolonial theory from the early 1930s which argued that miscegenation – cultural, sexual, botanical, artistic, racial – led to a 'cannibalistic' society that transcended the colonist/colonized binary. This discourse rejected the static idea of the wild jungle, outside the civilized garden, outside of time. Instead, Burle Marx searched for an 'authentic' Brazilian landscape through, for instance, reworking of jungle aesthetics using colour-blocked planting, abstract patterning and the transplantation of tropical plant. For Burle Marx, there was never an 'attempt to recreate the feel of a jungle or to provide the experience of an immersion in a tropical Eden' (Stepan 2002: 208) and his 'anti-tropical' garden for Edmundo Cavane that mostly resembles Watson's design for Sassou Nguesso. The indigenous forest forms a dramatic backdrop to a whimsical checkerboard lawn and abstract massed purple plants and ponds.

This notion of Lusotropicalism differs quite profoundly from an Anglo/French critique of tropical discourse and it is rarely applied to non-Lusophone colonies. It is, however, useful to read against the grain in this way, to consider alternative responses to the jungle. A Southern approach looks not only to obvious European colonial influences like Versailles or the eighteenth-century English landscape garden but (rather) to South Africa, Mauritius, DRC and Brazil for attempts at articulating kinds of postcolonial aesthetic.

Improvement and the Postcolony

The Lost City, Hall and Bombardella argue, was 'intended as an improvement on Africa, an experience without the distracting unpleasantness of the organic' (2005: 9). The paradox central to this discussion is the desire for nature but the requirement that it be clean, almost nonliving, static: the aesthetic of nature without the mud and labour. This is one of the key functions of the landscape: to naturalize and fix human–nonhuman relationships in such a way that the exercise of power seems inevitable and stable. It is the very instability of the gardens discussed in this chapter that make them fertile, as it were, for thinking through the operations of power in the postcolony.

It can be argued that ruination always haunts luxury in post-independence Africa; the threat of decadence – not necessarily (only) as moral decay or political obscenity – figures right from the start. This discourse is most compellingly exemplified in the tropical, especially as it is figured in the forest, or in the more problematic and anachronistic term, the jungle. The production of comparative scale, the articulation of affective ratio and relation: to be made small in relation to the nonhuman. The jungle threatens to enfold and consume the human scale, in a manner that is simultaneously desired and dreaded, and in a way that is always already going to happen. We can observe in the duality of the jungle discourse the delicious fear of being consumed by the jungle, and the greater fear, underlying the first: that the jungle might be impotent, too weak to swallow up humanity and civilization. The desire for and fear of being swept out of existence, overwhelmed, delirium, is at the core of tropical discourse.

The chapter asks whether luxury in organic form – botanical, animal, human – is substantially different for other modes or registers of luxury. In parallel and in addition, the chapter offers original empirical analysis of African gardening outside of the scope of farming, subsistence and unplanned 'vernacular' gardening. The chapter insists on addressing a dramatic, interesting and important garden of real aesthetic and political concern outside of the usual geographic focus for landscape studies.

Acknowledgements

The author acknowledges support from the Andrew W. Mellon Foundation funded through the Architecture, Urbanism and Humanities Initiative at Wits City Institute, based at the University of the Witwatersrand, Johannesburg. Opinions expressed in this paper and conclusions arrived at are those of the author and are not necessarily attributed to the Andrew W. Mellon Foundation or the Wits City Institute and Wits University.

References

Arnold, David (2000), '"Illusory riches": Representations of the tropical world, 1840–1950', *Singapore Journal of Tropical Geography*, 21:1, pp. 6–18.

Beauman, Francesca (2006), 'The king of fruits', *Cabinet*, 23, www.cabinetmagazine.org/issues/23. Accessed 18 September 2013.

Braithwaite, R. W. (1993), *Gardening as Environmentalism: A Wet-dry Perspective*, Darwin: State Library of the Northern Territory.

Cane, Jonathan (2012), 'The garden of melancholia and boredom', *Art South Africa*, 11:1, pp. 68–69.

Casid, Jill (2005), *Sowing Empire: Landscape and Colonization*, Minneapolis: University of Minnesota Press.

—— (2011), 'Epilogue: Landscape in, around, and under the performative', *Women & Performance: A Journal of Feminist Theory*, 21:1, pp. 97–116.

Coetzee, M., Van Averbeke, W., Wright, S. and Haycock, E. (2007), 'Understanding urban home garden design in Ga-Rankuwa, Pretoria', *Institute of Environment and Recreation Management Conference*, Pietermaritzburg, South Africa, 5–6 October.

Comaroff, Jean and Comaroff, John L. (1997), *Of Revelation and Revolution: The Dialectics of Modernity on a South African Frontier*, vol. 2, Chicago: University of Chicago Press.

Conrad, Joseph ([1902] 2005), *Heart of Darkness*, Delaware: Prestwick House.

Cosgrove, Denis (1984), *Social Formation and Symbolic Landscape*, Sydney: Croom Helm.

Creed, Barbara (2013), 'Apes and elephants: In search of sensation in the tropical imaginary', *Etropic*, 12:2, pp. 156–70.

D'Elboux, Roseli (2013), 'A promenade in the tropics: The imperial palms between Rio de Janeiro and São Paulo', *Studies in the History of Gardens & Designed Landscapes*, 33:3, pp. 148–56.

De Boeck, Filip and Baloji, Sammy (2016), *Suturing the City: Living Together in Congo's Urban Worlds*, London: Autograph APB.

De Boeck, Filip and Plissart, Marie-Françoise (2004), *Kinshasa: Tales of the Invisible City*, Ghent: Ludion.

Driver, Felix (2004), 'Imagining the tropics: Views and visions of the tropical world', *Singapore Journal of Tropical Geography*, 25:1, pp. 1–17.

Hall, Martin and Bombardella, Pia (2005), 'Las Vegas in Africa', *Journal of Social Archaeology*, 5:1, pp. 5–24.

Huntington, Ellsworth (1915), *Civilization and Climate*, New Haven, CT: Yale University Press.

Kirkby, David (2013), 'Sun City: Gardens & grounds management', instructional document.

Lagae, Johan and De Raedt, Kim (2014), 'Building for "l'Authenticité": Eugène Palumbo and the architecture of Mobutu's Congo', *Journal of Architectural Education*, 68:2, pp. 178–89.

Marriott, David (2017), 'On decadence: Bling bling', *e-flux* 79, http://www.e-flux.com/journal/79/94430/on-decadence-bling-bling. Accessed 15 October 2017.

McHale, Melissa, Bunn, David, Pickett, Steward and Twine, Wayne (2013), 'Urban ecology in a developing world: Why advanced socioecological theory needs Africa', *Frontiers in Ecology and the Environment*, 11:10, pp. 556–64.

Mitchell, W. J. Thomas (1994), 'Introduction', in W. J. T. Mitchell (ed.), *Landscape & Power*, Chicago: University of Chicago Press, pp. 1–4.

Mukerji, Chandra (1994), 'The political mobilization of nature in seventeenth-century French formal gardens', *Theory and Society*, 23:5, pp. 651–77.

—— (2012), 'Space and political pedagogy at the Gardens of Versailles', *Public Culture*, 24:3, pp. 509–34.

Naipaul, V. S. (1979), *A Bend in the River*, York: Vintage International.

Ndebele, Njabulo S. (1998), 'Game lodges and leisure colonialists', in I. Vladislavić and H. Judin (eds), *Blank: Architecture, Apartheid and After*, Rotterdam: NAi, pp. 119–23.

Pratt, Mary Louise (2007), *Imperial Eyes: Travel Writing and Transculturation*, London: Routledge.

Sacks, Ruth (2017), 'Congo style: From Belgian Art nouveau to Zaïre's *Authenticité*', Ph.D. thesis, Johannesburg: University of the Witwatersrand.

Stepan, Nancy (2000), 'Tropical modernism: Designing the tropical landscape', *Singapore Journal of Tropical Geography*, 21:1, pp. 76–91.

—— (2002), *Picturing Tropical Nature*, London: Reaktion Books.

Sun International Official Website (2017), www.suninternational.com. Accessed 4 October 2017.

Sutter, Paul S. (2014), 'The tropics: A brief history of an environmental imaginary', in A. Isenberg (ed.), *The Oxford Handbook of Environmental History*, Oxford and New York: Oxford University Press, pp. 178–216.

The Lost City (c. 1993), Johannesburg: Hooper Productions.

Walcott, Derek (1992), 'The Antilles: Fragments of epic memory', Nobel lecture, Stockholm, 7 December, www.nobelprize.org/nobel_prizes/literature/laureates/1992/walcott-lecture.html. Accessed 11 October 2017.

Watson, Patrick (2017), personal interview, Johannesburg, 2 August.

Wimmler, Jutta (2017), *The Sun King's Atlantic: Drugs, Demons and Dyestuffs in the Atlantic World, 1640–1730*, Boston: Brill.

Biographies

Editors

Mehita Iqani is associate professor in media studies at the University of the Witwatersrand in Johannesburg, South Africa. She is the author of *Consumer Culture and the Media: Magazines in the Public Eye* (2012) and *Consumption, Media and the Global South: Aspiration Contested* (2016), and a co-editor of *Consumption, Media and Culture in South Africa: Perspectives on Freedom and the Public* (with Bridget Kenny, 2015), *Media and the Global South: Narrative Territorialities, Cross-Cultural Flow* (with Fernando Resende, 2019) and *Media Studies: Decolonising the Discipline* (with Sarah Chiumbu, 2019). She has published in journals including *Consumption Markets & Culture, Feminist Media Studies, International Journal of Cultural Studies, Social Semiotics* and the *Journal of Consumer Culture*. She holds a Ph.D. in media and communications from the London School of Economics and Political Science.

Simidele Dosekun is assistant professor in media and communications at the London School of Economics and Political Science. She holds a Ph.D. in gender and cultural studies from King's College London. Her research centres black African women to explore questions of gender, subjectivity, power and inequality in a global context. Her work has been published in journals including *Feminist Africa, Feminist Media Studies* and *Feminism and Psychology*, and her first book, *Fashioning Postfeminism: Spectacular Femininity and Transnational Culture,* is forthcoming from the University of Illinois Press.

Contributors

Ndapwa Alweendo is a graduate of Rhodes University. Her master's dissertation focused on the 'Luminance woman' – a seemingly new iteration of black womanhood with access to a degree of class privilege and performance previously unimaginable for most black women in South Africa. Her current research interests include mental health and black womanhood and the varied misrecognitions of black women's participation in public and private spaces.

Jonathan Cane is a Mellon postdoctoral fellow at the Wits City Institute, University of the Witwatersrand. His Ph.D. thesis, 'Civilising grass', was about the politics and aesthetics of the lawn in South African visual culture. An art historian and practising artist, he is engaged with questions of modernity, sexuality and ecology.

Amah Edoh is a cultural anthropologist interested in the politics of knowledge production about Africa. Centring on material and visual objects traveling between African locations and Europe and North America, her work asks what the production and circulation of these forms makes visible about how Africa is made to mean in this moment. She earned her Ph.D. from MIT's programme in history, anthropology and science, technology and society. She is currently assistant professor of African studies at MIT.

Claudia Gastrow is a lecturer in anthropology at the University of Johannesburg, South Africa. Her research focuses on urban politics in Luanda, Angola, specifically exploring the role of aesthetic experience in the production of political belonging. Her interests include urban studies, the anthropology of the state and citizenship, aesthetics, material culture, informality, land and housing.

Pamila Gupta is associate professor at WiSER (Wits Institute for Social and Economic Research) at the University of Witwatersrand in Johannesburg, South Africa. She holds a Ph.D. in socio-cultural anthropology from Columbia University. She writes about Lusophone India and Africa, Portuguese colonial and missionary history, decolonization, heritage tourism, visual cultures and islands in the Indian Ocean. Her second book, *Portuguese Decolonization in the Indian Ocean World: History and Ethnography*, is forthcoming with Bloomsbury (2018).

Hlonipha Mokoena received her Ph.D. from the University of Cape Town in 2005. She is currently an associate professor at WiSER (Wits Institute for Social and Economic Research) at the University of the Witwatersrand, Johannesburg. Her articles have been published in: *Journal of Natal and Zulu History*, *Journal of Religion in Africa*, *Journal of Southern African Studies*, *Ufahamu: A Journal of African Studies*, *Interventions: International Journal of Postcolonial Studies*, *Image & Text* and *Critical Arts*.

Alexia Smit is a lecturer in television studies at the University of Cape Town. Her research focus is on popular entertainment television, with a particular interest in reality television. She has published on television and the body, feminist approaches to television and South African television. Her current research is concerned with transnational satellite television and women's genres in Africa.